The Woodbine Parish Report on the Revolutions in South America (1822)

The Foreign Office and Early British Intelligence on Latin America

Liverpool Latin American Studies, New Series 27

The Woodbine Parish Report on the Revolutions in South America (1822)

The Foreign Office and Early British Intelligence on Latin America

Mariano Schlez

LIVERPOOL UNIVERSITY PRESS

First published 2022 by
Liverpool University Press
4 Cambridge Street
Liverpool
L69 7ZU

This paperback edition published 2025

British Library Cataloguing-in-Publication data
A British Library CIP record is available

ISBN 978-1-80207-731-5 (hardback)
ISBN 978-1-83624-447-9 (paperback)

Typeset by Carnegie Book Production, Lancaster

Contents

Part II: Documents

Acknowledgements

This project was funded by the UK Arts and Humanities Research Council (AHRC) research project "Cross-Language Dynamics: Reshaping Community", hosted at the School of Advanced Study, University of London, within the framework of the "Open World Research Initiative" (OWRI). I would like to thank its co-director, Catherine Davies, for having translated and commented on this book and for offering me her generous friendship during these years. Likewise, my research visits in London were made possible thanks to the "OWRI Fellowship in Languages and Communities", awarded by the Institute of Modern Languages Research (IMLR), University of London, and by the Postdoctoral Visiting Fellowship of the School of Cultures, Languages and Area Studies, University of Nottingham, in 2014, under the supervision of Antoni Kapcia, who I also thank for his friendship and camaraderie. I would also like to mention Bernard McGuirk, John Fisher and Adrian Pearce for their conversations and advice, which were kindly offered to me in Nottingham, Liverpool and Mexico. This book is indebted, in particular, to the Royal Geographical Society (with IBG), and especially to their librarian, Eugene Rae, who gave me access to the Parish archive. Throughout these years, I have received the encouragement and collaboration of a group of researchers, now friends and colleagues, to whom I would like to express my gratitude: Juan Marchena Fernández, Manuel Chust, José Luis Caño Ortigosa, Tristan Platt, Osvaldo Coggiola, Daniel Gaido, Gustavo Burachik, Valentina Viego, Karen Racine and Gesine Brede.

My research is carried out at CONICET, in the Area of American and Argentine History, Humanities Department, National University of the South (Universidad Nacional del Sur), for which I thank especially Dr. Hernán Asdrúbal Silva, who not only served as my director until recently, but from the very start made me feel a part of his family.

And since no-one lives by work alone, I will end by dedicating this book to my "old" friends in Necochea, Marce and Meche; my new friends in Bahía, Valen, Gustavo, Gastón, Pame, Pali, Nati, Tincho, Marina and Ferni; to Maiu Fabris, who welcomed me into his home in London; to my comrades of the Workers Party (T) and to Stella (my first reader, critic and confidant),

Caro and Juli, who put up with my repeated absences and always gave me their full support. Without them, this research would not have been possible.

Mariano Schlez
Bahía Blanca, February 2022

Introduction

It is not difficult to explain, at a time when the 'end of history' was widely predicted, why in the late 1990s I decided to study history at the University of Buenos Aires: the 2001 upheavals in Argentina, just one episode in a process of continental scope, made it quite clear that, at least in Latin America, history was still moving on. As the twenty-first century unfolded, a sequence of crises, popular uprisings and wars, provided further confirmation. It soon became apparent that 'democracy' and neoliberalism were not about to offer the often-promised global peace and prosperity. And when a coalition of nations, led by the United States and the United Kingdom, invaded Iraq, debates around imperialism once more came to the fore.

Since then, my interests have focused on the study of colonial and imperial ties in Latin America as a means of understanding the increasingly strong and periodic economic and political crises experienced in my continent. For this reason, my doctoral studies centred on the economic and political relationships established between the Rio de la Plata region, the Spanish Empire and the dominant European powers, the aim being to explain the character of the revolutions and wars of independence, and the origins of the new states. My research therefore focuses on the political, economic and cultural relationship established between Britain and Rio de la Plata in the first half of the nineteenth century. By studying the historical connections between the various social subjects, I will engage with theories that have conceptualized this relationship as a *neo-colonial pact, Informal Empire, Imperialism of Free Trade,* or *dependent capitalism,* as well as theories that challenge these views.

The relationship between Britain and the Rio de la Plata was developed by historical social subjects. Therefore, to study the main features of this relationship entails consideration of connections established between the ruling classes on both sides of the Atlantic, classes consisting mainly of merchants, industrialists, financiers, politicians and diplomats. Within this framework, diplomatic relations are a particularly significant subject for research, as they encapsulate the political, economic, social, military and cultural aspects of the ties established between the two states (De Goey,

2014), a process which began in the 1820s when the first British consuls were posted to South America (Humphreys, 1940; Platt, 1971). It was during this period, in 1825, that the new Rio de la Plata state received its first loan from British capital (Baring Brothers), signed the Treaty of Friendship and Commerce with Great Britain (which lasted a century) and subsequently obtained formal recognition by His Majesty's government. Although the first British consul in Buenos Aires, Woodbine Parish, was mentioned in several studies (Busaniche, 1958; Ferns, 1960; De Gandía, 1968; Williams, 1972; Nicolau, 1990; Howat, 2019; Rock, 2019), researchers have yet to present a detailed and systematic analysis of his activities, and of the voluminous documentation his consulate bequeathed.

To address this gap, I undertook two research visits to London to locate and examine the available documentation relating to the first British consulate in Buenos Aires. This was housed mainly in the Foreign Office section of the National Archives (TNA), the western manuscripts collections of the British Library (BL) and, to a lesser extent, the Baring Archive (TBA).[1] During this research, I found a small, though no less important, Parish archive at the Royal Geographical Society (TRGS). Although used less extensively by historians, this archive is a source of important scientific and political documents, written in South America, including a notebook with the following catalogue reference: "South America. Volume containing printed and manuscript reports prepared for the Congress of Verona, 1822".[2] To adduce oversight in such a large volume of historiography is risky; nevertheless we have found only one mention of this report to date. It is briefly referred to in Nina L. Kay Shuttleworth's (1910) biography of her grandfather. We can only speculate as to why this document has been overlooked, but it is likely that the circumstances in which it was written and presented, during the one-month transition between Castlereagh's sudden death and the appointment of Canning, were important in this respect. And, as we have indicated, the manuscript has not been preserved in the Foreign Office documentation held in TNA, the major source used by historians, which may have contributed to it being overlooked.

At the time of its writing in 1822, Parish was a clerk in the Foreign Office and private secretary to the Foreign Secretary, Castlereagh, who requested the report in order to prepare for British negotiations at (what was to be) the final Congress of the Holy Alliance held in Verona. It was probably the first report on the revolutions in South America commissioned by the Foreign Office. As we will see throughout this book, an analysis of the report provides insight into the early stages of British intelligence and diplomacy

---

1　TNA, FO 354/1–9; 6/1–31; 6/499; 119/1–2; 446/3; 93/10/1; 95/661; 566/99; 566/100; 881/311; 118/1–30b; 97/76. BL, Add MS 32603–32609. TBA, HC4.

2　TRGS, The Sir Woodbine Parish Collection (SWP/3), South America. Volume containing printed and manuscript reports prepared for the Congress of Verona, 1822.

with respect to Latin America promoted from within the Foreign Office, and at the same time reveals the Foreign Office's powers and limitations. Likewise, the report will offer an overview of the information about the South American revolutions circulating in London at the time, as well as the mechanisms used by the British government to obtain and classify this information for political purposes. In this sense, the report makes evident the importance, for the British government in general and for the Foreign Office in particular, of knowing a specific historical and geographical reality in order to develop a political strategy. We will see how this knowledge is mediated by class antagonism and power relations (on a national and international scale) and determined by the stages of development of the productive forces in the regions involved. Studying the Parish family will allow us to more fully understand the role played by the rising social classes, in particular the merchants and manufacturers, in the development and implementation of a British foreign policy for Latin America.

The report was written during the second 'Latin American boom' experienced in Britain in the decades following the independence revolutions—an earlier 'boom' followed the news of the conquest of Rio de la Plata, sent by Home Popham in 1807 (Gregory, 1993). British interest in Latin America is evident in contemporary publications of all kinds—including a significant number of 'travellers' accounts (Pratt, 1992; Salvatore, 1999; Roldán Vera, 2003; Paquette, 2004; Heinowitz, 2010; Somarriva, 2016)—encouraged by growing economic ties with the new South American states which heralded an era of exorbitant economic profit for British capital, as well as the first capitalist economic crisis in 1825 (Dawson, 1990).

Parish's report can only be fully understood by taking into account the historical, geographical, social and economic context in which it was written and read. This book aims to present the necessary cultural coordinates which will enable the reader to reposition the report and, following Reeder, appreciate the ideas it puts forward as an expression of its material, social and economic existence (Reeder, 2020: 22). As we shall show, the historical context, the authors, and the content of this report make it a key document in British diplomacy on Latin America. It brings to light unknown aspects of the period, and illuminates with new information existing historical accounts of the events leading to the recognition of the South American states. We argue that Parish's report helps us to understand the principles of British policy towards Latin America in the 1820s.

Considering that Kay Shuttleworth (1910) fails to describe the report's content; that it is not mentioned in any of the biographies dedicated to Parish and Castlereagh, nor in the studies on British policy towards Latin America, nor even in studies dedicated to the Congress of Verona; and considering that the context of the report's production was a moment of immense significance in British and South American politics, we take the view that to photograph, transcribe, study and edit the entire document, and to thus make it available to historians and the general public, is a necessary and original contribution to the development of research on the *imperial question*, which has occupied historiography since the mid-nineteenth century and is still a major debate today.

Part I

History

CHAPTER 1

The Persistence
of the Imperial Question

Debates centring on modern imperialism appeared in tandem with the development of global capitalism at the beginning of the nineteenth century. The political, economic, military and cultural expansion of a limited number of states led to direct and indirect forms of domination, leading to new theories that sought to define these relationships. How should we conceptualize a nation-state which is independent but closely linked to a foreign government? What are the impulses that lead to this particular form of relationship and where do they originate? To what extent is this a form of domination, and does it imply violation of the sovereignty of the countries affected? The search for answers to these questions developed into what is known as *the imperial question*.

Although the debate is ongoing, four key moments may be identified: the rivalries between European powers leading to the division of Africa and the First World War (Day and Gaido, 2012); the decolonization of Asia and Africa, the crisis of the British Empire and U.S. ascendancy during the second post-war period (Jones, 2008; Barton, 2014); U.S. global interventions and Latin American politics since the 1959 Cuban Revolution (Owen and Sutcliffe, 1972); and the neoliberal crisis, which gave rise to new imperialist wars and new 'anti-imperialist' governments in twenty-first century South America (Brown, 2008). Evidently, the debate has continued on a par with two centuries of asymmetric relations between states.

Discussions have pivoted around two central axes: on the one hand, the extent to which state sovereignty is compromised by various forms of foreign intervention (political, economic, military or cultural) (Brown, 2008: 21) and, on the other, whether imperialism, and asymmetric relations between states, are inevitable. Although the debate at first focused on territorial conquests and invasions, it was soon recognized that capitalist imperialism was distinctive in its ability to impose hegemony indirectly by economic, diplomatic and cultural means.

The initial concepts seeking to account for this new kind of imperial domination were *semi-colony* and *dependence* (Lenin, 1960: 274).[1] Later, when decolonization led to forms of indirect control on a global scale, the concept of *informal empire* was formulated in Britain (Fay, 1940) and developed by Gallagher and Robinson (1953), resulting in a controversy that survives to this day. In a brief essay, Gallagher and Robinson maintained the continuity of nineteenth-century British expansionism and argued for an organic union between formal and informal empire, the visible and invisible parts of a unique iceberg. From their perspective, this was a policy of imperial security for which market access was both a means and an end. Their ideas resulted in a 180-degree change of perspective: direct and indirect governments were interconnected and interchangeable; they were different not in nature but in degree, according to specific historical contexts. Furthermore, the principal drive towards imperialism was no longer the demands of metropolitan capital, but the situation in the dependencies and inter-imperialist competition. Gallagher and Robinson (1953: 13, 11) thus concluded: "British policy followed the principle of extending control informally if possible and formally if necessary", the treaty of free trade and friendship being "the most political technique of British expansion".

In the 1960s several historians rejected the category *informal empire* (Ferns, 1960; Platt, 1968a; 1968b), some proposing a new concept seeking to account for the same reality: *neocolonialism* (Nkrumah, 1965; Guevara, 1967) or *neocolonial pact* (Halperín Donghi, 1967). These positions were hotly debated without reaching definitive conclusions (Owen and Sutcliffe, 1972; Louis, 1978). Spanish translations led to debates in Latin America dominated by confrontation between *dependency* and modes of production (Cardoso and Faletto, 1969; AA.VV., 1973).

Within this context, Robinson (1978) put forward his *theory of collaboration* or "excentric approach" to imperialism, which developed his previous position; imperialism was not a unilateral European imposition, implying oppression and domination of other countries, but a kind of marriage of convenience, a symbiosis or dance between partners to the benefit of both (Barton, 2014: 13–14). He thus provided the basis of postcolonial theory (Said, 1978) which developed some of these ideas around the ideological, psychological, cultural, discursive and political dimensions of the colonial encounter, replacing concepts such as oppression, exploitation, class and state antagonism with hybridity, mimicry, reciprocity and the 'other' (Young, 2001; Parry, 2004: 76).

The ascendancy of neoliberalism in the 1980s and 1990s, and capitalist expansion into former 'socialist' territories revitalized earlier positions, particularly regarding the British relationship with Latin America during the

---

1 Developed following Marx (1999: 378), who argued around 1866 that even the United States could be considered a colony of Europe given that its economic development was still a product of British industry.

nineteenth and early twentieth centuries. While Lynn (1999: 101–121) stressed the centrality of trade and capital in informal empire, Kennedy (2002: 17) argued that British hegemony was due to the competitiveness of its cheap manufactures, its abundant capital and its omnipresent naval power. Pratt (1992: 147) insisted on characterizing the British–Latin America relationship as "neocolonial" whereas Knight (1999) suggested the usefulness of dependency theory, criticizing the idea that Britain had a merely informal empire in the region. For his part, Thompson (1992: 436), who defined formal empire as control by annexation and subordination, concluded that in the case of Argentina imperialism was a "myth" because the relationship did not show a trade imbalance, did not compromise Argentina's autonomy, and Britain did not benefit from it disproportionately. Thompson was contested by Hopkins (1994: 483), who argued that the concepts of informal empire, semi-colony and invisible empire were still valuable for categorizing the conditions of domination and subordination imposed by a stronger state operating as an integrating force and exercising power in a way that infringes the sovereignty of smaller countries.

More recent historical research has confirmed Hopkins' view, although clarifying that British intervention in the 1840s was motivated principally by the conflict between Uruguay and the Argentine Confederation (McLean, 1995). Likewise, for Gallo (1994) British policy during the 1820s was founded on the Treaty of Friendship and Commerce signed by both governments, which protected Britain and offered a stable economic dominance but did not grant Britain extraordinary privileges. Unsurprisingly, Argentina, "the most precious possession" of the British informal empire, has played a central role in these historiographical debates. Nevertheless, most recent studies of Argentina in the first half of the nineteenth century have concentrated on political, military, social and cultural matters (Cibotti, 2006; Frega and Vegh, 2007; Somarriva, 2013; Hughes, 2013; Silveira, 2017), the exceptions being a few which have favoured an economic and social focus (Silva, 2001; 2008; Cámara de Comercio Argentino-Británica, 2014). This also applies to recent studies on the British community in the Rio de la Plata which highlight its cultural (linguistic and religious) unity rather than its social and economic interests (Graham-Yooll, 2000; Stewart, 2000; Hanon, 2005; Seiguer, 2009; Flores, 2011; Silveira, 2011; O'Brien, 2017).

Throughout these deliberations Atlantic trade has remained at the centre of research on post-conquest Latin American societies, notwithstanding the nineteenth-century revolutions (Topik, Marichal and Frank, 2006). New, detailed studies focusing on trade between Britain and South America show close connections existing since the mid-eighteenth century (Pearce, 2007; Llorca-Jaña, 2012; Camarda, 2013a) and recent case studies of British merchants in the Rio de la Plata have shed light on their business operations, networks and contacts (Böttcher, 2008; Silveira, 2015, Schlez, 2015; Besseghini, 2020a).

The debate today

Discussions around informal empire resurfaced in the twenty-first century with several attempts to revaluate its usefulness and limitations; some of the divergent, often opposing, views are outlined here.

A relatively new direction of research took a cultural studies approach to political economy (Howe, 2001), linking informal empire to the Latin American independence revolutions, and regional nation building and state formation (Brown, 2006). Economic and social relations are considered as fields of practice and cultural production; hence to understand imperialism fully not only must the official mindset of the metropolitan centre be taken into account but also, and more importantly, the daily interactions between the colonized, colonizers and their various mediators (Hunt, 1988). These issues were discussed at a 2007 Bristol conference that focused exclusively on informal empire in Latin America, bringing together those who rejected the concept, considering it a euphemism (Stoler, 2006), as well as those who continued to downplay and stereotype the role of South America within British imperialism (Bayly, 2004). For Matthew Brown (2008), informal empire implies the presence of trade, capital and culture as three interdependent influences that mutually reinforce each other to limit local sovereignty, shape political and diplomatic relations and influence the formation of a specific culture. Informal empire is an empirically demonstrable reality of asymmetric power, as well as measurable control that is exercised both in everyday reality and in the consciousness of the subjects involved. Brown examines the character of these incursions and controls and elucidates the extent to which they affected the sovereignty of Latin American states. His method involves a cultural dimension but without forfeiting socioeconomic and political anchorage. By analysing *contact zones* and *cultural encounters*, Brown studies in depth how historical relations between migrants and residents may be perceived as daily manifestations of the power asymmetries implied by the imperial connection.

Alan Knight (2008) differentiates imperialism (the practice or ideology associated with building and maintaining an empire) from empire (the sustained assimilation, asymmetrical exercise of power, and influence of one group of people over another). Although the threat to use, or actual use of, force may be widespread, he does not consider coercion a necessary or adequate feature of imperialism. He classifies the different categories of empire according to their form (direct or indirect) of extraction of surplus value, the character of their governments (direct and indirect, *de facto* and *de jure*), and the role of force, local crises, and metropolitan objectives (summarized as God, glory, gold and geopolitics) (Knight, 2008: 32). Citing the Argentine case as an example, Knight concludes that the mutual benefit of the ruling classes on both sides of the Atlantic did not nullify the asymmetric relationship or Argentina's economic dependence on Britain. In short, "no Argentine fleet had ever sailed up the Thames, blockaded London or engineered the creation of Belgium as a convenient buffer state" (Knight, 2008: 45–46). That said, however, it was not in the control of the metropolis to decide how the relationship developed: at a time when formal imperial government was pursued in Africa, no imperialist power could promote a similar policy in Latin America.

Charles Jones (2008) considers informal imperialism an oxymoron or tautology. For Jones, imperialism implies *agency*, and empire "merely structure"; the former is a *policy* or a *doctrine* and the latter a *constitutional order* (Jones, 2008: 142, 144). Imperialism implies direct control of a territory; hence to include indirect control broadens out the concept to encompass any manifestation of asymmetric power. Agreeing with Platt, Jones posits a *business imperialism*, which he defines as the deliberate use of market power by metropolitan corporations to circumscribe and shape the power of peripheral states without resorting to their parent governments. This does not imply the absence of the state: the British government and its agencies (such as the British Council) sought to protect connections between British businessmen and the local ruling classes. These activities (including those of historians), though related to informal empire, did not constitute an act of imperialism. In short, rejecting informal imperialism is not the same as rejecting informal empire which is not a doctrine or policy, but is created by men and women engaged in various activities, mainly trade and investment.

David Rock (2008: 50) has criticized the application of Gallagher and Robinson's ideas to Latin America on similar grounds, claiming their inconsistency led (as in the case of Argentina) to erroneous historical interpretations which underplayed the importance of local forces in the country's development. He disagrees with Platt, however, arguing that his superficial methodology and rigid definition of intervention led him to underestimate the disorder caused by British commercial penetration, fully described in the accounts of travelling merchants (Robertson and Robertson, 1843), and to minimize its importance before 1860, contrary to the views expressed by the British consul Woodbine Parish (1839). Rock takes a postcolonial approach and seeks to clarify the differences and specificities of Latin America, particularly the fact that, following the revolution, the creole liberals made the foreign imperialists redundant by themselves pushing the imperialist agenda. With respect to Argentina, Rock concludes, in line with Ferns and Platt, that although Britain played a major role in trade and investment, it is difficult to prove regular or prolonged infringement on Argentine national sovereignty (with the exception of the capture of the Falklands / Malvinas Islands in 1833 and the shipping blockade of the mid-1840s). The case studies and individual subjects discussed by Rock, however, are not always located in their specific historical–social context. For example, when referring to "Anglophile" Miguel Alfredo Martínez de Hoz Fernández, Rock does not mention that he was the grandson of Miguel Fernández de Agüero, representative at the Cádiz consulate and staunch defender of the Spanish monopoly against British trade towards the end of Spanish rule (Schlez, 2021a). This detail sheds light on Martínez de Hoz's ideology as a concrete and specific example of the transformations experienced in the spheres of production and trade in the immediate independence period. In his 2019 publication, Rock returned to "the nebulous issue of British power in Argentina" (2019: XII) and finally rejected the existence of an informal empire. He concluded that Argentina, a great centre of business, economic power and British settlement, was an independent republic not a colony.

A cultural studies approach is taken by Karen Racine (2008) and Fernanda Peñaloza (2008) who show how economics and culture were intertwined in the British Christian evangelization of South America and in the discursive ramifications of British imperial rhetoric focusing on Patagonia. Like Aguirre (2005), they take issue with historians who study the economics and politics of the relations between Britain and Latin America without taking into consideration the production, circulation and consumption of cultural forms.

The same questions have returned to the fore in Latin America. The seminar "The colonial question", held in Colombia in November 2009, aimed to clarify the differences between early modern colonization in America and later colonization "under the aegis of capital" in Asia and Africa. It was argued that "only an effort to understand the global dimension of colonization" can elucidate its significance, similarities and contrasts, and successfully account for its root causes rather than superficial developments (Bonilla, 2011: 16). The modalities and consequences of colonization have been diverse, depending on the specific contexts and moments in history which have shaped direct and indirect colonial governments and brought about the transformation and co-option of native authorities whose collaboration was crucial. These transformations were not only of a material nature but also occurred in the society, politics and cultures of the subjected peoples, including their religion and languages (Godelier, 2011). It was also agreed that the revolutionary wars in Latin America can be fully understood only by addressing the imperial question (Anderson, 2011). Recent interdisciplinary conferences have further developed these ideas by interconnecting the study of modes of production, revolutions and historical transitions, and by promoting global, long-term interdisciplinary historical research (Schlez, 2018; Marchena, Chust and Schlez, 2020).

Wider global research on South America has also re-engaged with questions of informal empire. For Barton (2014), informal empire was the means by which British and U.S. elites wielded control, powerfully influencing elites in the rest of the world and the structures of globalization. Its formal or informal character depended on the changing political and economic conditions, both local and global, that promoted, required or discouraged a certain structure rather than on the conscious intention of the imperial power. Following this line of enquiry, Baeza Ruz (2019) reconstructed the multiple "contacts, collisions and relationships" between the British and Chileans during the independence period, reprising the arguments presented at the Bristol conference. He explored not only the economic and diplomatic aspects of these relationships but also their cultural dimension, concentrating on the daily personal interactions of those affected by British expansion. In this way, he showed how the idea of Britain threatening Chilean sovereignty took on different meanings according to circumstances (Baeza Ruz, 2019: 219). The merchants' relationships, for example, evidenced their dual role as promoters of trade and agents of empire, on the one hand, and members of the local community, on the other. But the Chileans' need for Britain to recognize their independence demonstrated the asymmetric nature of the relationship. In short, British influence was undeniable but it was not unidirectional. It was expressed in different ways according to the context and local needs, as well as the class of the subjects involved. The fact that the British were rarely seen as imperial agents was of direct consequence for the process of nation-building.

For her part, Reeder (2020: 3–4) defines informal empire as the expression of the necessary unity of two pairs of superficially opposing concepts: freedom and empire; autonomy and submission. The concept of informal empire is important as it accounts for the contradictory character of Latin America—an example of self-government which was at the same time dependent on the British Empire. By means of a formalist analysis of British literature and imperial thought, Reeder elucidates the ways in which informal empire was perceived in the nineteenth century and concludes that this contradiction did not lead to a synthesis, but to an unstable and unresolved paradox.

Besseghini (2021: 140) argues that Britain exercised structural, relational and enabling power in the Rio de la Plata which contributed to the erosion of Spanish sovereignty and amplified ongoing conflicts between those competing for hegemony in the region. With regard to this, the plan for control issued from London, involving alliance with the creoles, helped lay the foundations of the region's new relations with Britain and made informal imperialism the external cause of Rio de la Plata independence; the market opening thereby assumed a "political function" (Besseghini, 2021: 62–63). Besseghini's argument reinstates metropolitan volition as the determining element in the relationship. The sources used (diplomatic and political) situate this study within the history of "great men", informed by statements rather than by historical social structures and relations. Paradoxically, this approach leads Besseghini to support Ferns' thesis that the British played a decisive role in the revolutionary outcome of May 1810 thus diminishing the role of local social subjects. Furthermore, by taking 1808 as his point of departure, the study overlooks the British invasions, leading to the erroneous conclusion that the British Empire in the region was born (in some way) informally. But historiography has already demonstrated that the opening of Rio de la Plata to British trade in 1809 cannot be explained without the invasions that prompted the formation of armed popular militias which then had to be sustained by an exhausted Spanish royal treasury (Schlez, 2020b).

Finally, in his discussion of South American capitalist development, Juan Iñigo Carrera (2022) objected to dependency and imperialist theories as well as to theories based on trade and unequal exchange. In his view, the concept imperialism does not explain the limitations faced by Latin American capitalisms. Instead of revealing their specificity, external causes, such as colonial oppression, are wrongly adduced (Iñigo Carrera, 2008: 19).

A theory for the study of capitalist imperialism in Latin America

In light of the above, this book takes the view that the political relationship between Great Britain and the nascent South American states was dictated by the interests of their respective ruling classes, who intervened according to the type of social relations they personified, and the degree of development attained by the productive forces in their respective spaces of capital accumulation. This does not imply the absence of internal conflict (as indicated throughout the book with reference to the disputes between landlords and capitalists over British recognition of the South American insurgent states). I contend that this political relationship was of a social character and was mediated by the exchange of commodities, the main objective being to increase the value of the capital assets for the ruling classes on both sides of the Atlantic. In short, the relationship was the historical form the capitalist mode of production developed in both spaces of accumulation. For this reason, the subordination of the Rio de la Plata economy to the requirements of British productivity did not mean that capitalist development was stalled or deformed in the region but, rather, that this was its necessary form of realization. I argue, therefore, that informal empire (and also semi-colony) indicates a direct historical connection, a contradictory alliance between independent capitals which are represented by their respective states and are thus the political expression of an asymmetric social and material relationship.

It follows that imperialism is the direct relationship established by the most developed capitalist countries with countries that are weaker or less developed, as a historical and necessary form of capitalist development on a global scale. Empire and imperialism, formal and informal, cannot be understood separately; they signify the unequal encounter or clash, in specific locations and historical periods, of two (or more) states which embody national processes of capital accumulation and class conflict with differing characteristics.

Consequently, economic structures do not 'influence' or 'determine' the action of individuals or social subjects, and cultural forms do not reinforce, support, lag behind or embellish material relations. On the contrary, economy, politics and culture constitute, like social reality, an inseparable whole. We understand politics and cultural forms as the specific way in which an economic structure develops, i.e. through the actions of historical social subjects, whose study is necessary to understand this development. Naturally, this definition excludes the existence of a predetermined metropolitan plan put into effect by the various agents involved. Empire and imperialism are objective social structures and relations, independent of the subjectivity of the people who embody and develop them (although their perceptions and experiences may be useful for studying the phenomenon) (Schlez, 2021a). In other words, the imperial relationship is not between territories or economic structures, but between social subjects who form part of a class, a culture and a state. Any analysis of empire and imperialism must take into account the types of connections established between people on both sides of the Atlantic and clarify the particular mix of trade, capital and culture (Brown, 2008).

This implies understanding the ways in which class relations have been embedded in social structures and the particular characteristics of the connections between creole and British capitalists (Thompson, 2008: 236–237), as well as reflecting on the impact of British material and symbolic influence (Vargas García, 2006).

With respect to periodization, the British informal empire in Latin America cannot be fully understood without taking into account the invasions of the Rio de la Plata in 1806 and 1807. Although it is generally agreed that the invasions lay the foundations for the future relationship between Argentina and Britain (Ferns, 1960; Rock, 2019), their continental scope is not always appreciated (Baeza Ruz, 2019). Their importance tends to be minimized by omitting them from the chronology of informal empire and assuming a starting point in 1808 or 1810 (Webster, 1938; Besseghini, 2021) or by describing them as marginal: a "filibustering expedition" (Gallagher and Robinson, 1953: 8); a "bizarre episode" (Lewis, 2008: 100); "a fiasco" (Darwin, 2013); and by absolving the British government of its responsibility (Barton, 2014: 112–113) suggesting military adventurism (Fortescue, 1921; Hugues, 2013).[2]

Although Gallagher and Robinson (1953: 8–9) sustain the colonialist objective of the invasions, they separate them from the revolutionary process of independence, concluding that the "British governments sought to exploit the colonial revolutions to shatter the Spanish trade monopoly". However, the invasions had already shattered the monopoly four years earlier. In fact, the "virtuous circle" of strategic hegemony coupled with trade began across all South America with these invasions which should be considered the British informal empire's "original accumulation" in the region. The political principle put forward by Gallagher and Robinson (1953: 13), according to which "it is only when and where informal political means failed to provide the framework of security for British enterprise [...] that the question of establishing formal empire arose" is exactly the reverse: the defeat and failure of territorial dominance led to the indirect or informal exercise of power. Similarly, to consider the question without taking into account the invasions invalidates the idea that the British informal empire in Argentina grew in strength once the threat of force decreased, or that the Anglo-Argentine

---

2 Although Rock (2019) presents one of the best and most detailed documented summaries of the invasions' importance, he discounts them from his argument because in his view they attacked Spanish rather than Argentine sovereignty.

relationship was largely consensual (Knight, 2008: 30, 44). On the contrary, the informal empire was the direct result of the British inability to 'formally' conquer South American territory by military invasion.

By analysing primary sources we can quantify the strength of the economic invasion and measure the extraordinary volume (of goods, traders and vessels involved) as well as the huge diversity of imperial trade routes (Schlez, 2019a). We have shown how and why the 1806–1807 invasions and the subsequent opening up of Buenos Aires to British merchants represented a mortal blow for the Spanish monopolists who still, in 1810, struggled to maintain their exclusive connection with Cádiz (Schlez 2020b; 2021c). We have also argued that the predominance of British mercantile capital depended on the power of social relations and capitalist productive forces, which expressed the necessary imposition of the laws of capital. The merchants, landowners and colonial state officials were fully aware of how capital worked. At the start of the nineteenth century, in the Rio de la Plata, we can clearly observe a transition from the Spanish commercial monopoly (governed by the Laws of the Indies) to a new, industrial monopoly, sustained by British and Rio de la Plata industrial capital (Schlez 2021a).

To further develop these ideas, research is still needed, especially in neglected archives (Brown, 2008: 3; Jones, 2008: 148). This is precisely the contribution of this book.

This book's contribution to the imperial question

The publication of the Parish report and an analysis of its immediate context will shed new light on the functions and interactions of the principal 'bridgeheads' operating between Britain and South America. We will more fully understand, therefore, what Darwin (1997: 641–642) referred to as the "informational environment" of the politicians involved, and how information on the imperial periphery was collected, processed, and disseminated in Britain. Knight's argument (2008: 29) that informal empire hindered the metropolitan government's 'cognitive power' with respect to the territories it sought to dominate, requiring it to appeal to native collaborators for information and intelligence, will also be evaluated. Drawing on unpublished Foreign Office documentation, we will uncover "the levels of ignorance" and "the barriers to communication ([...]) that disguised Latin American reality from the men charged with British relations with Latin America" (Brown, 2008: 19).

This book will also reveal the efforts made by the imperial authorities to monitor the relations between British and creole capitalists and show the situation to be quite different from the picture painted by those who deny this role (Platt, 1973; Peñaloza, 2008: 151). At the time, at least according to the Foreign Office officials, the keen interest shown by British industrial and commercial capital in Latin America far exceeded the excitement created by the conquest of Buenos Aires in 1806; there was little doubt that Latin

America had goods to offer Britain, even before the appearance of the railway (Platt, 1973: 88). Following the 'commercial boom' generated by the invasions, the presence of Latin America in total British exports grew from 2.3% in 1806 to 12.6% in 1826 (Miller, 1993: 73). These considerations are crucial for understanding who benefited (and who lost) with the empire (Knight, 2008: 26), without forgetting Peñaloza's reminder (2008: 151) about the class of those who benefited—the class which excluded (and opposed) the very existence of the indigenous peoples of Patagonia.

Similarly, the Parish case will allow us to penetrate the complex web of relations existing between the capitalist class and the British government. By studying in depth the social composition of the professional civil service at the Foreign Office this book will contribute to debates on the British ruling class in the early nineteenth century and its role in imperial expansion (Barton, 2014: 18). We will also reconsider the reason for Parish's appointment as British consul to the Rio de la Plata, which is usually attributed to his connections with Canning and government colleagues and with the Parish and Parish Robertson merchants in Bath (Rock, 2019: 54).

In addition, this book will shed light on the "close encounters" (Joseph, LeGrand and Salvatore, 1998) between the governments of North and South America in the 1820s, and how these shaped British policy in the region in order to attain commercial predominance (Rippy, 1972). Following independence, Latin America became a territory disputed between Britain, the United States and France (Barton, 2014). In this respect, the book contributes to historiography that seeks to dismantle the disciplinary limitations of Area Studies by incorporating Latin America into the history of the British Empire and the global history of capitalism.

We can therefore question some of the assumptions regarding the British 'official mindset', such as the suggestion that, before 1860, Latin America was of strategic rather than commercial and political importance; or that British recognition of independence was the 'high point' of informal political influence as demonstrated in the treaties of recognition designed specifically in accordance with British interests (Smith, 1978: 3, 7). By reviewing these historical events from a new perspective, we will show that attributing the institutional framework established between Britain and the major South American republics to Canning's strategic and creative brilliance alone (Gallagher and Robinson, 1953: 9) is incorrect. In the same way, the fight waged by Latin American revolutionaries against the Spanish Empire and the efforts of Latin American capitalists to trade with their British counterparts, outside the Spanish monopoly, indicate that the relationship cannot be attributed exclusively to European economic and strategic ambitions which relegate Latin American societies to the role of passive acceptance or rejection (Robinson, 1978: 187).

The material basis of our concept of informal empire allows us to explain, from a different perspective, that imperial formations constitute "states of becoming" (Stoler, 2006: 135–136) as well as the incomplete and disputed character of imperial authority (Cooper, 2005: 11). It also supports Thompson's (2008: 231) approach to the continuum between formal and informal empire, modified temporally and geographically according to the nature of the relationship with Britain. We agree, finally, with Reeder (2020: 8) in rejecting a transhistorical or transgeographical theory of informal empire.

This book argues that the intervention in Latin America was also politically important in Britain; the Tory government was required to recognize states and political sovereignties that had come about following social revolutions, revolutions that undermined the very foundations of monarchy by contesting the legitimism advocated by the Holy Alliance. This was at a time when the British working class was beginning to wage its own struggle and the Irish question becoming increasingly fraught. British economic priorities did not imply, therefore, a relative indifference to geopolitical issues (Ferns, 1960: 164), and their tolerant view of Latin American politics was the result of a correlation of forces leading to the defeat of the formal empire in the battle of Buenos Aires. In this sense, this book challenges the view that Latin Americans' resistance to colonialism and imperialism (formal and informal) was the resistance of pre-capitalist sectors to "rationalization" (Barton, 2014: 186).

Studying the Parish report will help historians to continue delineating the cartography of changes in British imperialism following its encounter with the Latin American revolutions (Brown, 2008).

CHAPTER 2

Understanding the Latin American Revolutions

Recent historiography has emphasized the importance of information processing and the acquisition of knowledge for the development of a successful global strategy. It has sought to understand the systems and technologies devised in the eighteenth and early nineteenth centuries to collect, classify and use this information (Headrick, 2001; Miller, 2020). As Jeremy Black (2014: 244) points out, information and power were closely linked, and "the processes of imperial expansion involved both and tested both". The state's 'need to know' led to the creation of an extensive bureaucracy which, by validating reports, sought to ensure the accuracy of the information that would later serve as the basis for political intervention. As Salvatore argues (2003: 67), to establish hegemony an informal empire requires the production and circulation of accurate information about the regions under its influence; reliable regional knowledge (geography, resources, production, culture and history) allows it to conquer markets and exploit resources. Information gathering expresses the centre's 'will to know' and its willingness to incorporate the peripheral region into its overall design. The new research area, labelled Science Diplomacy, refers to the "professional practices at the intersection of the world of science and that of diplomacy" (Krasnyak and Ruffini, 2020). In other words, the role of knowledge in diplomacy and political strategy became a problem of the first order.

Reports that offer a specific type of information and knowledge about the political, economic and social life of a country or region at a particular moment in history (which implies objective or scientific knowledge) have historically been referred to as *intelligence* reports. According to Herman (1996: 9), intelligence is a form of state power, but "as a set of permanent institutions dates back only to the second half of the nineteenth century. But as information and news -in the dictionary meaning used in English since the middle of the fifteenth century, of 'knowledge as to events, communicated by or obtained from another, especially military'- it has always been collected as part of warfare".

In eighteenth-century Britain, although intelligence was a top priority, it had not yet developed into a specific function of the state. It was produced in various departments and areas of government, mainly in relation to diplomacy and warfare (Maffeo, 2000). Deciphered diplomatic dispatches were known as 'The Secrets', but the state had also set up the Secret Service Fund which was used to finance British propaganda, part-time informants, operations of 'freelance' agents and a system of political and diplomatic bribery (Herman, 1996: 12). The development of British state structures regulated the use of the Fund, with a large part of its expenditure falling to the secretary for foreign affairs. In the first decades of the nineteenth century, acquiring knowledge of the various foreign countries was largely delegated by the British government to the Foreign, Home and War Offices (the Department of Military Knowledge was specially created in 1803), though the Fund's budget dropped sharply after Waterloo (Andrew, 1987: 26).

During this period, British intelligence grew in response to the French Revolution, prompting not only espionage activities but also covert political intervention such as plans for a royalist uprising to be carried out through William Wickham, British *chargé d'affaires* in Switzerland (Durey, 2009). British intelligence achieved resounding triumphs, such as the discovery of the secret Treaty of Tilsit, in which France and Russia agreed an alliance against Britain (Munch-Petersen, 2013). Diplomacy, first deployed against the American Revolution but redirected against revolutionary France, particularly after 1792 (Black, 2010: 120), was equally successful.

However, intelligence did not lead immediately to objective or scientific knowledge of the various situations from which a univocal policy might be formulated. On the contrary, intelligence became a subject of contention between the different components of the state, an understanding of which will require consideration of the conflicting interests of the social classes involved in the production and use of that knowledge. Understanding how and who obtains, processes and presents information and is aware of its content and orientation, and ascertaining what was actually done with the information will provide key insights into the major shifts experienced in British society at the time. For this was a society experiencing class contradictions from "above" (the confrontation between the old ruling classes and the rising "middle classes") and "below" (the growing antagonism between the ruling classes and the increasingly large and pauperized working classes) (Hobsbawm, 1962; 1968).

Although a study specifically dedicated to British intelligence on Latin America in the first half of the nineteenth century has yet to be published, the subject has been raised with reference to political and diplomatic relations (Webster, 1938; Kaufmann, 1951; Lynch, 1969; Bulmer-Thomas, 1989; Knight, 1999; Blaufarb, 2007; Silva, 2008; Robson, 2009; Racine, 2010; McCarthy, 2013; Somarriva, 2013); commercial and financial ties (Platt, 1972; 1977; Reber, 1979; Lewis and Abel, 1985; Miller, 1993; Pearce, 2007; Llorca-Jaña, 2012; Schlez, 2017); the political action of Castlereagh and Canning (Stapleton, 1831; 1859; Lloyd, 1904; Temperley, 1925; Bew, 2012); the several congresses of the Holy Alliance, in particular, the congress held in Verona (Webster, 1912; 1915; 1925; Green, 1913; Nichols, 1971; Yamada, 2004; Jarret, 2013); Anglo-American competition (Humphreys, 1966; Rippy, 1972; Besseghini, 2020b), and British recognition of the independent Spanish American states (Paxson, 1903; Rydjord, 1941; Metford, 1952; Van Hulle, 2014). These studies reveal the mechanisms and sources used by the British government to obtain information about the various situations of the former Spanish colonies of South America at the time.

In this chapter we will present an overview of some key considerations: when, how and why the British government found it urgent to *know* the situation in Latin America; the forms and mechanisms of the circulation of information; the social subjects involved in sourcing intelligence in the region; the production of the first reports, and the links between intelligence, the British industrial, commercial and financial bourgeoisie, and successive government strategies towards Latin America.

I. Understanding Latin America revolutions: from the "Parry Report" (1962) to the "Parish Report" (1822)

The global repercussions of the Cuban Revolution of 1959 had a major impact on higher education in Britain and the United States, resulting in the rapid growth of Latin American Studies (Schlez, 2018). In the United States, the Director of the Hispanic Foundation of the Library of Congress suggested that the U.S. Latin American Studies Association (LASA) "might well erect a monument to Fidel Castro, a remote godfather" (Cline, 1966: 64). Likewise, the crisis of the British 'Informal Empire' played a role in the development of Latin American studies in the United Kingdom (Elliott, 2012). In 1962, in order to better understand political conflict in Latin America, the University Grants Committee, the UK government body charged with distributing funds to universities, established a "Parliamentary Committee on Latin American Studies" to evaluate the situation (Paquette, 2019). In 1965 the Committee presented its report on Latin American Studies, known as the "Parry Report", which concluded there were serious deficiencies in British knowledge on Latin America and advised the government to set up specialist research centres.[1] Between 1964 and 1967 six Latin American Studies centres were founded in the universities of London, Oxford, Cambridge, Glasgow, Liverpool and Essex, giving the United Kingdom global status in Latin American studies.

However, this was not the first time the British government had needed to react to revolutionary processes in Latin America and to improve its knowledge of the region. As Robin Humphreys (1940: XVIII–XIX), one of the historians who sat on the 1962 committee pointed out, 140 years earlier

---

1 *Report of the Committee on Latin American Studies.* London: Her Majesty's Stationery Office, 1965.

the British government had requested the British consuls and commissioners in Buenos Aires, Santiago de Chile, Lima, Bogotá and Mexico to send in regular reports on the political and economic situations in those parts of the Americas. As George Canning's instructions to James Henderson make clear, reports were necessary due to "the growing importance of the States of Spanish America and the unsatisfactory nature of the accounts which are derived from accidental sources of intelligence".[2] There were serious deficiencies in British intelligence which had to be corrected immediately due to the pace of the revolutionary change in the former Spanish colonies and the need for a decision by His Majesty's government on whether to formally recognize their independence.

The intelligence deficiencies indicated by the Foreign Office did not imply an absence of communication with the region or ignorance of the main events. There were numerous informants (military, agents, consuls, merchants and propagandists) who more or less regularly sent the British government all kinds of news and information from the major South American cities.

II. How did the British government *know* Latin America?

Between 1821 and 1822 a series of events, with political impact on a global scale, confirmed the end of Spanish domination in the Americas. The advance of revolutionary forces from Rio de la Plata and Chile into the Spanish stronghold, Peru, which ended in the taking of Lima; the Córdoba treaties between Agustín de Iturbide in Mexico and Juan O'Donojú, sent from constitutional Spain, which signalled a further step towards the independence of Mexico; and the much celebrated meeting of Generals José de San Martín and Simón Bolívar, in Guayaquil, were all evidence of the general crisis of Spanish colonial power in the Americas (Chust and Frasquet, 2013).

This succession of events, which today appear clearly linked and which we now know in detail thanks to the passage of time and historical research, were not presented so unequivocally to European contemporaries. The geographical distances, the way information was circulated and the political tensions in the territories where intervention was sought, as well as the nature of their relationship with the United Kingdom (were these to be independent states or colonial/semi-colonial territories within a British 'Informal Empire'?), were some of the obstacles to understanding the political processes unfolding in those distant regions (Bayly, 2000; Laidlaw, 2005; Hevia, 2021). Despite the many studies on British intervention in Latin America at the beginning of the nineteenth century, there are still important gaps in our knowledge on the precise mechanisms devised by the British government to be apprised of the complex, ever-changing situation in the region. A full understanding of how intelligence was gathered is necessary to contextualize and fully appreciate

2 TNA, FO 18/1.

the significance of the Parish report of 1822. We will first consider the various kinds of informants operating at the time.

a. The circulation of information between Latin America and Great Britain

At the beginning of the nineteenth century, an important factor determining the flow of information was the relationship between geographical distance and transport technology. A ship took approximately three months to connect the South American subcontinent to the British Isles. The ships that crossed the Atlantic on a regular basis did so for political, military and commercial purposes.

The constant movement of maritime trade was one of the first and most regular sources of information in all the main markets of the world. Merchant ship officers were often the first to bring news from their ports of origin and to their ports of destination. Similarly, the complicated logistics required to promote commercial traffic forced merchants to establish a large, ongoing correspondence informing their trading partners about the latest events in distant regions.[3] The detailed knowledge long-distance merchants possessed of political events across the globe is a proven fact. As an example, in 1819, Brade, Moore & Ashcroft, in Liverpool, informed Hugh Dallas, in Buenos Aires, of the forthcoming Foreign Enlistment Act (preventing British subjects from enlisting in foreign militaries) and the preparations for a military expedition against the revolutionary governments about to set sail from Cádiz, but whose departure was prevented by the Spanish revolution of 1820.[4]

In addition, militants, political agents and 'spies' travelled back and forth on military and commercial ships. They could be revolutionaries or counterinsurgents, moving in both directions across the Atlantic, with competing objectives but with a common purpose: to transfer information between Europe and the Americas. Among the more noteworthy was Manuel Aniceto Padilla who, after helping General Beresford flee Buenos Aires in 1807 (Beresford had been imprisoned in Luján, Buenos Aires, following the failure of the British invasion), escaped to Rio de Janeiro, where he became an assistant to Lord Strangford. Padilla eventually moved to London and was awarded a government salary for his services (Williams Álzaga, 1965). Saturnino Rodríguez Peña followed a similar path. Based in Rio de Janeiro, he corresponded with Padilla and Miranda as well as with the Creole revolutionary party. In 1808, Juan Martín de Pueyrredón, who was in Spain, heard rumours about a new British expedition to America and sent José Moldes and

---

3 TBA, Buenos Aires and London: Letters from William and John Parish Robertson, 1817–1827.

4 Brade, Moore & Ashcroft to H. Dallas, Liverpool, 13/6/1819, Archivo Comercial de Hugh Dallas, Archivo y Museo Históricos del Banco de la Provincia de Buenos Aires, Box 1.

Manuel Pinto to London to gather information.[5] Likewise, Princess Carlota
Joaquina of Portugal sent letters from Brazil to those involved in the 'Carlota'
conspiracy in Rio de la Plata via the English surgeon, James Paroissien (an
acquaintance of Rodríguez Peña).[6] In the opposite direction, on their return
from the Iberian Peninsula, officers Matías Zapiola, Carlos María de Alvear
and José de San Martín stayed in London, where they forged a relationship
with López Méndez, Andrés Bello, the Mexican Mier, and Francisco de
Miranda (Davis, 1964). As is frequently pointed out, London became one of
the main 'headquarters' for the South American revolutionaries (Bonpland,
1940; Berruezo León, 1989). New arrivals included Francisco de Miranda,
Bernardo O'Higgins, Simón Bolívar and José de San Martín who, with other
important revolutionaries, created a Latin American interest group that
proved crucial for the triumph of Independence (Jaramillo, 1983; Racine,
2003; Terragno, 2013).

After revolution had broken out in 1810, communication was the responsibility of the diplomatic envoys sent to England by the new South American
states, mainly by Rio de la Plata and Colombia, where the revolution was
most successful. Their aim was to obtain political, economic and military
support in the war against Spain. They represented an important source of
information (and lobbying) for the British government, though they were not
entirely reliable because their versions of events were intended to justify the
soundness of their governments.

From the earliest stages, throughout the entire revolutionary process,
extensive communication existed between the South American envoys and
the British government. In 1810, Richard Wellesley met with the delegates
from Venezuela and Colombia, Luis López Méndez, Andrés Bello, and
Simón Bolívar himself (Lynch, 1982; Waddell, 1983). Later, in January 1817,
after the revolution thwarted the first Spanish counterattack, López Méndez
and Bello were appointed the 'agents and special commissioners' of Venezuela
in London. From 1819, the Republic of Colombia was represented successively by López Méndez (1819); Francisco Antonio Zea (1819–1821); José
Rafael Revenga (1822–1824); Manuel José Hurtado (1824–1827) and José
Fernández Madrid (1827–1830).[7]

Likewise, between 1810 and 1824, seven diplomatic missions were sent
from Buenos Aires to London, the main objectives of which were to obtain

---

5 They met Miranda and also the prime minister who offered them details about the
   expedition that was being prepared (Roberts, 2006: 36).
6 Some authors state he was Rodríguez Peña's friend and belonged to the group who
   promoted the 'Carlota' plan. However, others maintain he was duped by Carlota,
   having no idea when he set out that he was carrying letters on her behalf. See
   Humphreys (1952); Heredia (1977); and Ternavasio (2015).
7 As demonstrated by Gutiérrez Ardila (2012: 54–55), the choice of agents depended
   on the political and economic aims of the Colombian delegation.

political recognition of the new state and to acquire arms:[8] Wellesley met with Matias Irigoyen in June 1810, with José Agustín de Aguirre and Thomas Crompton (an English merchant) in August 1810 (Guastavino, 1918; AGN, 1937; Cárcano, 1972; Escudé and Cisneros, 1998; Harari and Flores, 2017; Pasino, 2017), and with Mariano Moreno, Manuel Moreno and Tomás Guido at the end of 1810;[9] Manuel de Sarratea travelled to London in 1812, seeking to prevent a Spanish reconquest of the Americas, as did Manuel Belgrano and Bernardino Rivadavia, who arrived in April 1815.[10] Meanwhile, Manuel García was sent to Rio de Janeiro, with a letter from Carlos María de Alvear to Lord Strangford in which Alvear ceded Rio de la Plata to the British government.[11] After the crisis of 1820, in June 1824 the Rio de la Plata government sent Alvear to London and, again, in November, also Rivadavia, who despite having the position of Rio de la Plata's *chargé d'affaires*, dedicated himself (much to Canning's annoyance) to running his own businesses in partnership with British capital (Piccirilli, 1952; Rosa, 1964; Rees Jones, 2008).

London not only received envoys from Buenos Aires, Caracas and Bogotá. Santiago de Chile and Mexico also deployed intense diplomatic activity in the United Kingdom, collaborating with the same general objective: formal recognition of the new states (Montaner Bello, 1961; Jiménez Codinach, 1991). In the case of Chile, the first diplomatic envoy to London was Francisco Antonio Pinto who arrived in London in 1813; followed by Antonio José de Irisarri, in November 1818, and Mariano Egaña, who was active in Europe between 1824 and 1827. The aim of Egaña's political activity was to achieve British political and financial support. Irisarri tried to convince Castlereagh to send British commercial consuls to Chile in mid-1819 (Baeza Ruz, 2019: 193–194). In 1818, at the height of the independence struggle, San Martín himself wrote directly to Castlereagh (Webster, 1938).

One of the most significant means employed by South American diplomats to achieve their objectives was to promote a vigorous propaganda campaign

---

8 Some included other destinations such as Rio de Janeiro, Madrid, Paris and the United States.

9 Although Mariano Moreno, the only official envoy, died at sea, his brother Manuel was able to continue the mission and met with Wellesley in June 1811.

10 It appears they had no contact with members of the government. Belgrano returned home soon after. Sarratea and Rivadavia remained in Europe to observe the formation of the Holy Alliance. Rivadavia criticized Lord Liverpool's government, including Castlereagh, for not receiving the South American envoys. He distinguished the government from the "Nación Inglesa", which was in favour of independence, and praised the role played by the Whig opposition in Parliament (Gallo, 1994: 175).

11 There continue to be different views on Alvear's order. Gallo (1994: 160) argues that neither García nor Rivadavia (who had received the same letter) obeyed these instructions in their respective missions. On the subject, see Rosa (1951) and Piccirilli (1969).

which aimed to justify the historical foundations of the independence movements and explain the political situation they were experiencing. They collaborated with British publishers and the press, thus creating an "English public opinion" and a "public space" for news from Latin America (McFarlane, 2016), which also represented class interests making it possible to intervene politically through parties and politicians and to influence and challenge government policy.[12] *The Morning Chronicle* and the *Edinburgh Review*, for example, were organs of the Whig (reformist) party and gave ample space to its main leaders and intellectuals, such as Henry Brougham, Jeremy Bentham, James Mill and Francisco de Miranda himself (Asquith, 1975; Alberich, 1982). In contrast, *The Times*, was closer to the positions of the Tory government of Lord Liverpool (and Castlereagh). As stated by David Brown (2011: 37), at the start of the nineteenth century, "journalists were coming to be seen in the diplomatic sphere as something more than passive narrators or commentators and instead as potentially having a real impact on international relations". Also, Gutiérrez Ardila (2012) has demonstrated that the Colombians subscribed to the most important international newspapers and also paid British and French commercial enterprises to promote the South American 'cause' in their publications. In other words, the press offered a valuable and essential tool and source of information about events in distant parts of South America, and this information became part of British political and intellectual debate.[13] In this way, the authors, editors, articles and newspapers of the time became active subjects of the process they scrutinized, which gave rise to a strong and long-term bond with South American politicians and diplomats.[14]

These diverse sources of information, though crucial for British intelligence, were politically deficient in two important ways: first, they were fragmented and disperse, making it necessary to use various sources to obtain a general overview; second, the informants shaped the information according to their own interests. No government could simply accept their information at face value, on any subject. These deficiencies prompted the

12 According to Kennedy (1981), these issues could be discussed in more detail in the periodical press than in the House of Commons and for this reason the press played a significant role in the debate on foreign policy, even when dominated by political party interests. The most recent study of the British press is Black (2019).

13 According to Gallo (1994: 147), Manuel Moreno established links with Blanco White and William Walton, a publicist who wrote for the *Morning Chronicle*. Jeremy Bentham corresponded with Rivadavia, San Martín and Bolívar (Williford, 1980; Paquette, 2011).

14 A particularly strong collaboration was that between the South American diplomat Francisco Antonio Zea and the publicist William Walton as evidenced in their joint publication *Colombia: being a geographical, statistical, agricultural, commercial, and political account of that country: adapted for the general reader, the merchant, and the colonist.* London: Baldwin, Cradock, and Joy, 1822.

British government to obtain and process its own information, which was not coloured by the immediate interests and views of the informants, and which offered as far as possible an objective or scientific assessment of the Latin American situation.

The British government, therefore, began to train up special political staff to carry out the tasks of acquiring and processing information. The intervention of spies, military officers, diplomats and commercial agents on the subcontinent would provide more systematic intelligence. Their task was to produce a specific type of historical and political document which was essential for informed political decision-making: the intelligence report.

b. Spies, military, diplomats and merchants: the origins of British Intelligence on South America

Since the 1806 invasions of Rio de la Plata, the British War Office received regular information from South America through its naval vessels stationed in the South Atlantic (Grainger, 2015). But the failure of the invasions forced the British government to assess the causes of defeat and to reconsider any ambition it might have had of territorial conquest. The Popham and Whitelocke trials revealed the close relationship between British capital (especially merchant capital), the Admiralty, and the government, in particular the Foreign Office (*A Full*, 1807; *The Proceedings*, 1808). The trials also showed up serious deficiencies in British intelligence on Latin America. Certain reports (some of them written by Francisco de Miranda, others anonymous) has assured the British government that an invasion would have the support of the local population, supposedly anxious to free themselves from Spain.[15] Although faulty intelligence was not entirely to blame, from then on the British government made rapid progress establishing its own diplomatic and intelligence channels across South America.

Recent research has shown that during the Peninsular War British intelligence was not limited to Wellington and his one-man intelligence department, but that the British government also acted to establish a civilian network of correspondents and agents communicating with the British ambassadors to

15 Various documents deal with this question. Among the lesser known is the MSS *A concise account of the present state of the Spanish colonies of America* (MS149, Senate House Library, University of London), which appears to be a copy of a document written by a Spanish American in 1805, with a view to invoking British intervention as a means to escape the oppressive Spanish colonial policy it describes. According to Mikaberidze (2020: 451–452), the decision to invade the Rio de la Plata was not taken in London, but Popham "was clearly influenced not only by the exaggerated rumours of disaffection in Spanish colonies that Miranda had spread but also by long-standing British imperial aspirations to penetrate Spain's South American colonies with a view toward obtaining a position favourable to British trade; between 1702 and 1783, Spain had repelled no fewer than six such attempts by Britain".

Spain and Portugal. In this sense, as Huw Davies (2006: 202) has pointed out, "Wellington's main priority was to integrate the 'strategic intelligence' collected by government agents with his own 'operational intelligence'. Instead, analysis was conducted more by Wellington's subordinates in the field, applying their personal localized expertise to the information they received". Nevertheless, throughout the Napoleonic wars, British intelligence, which was inseparable from secret diplomacy, had limited effectiveness due to its lack of professionalism and institutionalization (O'Connell, 2019). In 1808, during preparations for an expeditionary force destined for Sweden, Castlereagh, Secretary of State for War and the Colonies, admitted to almost complete ignorance of the region in which it was to operate and his lack of knowledge included questions relating to the strength, positions and morale of the Swedish, Norwegian and Russian armies (Hall, 1992: 49).

After the defeats of 1806 and 1807 in Rio de la Plata, and following the French invasion of the Iberian Peninsula in 1808, the British sought to gain a footing in South America in a different way, and signed a political and military alliance with Spain, its erstwhile enemy, to confront Napoleon. Captain James Burke was sent by Castlereagh as an agent to Buenos Aires, in order to find out "as much as possible about the feelings of the people of the River Plate" and to inform the Spanish authorities there of the unexpected sudden alliance between Spain and Great Britain against the common enemy, France.[16]

The officers at the British naval stations in South America also sent out regular information (Ratto, 1945; Graham and Humphreys, 1962). These showed their collaboration—and, sometimes, open disputes—with British diplomatic agents and merchants based in the region. Such conflicts indicate the problem facing the British government which was forced to intercede in internal disputes proposing different courses of action.[17] Of course, the ships based at British naval stations did not transmit information in one direction only, from South America to Europe; they also reported the latest European events to those in South America, especially when this news affected local

16 TNA, Secret, Colonel James Burke Papers, 1809, FO 72/81. On this subject, see Pyne (1998) and Gallo (1994: 127).

17 The disagreements between Sir Sidney Smith and Lord Strangford over Rio de la Plata politics led to the direct intervention of Castlereagh, who convinced Joao VI to ask Smith to step down from his post. Smith was replaced by Rear-Admiral De Courcy. In 1810, the River Plate station was under the command of Captain Elliott, whose principal duty was to defend British commerce, but after the commercial agents' complaints, he was replaced by Ramsay accompanied by Captain Fabian. The authority of these naval officers was so significant that in 1818 the British government recommended that they should not be involved in commercial matters but should liaise with the consuls instead—the problem being that at the time there were no official British consuls in post in South America. See Fitte (1965: 181) and Street (1967: 179).

interests. News of the French conquest of Seville on 1 February 1810, for example, reached Rio de la Plata, delivered by HMS *Mistletoe*, on 14 May.

In 1808, Lord Strangford was appointed British ambassador to the Portuguese royal court which had fled Lisbon under British protection and relocated to Rio de Janeiro. He held the position until 1816 (Ruiz-Guiñazú, 1937; AGN, 1941; Rosa, 1951; Street, 1953) but fulfilled his duties during the first stage of Rio de la Plata revolutions without instructions from Foreign Secretary Richard Wellesley. Many of the official communications from South America to Britain passed through Strangford's hands. In 1811, Strangford arranged for Manuel Aniceto Padilla to go to London and, in 1812, on resuming his post as Foreign Secretary, Castlereagh finally sent Strangford instructions. These were relayed to Rio de la Plata through Captain Heywood. Castlereagh communicated to the Buenos Aires government that Britain expected it to remain loyal to Spain, a British ally, in their common battle against France. In 1816, Henry Chamberlain was put in charge of the British diplomatic mission in Rio de Janeiro and likewise maintained direct contact with Castlereagh. For example, when he learned of San Martín's victory at the Battle of Maipu, Chamberlain immediately informed Castlereagh of the political implications.

Finally, British merchants sent regular information from Rio de la Plata to the Foreign Office, the government and the king.[18] But as they appealed to the British government to promote and protect their businesses, their 'information' was usually accompanied by joint petitions or requests.[19]

In short, the British government had an important mass of information at its disposal, gathered by its own officials (spies, military officers and diplomats). Merchants and company agents (frequently incorrectly labelled 'travellers') were another significant source of information. However, these were all individuals with a stake in the political process they sought to know, and their information had to be analysed objectively if the government was to access knowledge on South America beyond the ideological biases, aims and interests of its sources. To help develop a political strategy, this voluminous wealth of information had to be compiled and analyzed in order to produce an overview of the political situation across the region.

---

18 Between 1809 and 1813 the Foreign Office received reports from the merchant Alexander Mackinnon in Buenos Aires and later from Robert Staples and the Parish Robertson brothers: TNA, FO 72/90; FO 72/107; FO 72/126; FO 95/7/7; FO 72/157; FO 72/171; FO 72/202; Robertson and Robertson (1838; 1843). On the activities of British merchants in Rio de la Plata see Humphreys (1965); Fitte (1967); Böttcher (2008); Silveira (2015) and Rock (2019).

19 "Memorial from British Merchants resident at Rio de Janeiro (March 1809)", TNA, Board of Trade, 1–89. The British merchants in Buenos Aires wanted Staples to be named consul for the River Plate. The government's refusal led to them naming him commercial agent in 1818 (Ferns, 1960: 91; Gallo, 1994: 180).

c. Knowledge and political action: intelligence reports on revolutions in South America

The need to know what was happening in the former Spanish colonies in the Americas was a problem not only for the British government, but for all the European powers. The Holy Alliance (Austria, Prussia and Russia) had a system of information gathering established by the Austrian and Prussian consuls in Washington, Rio de Janeiro, Madrid, Paris and London.[20] With increasing regularity, reports specifically dedicated to the South American question were commissioned due to the new states' demand for the recognition of their independence.

One of the first and best-known reports was written in 1818 by the U.S. commissioners to Rio de la Plata and served as the basis for the official recognition of independence by President James Monroe in 1822 (Graham and Rodney, 1819).[21] Later, after Fernando VII's constitutional government proclaimed the *Manifesto of the Spanish government to foreign powers on the Independence of the Americas* in April 1822, the Spanish ambassador in Berlin presented to the Prussian cabinet a report on Latin America which underplayed the strength of the revolutionary forces and described the conditions of the unemancipated regions, such as Mexico under the Iturbide government, as "so desperate that it would take little time to achieve its reconquest" (Kossok, 1968: 129).[22] Similarly, after Chateaubriand sent a questionnaire on the subject to the governments of the Holy Alliance, Metternich's response at the end of 1823 demonstrated the importance of knowing and evaluating events in Latin America. From his perspective Spain had not yet totally lost power in the Americas, so the Holy Alliance could not proceed to establish formal ties with the insurgent governments.

However, according to Friedrich von Gentz in his *Memoire sur le discours du Président des Etats Unis d'Amérique* of February 1824, there was little consensus within the Holy Alliance on events in South America.[23] In practical political terms, von Gentz recognized the inevitability of independence, rejected a new congress of the Holy Alliance to discuss the issue, and advocated Spain's decorous withdrawal which would protect, as far as

---

20 Austrian and Prussian statesmen were briefed by their consular and diplomatic representatives in Washington, Rio de Janeiro, Madrid, Paris and London on American tactics in Latin America. In fact, Metternich received information directly from Washington, through Lederer, Consul General of Austria (Kossok, 1968: 126).

21 See the documentary appendix, in Part II of the book.

22 My own translation from Spanish.

23 In this memoir, Gentz summarized his proposals. As Manfred Kossok (1968: 148) sums up, Gentz "started from the irreversible situation in which Latin America found itself in 1823 [making] clear, down to the last detail, the insoluble crisis and the dissolution of the Spanish colonial empire", affirming that "it was not up to the will of the Holy Alliance to change the course of events".

possible, the authority of the sovereign, obtaining, in exchange, financial compensation. As Metternich's assistant, von Gentz had political authority as well as excellent language skills which equipped him to become head of translation for the British delegation in Vienna, appointed by Castlereagh; he was "on equally good terms with the British, the French and the Austrians, equally privy to the affairs of all and fully trusted by none of them" (Roland, 1999: 53).

Ferdinand VII (restored to absolutism by the French invasion of Spain in 1823) insisted on the Holy Alliance's military invasion of South America and sought their support by calling for a new congress and the sanction of a 'Free Trade Decree'. At such a critical moment, up-to-date intelligence of events in South America was an essential political tool.

By 1824, the Foreign Secretary, George Canning, had already sent consuls to the main South American ports. He responded to the Spanish king that the *de facto* recognition of the new governments depended on the consuls' reports which would assess, first-hand, the different political situations they were experiencing:

> "That as to any further step, (beyond that of sending Consuls, which had already been adopted,) to be taken by His Majesty towards 'the acknowledgement of the de facto Governments of America, the decision must (as has been already stated more than once, to Spain and other powers) depend upon various circumstances, and among others, upon the reports which the British Government might receive of the actual state of affairs in the several Spanish American Provinces'."

> (Stapleton, vol. 2, 1831: 40)

In May 1824, Count Ophelia tried to counter Canning's position and bring Britain closer to the Paris conference, "detailing at great length the state of each separate Province in Spanish America, and representing the condition of all, and each of them, to be one of complete anarchy, and confusion" (Stapleton, vol. 2, 1831: 53). But this version did not correspond with the reports arriving in London from South America. In this regard, Stapleton points out that:

> "If this description had been borne out by facts, it would indeed have been out of the question for England to have taken the step which she meditated; but it so happened that all the reports received in England of the condition of those countries, whether official or private, went to prove the erroneousness of the data from which the Spanish Government professed to have drawn these conclusions."

> (Stapleton, vol. 2, 1831: 53).

The debate continued even after Britain formally recognized the new states: in March 1825, the English ambassador in Berlin, the Earl of Clanwilliam, informed Canning of the difficulty of arguing with the Prussian government, while

"Count of Bernstroff is, on this matter, equally deaf to undeniable facts and the clearest arguments. For example, nothing about what he can say succeeds in shaking S.E.'s conviction that the new transatlantic republics are still in an anarchic state and still contain the elements of a pro-Spain reaction. The fact is that while S.E. has taken little care to find out, considering and comparing the different reports, what is the true state of these distant countries, it can be said rather that he has followed in the footsteps of Prince Metternich than to trace his own path."

(Webster, vol. 2, 1938: 380)

In fact, until the late 1820s, Spain still seriously considered the possibility of a violent reconquest of its colonies according to the information it received from disgruntled Spanish Americans, who assured Spain that in view of the prevailing social disorder Spanish troops would be welcomed as liberators (Fontana, 2006). Gentz himself reported on the situation, and was not opposed to the idea, assuring that

"la conclusion de traités de commerce avec les nouveaux États du Mexique, de la Colombie et de Buenos-Ayres [...] peu différent d'une récognition formelle de l'indépendance de ces États, est une véritable hostilité contre le Roi d'Espagne, qui, loin d'avoir renoncé à sa souveraineté sur les colonies, semble vouloir ramasser tout ce qu'il lui reste de forces pour envoyer des expéditions en Amérique."

(Gentz, 1877: 439–440)

As the frequency of these reports intensified, a new genre emerged which sought to actively intervene in the political struggle: historical narratives focusing on the independence revolutions, written not only by South American militants and intellectuals but also by the British and French. These texts, which range from the simple presentation of official documents and the defence of the new states, to published essays and books, played a major part in the political debate (Gutiérrez Ardila, 2012).

In summary, throughout the 1820s, acquiring accurate information about the specific political situations of the new Latin American states, their relationships with Spain, and the persistence of support for Spain in the Americas, became a major challenge in any attempt to devise a successful policy in the region. How did the British government seek to resolve this political and empirical challenge?

III. British strategies towards Latin America: from conquest to recognition (1806–1822)

In less than two decades, British strategy with respect to Latin America had shifted from an attempt at territorial conquest to the recognition of the independence of the republican states which had emerged in the heat of revolution. In the intervening years, Britain took on the role of 'mediator' between Spain and its rebel colonies, with the aim of hindering French advances in the region and preventing a Spanish reconquest that would restore Spain's commercial monopoly and threaten British commercial gains.

These changes of strategy responded to an international situation confronting Britain, one which involved a succession of revolutions—from the 1776 revolution in the British North American colonies, the French Revolution of 1789 and the South American insurgency beginning in 1810. Having quickly abandoned any attempt to retain its North American empire in the wake of the Anglo-French war of 1793–1802, from 1803 the British war effort had to focus on confronting the advance of Napoleon on a global scale until 1815 and thereafter a powerful competing bourgeoisie in continental Europe. British diplomatic strategy responded to a correlation of forces, at home and on a global scale.

Historiography has focused repeatedly on the so-called "Castlereagh Memorandum" of 28 August 1817. This memorandum responded to British power, but also potential weakness. Britain used its authority, gained by victory over Napoleon, to obtain from the Holy Alliance a commitment to neutrality in the war between Spain and its colonies, without denying Spain the right to attempt a reconquest. At that point, British intervention was not intended to promote South American independence but to collaborate in a restoration of the Spanish Empire which would protect British mercantile interests.[24]

This mediation was not only the result of the Napoleonic wars but also due to tensions within British society driven by the economic and political ascendancy of industrial and commercial capital. An indication of this was the immediate reaction to the restoration of Ferdinand VII to the Spanish throne in March 1814: between May and June 1814, the merchants, manufacturers and industrialists of London, Liverpool, Manchester, Exeter, Sheffield and Nottingham (who included in their documentation manufacturers in Glasgow, Paisley, Birmingham, Yorkshire, Staffordshire, Essex, Norwich and Devon), all interested in trade with South America, presented simultaneously and with similar content six petitions to George III raising their concerns about the danger of losing their businesses and capital in the event of a violent restoration of Spanish power in the Americas and the restoration of the old commercial monopoly.[25]

The petitions give a reliable estimate of the level of British economic interest in South America at the time; more than 300 companies, led by those in Liverpool, Manchester and Sheffield, had business interests in the region. Additionally, the petitions reveal the core problem facing British industrial and merchant capital in 1814, as well as the solution to which

24 In fact, Castlereagh urged the United States not to recognize independence, recommending that the United States should allow the British to mediate, to attempt to restore Spanish control (Nichols, 1971: 138–139).
25 TNA, Board of Trade, 1–89.

they aspired. Whereas the Spanish monopoly had practically prohibited the consumption of British goods in the Americas, these were now distributed right across the region to the benefit of British industry. The Spanish king's return to power raised the possibility that the old laws would be restored, thus reducing the region to its former colonial status. This would expose the merchants established in the Americas to ruin, and the British 'middle classes' (and the whole of the British nation) to the loss of the enormous amount of capital accumulated in South America if there was a reduction in the export of manufactured goods. A merchant from Exeter described the "fear entertained by the merchants of Exeter, respecting the safety of their property now existing in South America", warning that British property could be the "object of confiscation".[26] The petitions concluded that the best way to guarantee conditions for trade was a treaty between Great Britain and Spain that guaranteed British capital the possibility of continuing their business interests in South America. In other words, they did not propose at that time (1814), recognition of the revolutionary states but rather recognition of Spanish sovereignty, and even referred to South America as the Spanish colonies.

Although the United States pushed for recognition of the new states, the Spanish refusal to cede control of their colonial trade in favour of British mediation drove European diplomacy to an impasse and the British strategy, agreed by the Holy Alliance at the Congress of Aachen in 1818, came to nothing (Nichols, 1971: 140). The outbreak of revolution in Spain, sparked by General Rafael del Riego's military uprising in Cabezas de San Juan (Cadiz) in 1820, the strengthening of the revolutionary forces in South America, and the 1821 struggle for independence in Greece, gave rise to a new scenario which revealed the limitations of a strategy of mediation and the Holy Alliance's inability to counter "the badly extinguished bonfire of revolution" (Fontana, 2006: 14).

The fact that the "Counterrevolutionary International" (the Holy Alliance) was dealing with a global situation was noted by Castlereagh, who assured the British ambassador in the United States in late 1821 that, unlike the Holy Alliance, Britain would not get involved in other countries' domestic affairs:

> "The wide and increasing spread of the revolutionary movement throughout the American as well as the European Continent. The events of the last few months in Mexico, Peru, the Caraccas, and the Brazils, have nearly decided that both the Americas shall swell the preponderating catalogue of States administered under a system of government, founded upon a Republican or Democratic basis. The like spirit has been advancing in Europe with rapid strides; Spain and Portugal are in the very vortex of a similar convulsion [...] The same spirit has deeply mixed itself in the affairs of Greece. The insurrection throughout European Turkey, in its

---

26 TNA, BT 1–89, J. Buller Esq. Transmitting letter from Mr. Kennaway, 13 June 1814.

organization, in its objects, in its agency, and in its external relations, is in no respect distinguishable from the movements which have preceded it in Spain, Portugal, and Italy... [...] In short, it is impossible that the Emperor should not see that the head of this revolutionary torrent is in Greece, that the tide is flowing in upon his southern provinces in almost an uninterrupted and continuous stream from the other side of the Atlantic; and it is upon this principle, and not upon local views of policy, that his Imperial Majesty will, I doubt not, as a statesman, regulate his conduct."[27]

This was Castlereagh's policy of 'non-intervention' or non-interference with the independence of foreign states, as outlined in the State Paper of 5 May 1820, and later adopted by Canning. Gradually, the political forces realigned.

In Britain, the 'fear' of revolution was not limited to unease caused by the ascendancy of the commercial and industrial bourgeoisie but extended to the rapidly growing working classes. The first indications of radical and potentially anti-capitalist theories, plus the Irish question, made it necessary for the ruling class to smooth over its difficulties and internal differences in order to contain the growth of a social subject which might undermine the entire system of capitalist production. The war cry, "This is Waterloo for you—this is Waterloo!", shouted by the local militia charging a crowd demanding parliamentary representation in St Peter's Field, Manchester, in 1819 (subsequently known as the Peterloo Massacre) sums up perfectly this moment in history when the traditional British ruling classes (nobility and landowners) confronted both an aspiring middle class and at the same time early signs of an independently organized working class (Poole, 2019). It was in this context that Shelley's poem "The Mask of Anarchy" personified Lord Castlereagh as 'Murder' (Cozens, 2018: 44), and attacks on Wellington and the British army as instruments of oppression and despotism greatly increased (Muir, 2015: 150).

In March 1822, the United States recognized the independence of Rio de la Plata, Colombia, Chile and Mexico, a policy consistent with U.S. strategic objectives for territorial expansion in North America and economic intervention in the Americas more widely (Robertson, 1918; Whitaker, 1941; Gleijeses, 1992; Zoellick, 2020). For the British government, this meant that any counterrevolutionary agreements with the Holy Alliance would threaten its gains in the South American markets. In this context, the strategy adopted by British industrial, commercial and financial capital, increasingly linked to the South American markets through trade and loans, changed direction: British mediation no longer had any support, consequently progress had to be made to recognize the political independence of the South American states. In October 1822, John Parish (from Bath) wrote to James Paroissien:

---

27 The Marquess of Londonderry to Sir Charles Bagot, Foreign Office, 14 December 1821, in Castlereagh (vol. XII, 1853: 443).

"I have seen by the papers not only your arrival, but that you had succeeded in a Loan for the Peruvian Government, and I would fain hope before you again leave us, that you may find our Government disposed to acknowledge the Independence of South America, and thereby open a field of commerce, to both countries, to feed and fasten on."[28]

As Miller (1993: 37) points out, however, "while public opinion favoured recognition, the King and some of Castlereagh's cabinet colleagues were still strongly opposed to the idea of giving approval to countries born in rebellion against a monarchy". For this reason, Castlereagh adopted a different strategy which, though breaking the commitment with Spain, sought to sustain the unity of the Holy Alliance by establishing in South America not republics but constitutional monarchies (Kaufmann, 1951: 129). To this end, he took a series of initiatives and the upcoming congress of the Holy Alliance, scheduled to be held in Vienna in September 1822, was to be the scenario in which the details of this policy would be discussed.

First, he ordered his young secretary, Woodbine Parish, to draft a report on the state of the revolutions in South America and, based on the latest information available, to assess whether any political attachment remained between the revolutionary governments and Spain. He also requested assessments of the political situations in the new states (Kay Shuttleworth, 1910: 232).[29]

Later, between April and May 1822, he met the French ambassador in London, François-René de Chateaubriand, to whom he confessed that, although he did not wish to recognize revolutionary governments, he was unable to resist the forces that required him to send commercial agents to South America to protect British trade, and to recognize the flags of insurgent ships arriving at British ports. He presented his plan that, in exchange for recognition and commercial privileges, the new states should adopt monarchical forms of government (Kaufmann, 1951: 130).

In April 1822, as mentioned, the constitutional government of Fernando VII presented its *Manifesto of the Spanish government to foreign powers on the Independence of the Americas*, according to which Spain sought a peaceful reconciliation with its colonies which would lead to "a more free and liberal system for the American provinces" (Kossok, 1968: 128). In turn, Spain demanded that the European powers should not recognize the insurgent colonies as independent states and should respect the principles underpinning "the basis of the integrity, tranquillity and moral reputation of governments". Castlereagh immediately enquired how the Spanish king would implement this

---

28 John Parish to James Paroissien, Bath, 14 October 1822, James Paroissien Papers, Essex Record Office D-DOb C1–25. I thank Karen Racine for sharing this documentation with me.

29 According to Kaufmann (1951: 133), Castlereagh worked on the agenda of the Verona Congress from early 1822.

plan, how Spain would achieve this objective and obtain reconciliation with the colonies. He tried to pin down this new policy in order to evaluate the extent to which it was possible to re-establish his former strategy of mediation.

However, two pieces of news reached London in May 1822 which thwarted Castlereagh's strategy. One was the French refusal to promote constitutional (rather than absolutist) monarchies in South America, and the other was the U.S. recognition of the independence of the new republics.[30] The British government, forced to concede to these events and to increasing pressure from the British middle classes, finally took its first step in the *de facto* recognition of the South American states. On 20 May, Thomas Wallace, Vice President of the Board of Trade, presented to the House of Commons a bill that modified the Laws of Navigation, including a clause introduced by Castlereagh that admitted insurgent vessels to British ports, that is, recognized the flags of the new South American states (Kaufmann, 1951: 132). The government wanted this measure to attract as little publicity as possible, as it still aimed to deal with the issue at the forthcoming Vienna congress. Joseph Planta described this policy to Stratford Canning:

> "If I were to describe our line, I should say it would be one of as little *overt act* as possible, but one of securing to our subjects all the commercial advantages enjoyed by any other nation with the South American Provinces. For this object we shall insert a clause in one of our acts of Parliament, I believe the Navigation Act, to permit and protect this trade [...] But we shall make as little fuss about it as we can, and reason and defend the matter with Spain as absolutely required from us under the circumstances."[31]

This strategy was undermined by renewed pressure from the South American diplomats and the British middle classes, channelled through the Whig opposition in Parliament. In June, in Paris, the Colombian agent Francisco Antonio Zea announced that Colombia would close its ports to ships from countries that did not recognize its independence (Webster, 1938). Shortly after, he repeated this warning in London, where he was feted and honoured

---

30 In the revolutionary capitals, the news of U.S. recognition was widely celebrated which left the British in an uncomfortable position. When the news reached Buenos Aires, Rivadavia gave a reception at the University of Buenos Aires and, according to Consul Forbes's report, "in an animated speech of half an hour, spoke in terms of enthusiastic eulogy of the United States, which he declared to be greater than that of any other government in the world". Forbes also reported that foreigners from Buenos Aires, unable to gainsay US recognition, "made every possible suggestion to depreciate its importance, particularly the English, who asked, in the spirit of their own selfish policy, what the United States were to receive in payment of this Act of nugatory protection [...] Not a solitary Englishman had the generosity to offer me his felicitations on the concession": quoted in Pratt (1931: 315–316).

31 Planta to Stratford Canning, 11 May 1822, in Webster (1925: 584).

by British merchants. At the same time, the Baring Brothers, Barclay and other important bankers in the City of London lobbied Parliament for recognition of the South American states.

Although the plan to promote constitutional monarchies was no longer feasible, the British government still resisted immediate recognition of the revolutionary states and insisted on a common policy, to be presented to the Holy Alliance at the Congress of Vienna. At the beginning of June 1822, Castlereagh met with the ambassadors of Austria, Prussia and Russia, and informed them of the advances of the South American revolutionaries. As with Chateaubriand, he informed Count Lieven of his intention to send consular agents to South America, as well as the failure of the talks with France. The Russian ambassador's report to his government was terse: Castlereagh, he wrote, was a prisoner of the British commercial classes.[32] But commercial pressure was not only felt in Britain. On 3 June 1822, 42 merchants from the Hanseatic cities presented a request to the Commercial Deputation for "public relations [to] be established with the free states of South America", considering it "highly advisable, to install at least commercial agents" (Kossok, 1968: 109).[33]

The inability of the Spanish government to implement a policy of 'reconciliation' with the insurgents, expressed in its silence regarding Castlereagh's proposal, prompted a harsh response. On 28 June 1822, Castlereagh warned the Spanish ambassador in London, Luis de Onís, that some kind of recognition of the South American states by Great Britain was imminent, basing such a decision on "the overruling necessity of the case".[34] In view of Spain's apparent loss of control over its colonies, Castlereagh advised the Spanish government to recognize their independence. He sent his communication to the Holy Alliance, attaching a note in which he stated: "the approaching meeting at Vienna will afford me an opportunity of fully explaining to the allied Cabinet the sentiments of His Majesty's Government upon this important question" (Webster, 1925: 433).

The two revolutionary leaders, Bolívar and San Martín, met in Guayaquil on 26 July 1822 to coordinate a definitive victory over the royalists. Meanwhile British commerce pressed further for recognition of independence. On 20 July, John Lowe, one of London's most powerful merchants, wrote to Castlereagh indicating that he

"look[ed] forward with interest to the prospects of new openings for any interchange of our industry with the products of other countries, and

---

32 Lieven to Nesselrode, 10 June 1822, in Webster (1925: 578).

33 The proposal suggests that public recognition could be dispensed with and that an agent could be dispatched to communicate the desire to initiate commercial relations based on the established tradition of trade between both regions, particularly the port of Hamburg and linen fabrics. See König (2007) and Ott (2008).

34 Castlereagh to Onis, 28 June 1822, in Webster (1925: 423–433).

[the British merchants] feel much anxiety that any advantage now in our reach should not be lost by vacillation or delay [...] And, above all, I would now entreat you to reflect how important it is to be prompt in every measure which can secure to us any lasting trade. Our manufacturers possess everything necessary to maintain their position, if protected and left to themselves; and the country has enterprise and capital enough to maintain its advantages, if not thwarted by inactivity or impeded by restrictions [...] if we are convinced that the power of Spain has ceased to have effect, to what system of politics, to what interests, to what feelings are we subscribing, in not acknowledging the independence of Columbia; Spain may say, I had a right - but can she exercise it? Spain may say Columbia was hers - but Columbia says, We now belong to no one: and can Spain, by efficient force, show to the world that she can enforce her laws, produce obedience and a conformity to her dictates? [...] We may, my lord; continue to subscribe to the wishes of Spain; but Columbia and the free States of South America will adhere to their independence; and we may gain the palm of fealty to old opinions, but we shall be deprived of the riches and the abundance which may be derived from cultivating the friendship of those who have an interest in our friendship, and who have a sincere wish to cultivate it."[35]

On 23 July, the Whig opposition took the industrialists' and merchants' complaints to the House of Commons and demanded the recognition of the South American states. A heated debate followed. Their demand was, once again, rejected with few convincing arguments (Kaufmann, 1951: 132). Castlereagh assured the House of Commons that "he had no hesitation in saying, that he did not think Spain was entitled to detain British vessels, trading with those parts of South America which had declared themselves independent and had obtained a recognition of their independence from other nations" (Ferns, 1960: 106). He wanted to buy time to try to impose the British strategy at the next congress of the Holy Alliance.

a. Castlereagh's instructions for the Vienna–Verona Congress
In late July 1822, just weeks before his suicide and with Woodbine Parish working at his side, Castlereagh drew up a memorandum synthesizing British policy to be discussed at the next congress in Vienna (relocated to the city of Verona). Since he himself would head the delegation, he drafted the text for his own use, and probably to present his strategy to George IV (Nichols, 1971: 21).

The Castlereagh Memorandum has been the subject of numerous historiographical analyses. Here we will mention its most salient points.[36] For

---

35 John Lowe to the Marquess of Londonderry, 27, New Broad Street, July 20, 1822, in Castlereagh (Vol. XII, 1853: 476).
36 Castlereagh's memorandum was sent to the Duke of Wellington on 14 September 1822, the Duke having been appointed the British representative in Verona following

Castlereagh, the three issues that shaped world politics in 1822 were "1. The Turkish question, internal and external. 2. The Spanish question, European and American. 3. The affairs of Italy".[37] The "Spanish question" was divided into two parts, the peninsular and the American. With respect to the first, Britain would remain neutral regarding Riego's liberal uprising in 1820 and, unlike the Holy Alliance, refused to intervene. However, he considered that "the present state of South American affairs is of a more serious nature".

If the current governments of South America remained in power and Spain did not establish its authority, it was inevitable that other countries (apart from the United States and Portugal) would formally recognize them, sooner or later. Castlereagh considered recognition as "more as a matter of time than of principle". The "question of time" had to take into account the political forces within the South American states and, crucially, the existence or otherwise of their relationship with Spain. He classified these states into three types: those which were still fighting; territories where the fighting had ended and new governments were fully established, and those which were still negotiating (or trying to) with Spain. In the first and third cases, no recognition could be forthcoming and the Holy Alliance would have to await the results of the confrontations and negotiations. Obviously, "the real question" was policy towards the states in the second category, to be discussed at Verona. For Castlereagh it was imperative that any discussion should focus on how relations with these states could continue legally, rather than whether they should exist or not; otherwise British trade with South America might be interrupted thus provoking discontent among the mercantile classes.

He proposed three types of possible recognition: *de facto* recognition, which was already in force in Great Britain given the recent modification of the Navigation Laws recognizing the flags of insurgent states; a *more formal* recognition, enacted and communicated by diplomatic agents (which he had already decided to send to the main South American cities); and *de jure* recognition, the only kind of recognition that clashed with the rights of the "former occupant", the king of Spain. Britain would not proceed with *de jure* recognition, as it was up to the two disputing parties to resolve this issue and British *de jure* recognition would amount to interference in domestic affairs.

In conclusion, while the *de facto* recognition had already been implemented, and the resolution of a *de jure* recognition corresponded to Spain, the only

Castlereagh's suicide: "I have the honour to transmit, for your Grace's guidance in the execution of the commission with which his Majesty has been pleased to entrust you in consequence of the lamented death of the Marquis of Londonderry, a Memorandum which was originally drawn up by his Lordship, and having been approved by his Majesty's confidential Servants, was submitted to his Majesty and received his Majesty's sanction ...": Earl Bathurst to Field Marshal the Duke of Wellington, Downing Street, 14 September 1822, in *Despatches* (1867: 284).

37 "Fair Draft of Memorandum. Instructions for the Duke of Wellington", in *Despatches* (1867: 284–288).

practical question remaining was to decide how to advance diplomatic recognition, that is, the appointment of official consuls. Having already suggested this to the Spanish ambassador, the British envoy to Verona had to convince the member states of the Holy Alliance to agree to this policy. Under no circumstances could the British government commit to a common policy that was contrary to these principles.

In summary, the Castlereagh Memorandum openly stated Britain's intention to implement diplomatic (and commercial) recognition of the South American states. This implied a substantive change with respect to the three earlier strategies: territorial annexation; reconciliation between Spain and its colonies, without affecting British trade; and the imposition of constitutional monarchies in the new South American states in exchange for recognition. The factors influencing this political course of action, particularly the strategic objective to protect and develop commerce with South America, have been amply studied. What, then, was the empirical evidence taken into account by the British government, by Castlereagh in particular, to decide on this policy to push for the diplomatic recognition of the South American insurgent states? We can now answer this question in the light of an unpublished document, overlooked by historians to date: at some point in July 1822 Castlereagh's young secretary, Woodbine Parish, presented to him the results of his findings on the current state of the revolutions in South America. As we will see in the next section, an analysis of his report will allow us to more fully understand the memorandum prepared for the Verona congress and, in addition, the policy promoted by George Canning with respect to Latin America.

CHAPTER 3

The Foreign Office Social Class

This chapter describes the historical, social and institutional framework in which Woodbine Parish wrote his 1822 report on the revolutions in South America. We begin by outlining the origins of the Foreign Office, principally during the first three decades of the nineteenth century, attending particularly to its functions, objectives, structure, the role of its employees, social composition, and financing. We then introduce the Parish family to ascertain the social relationships that structured their personal lives and their incorporation into the British diplomatic service.

I. The Foreign Office in the first half of the nineteenth century

a. Origin and functions

The Foreign Office (FO) was created as a state department, independent of the Diplomatic Service in 1782 (Jones, 1971: 11). The Secretary of State for American or colonial affairs had already been abolished, and the FO was created by the union of the former 'Northern Department' (which dealt with questions concerning countries such as Germany, Denmark, Sweden, Poland, Russia, etc.) and 'Southern Department' (dedicated to France, Switzerland, Italy, Spain, Portugal, Turkey, etc.). The Northern Department became the FO and the Southern Department took the name of the 'Home Office' and included the British colonies within its remit (*The Foreign Office*, 1857: 3). On 17 July 1794 a Principal Secretary of State for War was appointed; and to him the business of the colonies (which was carried on at the Home Department) was transferred on 17 March 1801, when the Secretary of State for War had been awarded formal responsibility for colonial matters.

After relocating to two premises on Cleveland Row, St. James's, formerly occupied by the Secretaries of State for the North and South Departments, the FO had to again relocate due to an increase of staff and political importance—first to Cockpit, Whitehall, in 1786 and, finally, to Downing Street, in 1793 (Steiner, 1981: 177; Historians, 1991: 11). According to Southern (2020: 16), "The Foreign Office was created in, and by, a world of social and political turmoil [...] in a world of strict social hierarchy, but one which was beginning to fall apart", in which the British ruling classes, concerned about the development of the social revolutions in the United States and France, understood the need for a formal and centralized direction of foreign affairs in order to suppress any attempt at sedition. In addition, the British defeat in the American War of Independence represented a turning point in the FO and in foreign policy in general, from an aristocratic practice that required minimal bureaucracy to an affair of the first order in the modern state (Dittmer, 2017: 26).

In this sense, the main task of the FO was to carry out, as far as possible, the foreign policies of the British government, which was established by parliamentary majority. The government was derived from that majority, the cabinet heading up the government, and the Secretary for Foreign Affairs (the Foreign Secretary) the minister of state in the cabinet with this responsibility. Accordingly, "the foreign secretary enjoyed a very special place in the British ministerial structure and the Foreign Office was given a degree of Independence unique among other domestic departments. For most politicians only the office of Prime Minister ranked higher that of foreign secretary" (Steiner, 1981: 179).

The various matters dealt with by the FO usually required the attention of other government departments, particularly the War Office, the Treasury and the Board of Trade. The role of the FO in promoting British trade and investment abroad during the first half of the nineteenth century is much debated by historians. Strang (1955: 38) argues that the FO did not understand, or did not take into account, the importance of high finance and commerce in foreign policy, although there were connections between diplomacy and economics. Conversely, Tilley and Gaselee (1933: 227–229) reject the accusations asserting that "the Foreign Office was always concerned for the promotion of trade" referring to "the fact that Chatham [Pitt the Elder] founded an Empire for the benefit of British trade" since "excessive regard for the wishes of British traders lost us the American Colonies, and Canning's South American policy was inspired largely by anxiety for the promotion of British trade, and was strongly supported by the City and other commercial interests". As Otte (2016: 25–26) has pointed out, British business diplomacy in the nineteenth century is the 'Cinderella' of historiography and, with few exceptions (Platt, 1968b), has not been systematically addressed.

The way the nineteenth-century FO operated is also widely debated. Strang (1955: 18–19) argued that the FO became an active and necessary participant in the process of developing international policy, as it could not carry out its obligations without acquiring information on the countries where it was seeking to intervene. The contribution of the FO, in general, and of its diplomats and consuls abroad in particular, was vital. In fact, as he points out, simply acquiring information was not enough. The data had to be correctly summarized and evaluated, to understand the underlying causes of historical events and to come to a decision on a political recommendation which might not always be self-evident. In this way, the reports prepared by the FO, requiring an attentive and thorough consideration of the various world realities, were a key element in the making of state policies and a major contribution to British government. As Dittmer (2017: 32) points out, "what made paper crucial to the practice of foreign policy was not just its ability to circulate widely, but more specifically its ability to circulate *and then accumulate* in an archive that could be accessed by policy makers". In this regard, James Bandinel testified, in 1839, that access to the last 20 years' worth of paper was necessary for the everyday formulation and conduct of British foreign policy.

Nevertheless, the FO in the twentieth century was quite unlike that of the first half of the nineteenth century, and the history of the development of its research department has been thoroughly studied. For Tilley and Gaselee (1933: 42–43, 47), both Castlereagh and Canning gave little importance to the organization of staff. From Strang's (1955: 38–39) perspective, the nineteenth-century FO "was not recognised as having any advisory function" and "British foreign secretaries sought the advice of their officials very much less than they came to do in later times". Steiner (1981: 183) argues that the evolution from a bureaucratic secretariat to a political organ of government was gradual and may be traced in the increasing numbers of staff. Growth was due to the rapid rise in the number of dispatches received: in 1821 the FO received 6,193 dispatches, in 1826 it received 12,402, twice as many. There is no doubt that the age of revolution resulted in the development of the FO (Middleton, 1977: 176). As Joseph Planta testified to the first select committee, in 1839:

> "When I first knew the office there were not above three or four foreign ministers accredited to this country; the number has now increased at least to four or five times that amount. Likewise, our relations with foreign countries were by no means as considerable as they are now; and latterly, in Mr Canning's time, the whole of South America was thrown open too, which almost doubled the business of the foreign office."[1]

During the first half of the nineteenth century the work of the FO would have been mainly bureaucratic, dedicated primarily to maintaining correspondence between the British and foreign governments, and between government departments, in order to assist the Foreign Secretary in his negotiations with ambassadors and ministers (Steiner, 1981: 178). From this perspective, bureaucratic disorganization contributed to potential intelligence failures and often involved the simple neglect of routine business. In this sense, the FO was so slothful and inefficient that many intelligence reports went unread for years (Deacon, 1969; Maffeo, 2000).

Recent studies return to this debate around new and 'old diplomacy', suggesting that such epithets cannot be applied to the nineteenth-century FO which Otte describes as "a knowledge-based organization with efficient information management procedures geared towards informed policy-making",

---

1 *Report from Select Committee on Public Offices (Downing-Street)*. London: Her Majesty's Stationery Office, 1839, 28), quoted in Dittmer (2017: 32).

supported by a homogeneous small elite of officials giving rise to what he refers to as the "Foreign Office mind" (Otte, 2004: 31). In this way, "professional diplomats provid[ed] the strategic basis of British foreign policy" and "understood the reality of power, and for the most part produced effective diplomatic strategy. Such strategy merely reflected the goal of Realism to see the world as it is, not as it should be" (Krasnyak 2019: 44). Scientific knowledge in foreign policy sustained British hegemony during the Victorian era (Krasnyak, 2019: 46).

An analysis of the internal structure of the FO in the first half of the nineteenth century, the functions and social backgrounds of its personnel, as well as its relationship with the other state departments, will illuminate some of these considerations and more fully elucidate the administrative and political framework in which the Woodbine Parish report was produced.

b. The structure: employees and functions

Originally the FO was the responsibility of a secretary of state, a government minister who was assigned to carry out daily tasks, an under-secretary, and ten clerks directed by the chief clerk. These were joined by the staff of the State Paper Office—which not only served the the FO—, comprising a keeper of state papers, a transmitter of state papers and secretary of the Latin language, two commissioners of state papers and one gazette writer and his deputy. In addition, a corps of messengers served the three secretaries of state until 1822, when the FO had its own staff under the control of the librarian (Tilley and Gaselee, 1933: 27, 204). From 1786 a permanent under-secretary assisted the minister, to ensure that administrative reforms would not create problems, and a private under-secretary was to be appointed by the minister, to handle the most confidential matters (also called parliamentarian, although he did not necessarily have to occupy a seat in parliament).[2] The Ministry of Foreign Affairs grew slowly, and its basic structure was retained over time, despite a growing mass of work and increasing political importance (Steiner, 1981: 178). In 1821, the FO staff did not witness great changes, and consisted of two under secretaries, a chief clerk, three senior clerks and 13 junior clerks, a librarian, a sub-librarian, a clerk in the chief clerk's department, a private secretary and a precis writer, a translator, Turkish interpreter, a collector and transmitter of papers (Tilley and Gaselee, 1933: 48).

---

2 Steiner (1981: 183) affirms that, although initially both under-secretaries held the position due to political favour, after 1795 it became customary to replace only one of the two when the minister in charge was changed, so that the parliamentary undersecretary identified more closely with the minister and left office when he did. According to Otte (2009: 2–3), following the formation of the FO, the new ministry adopted the practice of the old Northern Department of having two under-secretaries: "Joseph Planta, an Under-Secretary from 1817 until 1827 and in many ways much more akin to a modern PUS (Permanent Under-Secretary) than any of his predecessors, still regarded himself as a 'political gentleman' rather than a permanent official".

Table 3.1: The FO during the Castlereagh and Canning administrations (1812–1823)

Secretaries of State	Under-Secretaries of State		Private Secretaries to the Secretaries of State	Precis Writers	Chief Clerk
	Permanent	Parliamentary			
1812, 4 March Robert Henry Stewart (Viscount Castlereagh)	1809 William Richard Hamilton	1812, 28 February Edward Cooke	1812, 10 October Edward Michael Ward 1814, 5 July Joseph Planta	1809, 5 January Joseph Planta	Apr. 1792 – September 1817 Thomas Bidwell
		1817, 25 July Joseph Planta	1817, 5 January Richard Meade	1817, 5 January George Lenox-Conyngham 1817, July Thomas Cartwright	
			1819, 5 July John William Robert Kerr	1819, December Sir G. Hamilton Seymour	September 1817 – January 1824 Stephen Rolleston
1822, 16 September George Canning	1822 Joseph Planta	1822, 22 January Richard Charles Francis Meade	1822, 29 January Sir George Hamilton Seymour, G. C. B.	1822, 29 January Lord Arthur Marcus Cecil Hill	
		1823, 6 January Lord Francis Nathaniel Conyngham	1822, 10 October Lord William George Frederick Cavendish Bentinck	1822, 11 October George Augustus	

Treaty Department: John Brodribb Bergue (1817, 5 January); Librarian: Lewis Hertslet (1810, 6 January)

Source: My own table based on *The Foreign Office List* (1857) and Historians (1991).

In 1822, when Canning took office, their salaries were as follows: at the head, the Secretary of State for Foreign Affairs received a salary of £6,000; two under-secretaries, each received £2,500/£2,000 (the chief assistant secretary £2,500 and the other £1,000 each); the chief clerk, who followed in seniority, earned a salary of £1,811; the 12 senior clerks between £1,149 and £314; finally, the three supernumerary clerks from £100 to £180, although the librarian had another income, as 'Superintendent of the Establishment of Foreign Service Messengers', a corps of 38 messengers, of which 18 were in the service of the FO, dedicated to the safe delivery of state papers that passed between the Secretary for Foreign Affairs and British representatives abroad (Cecil, 1923: 557–558; Jones-Parry, 1934; Bindoff, 1935: 317).

In short, throughout the first half of the nineteenth century the FO remained "an uncomplicated, compact organisation easily controlled by the Secretary of State" (Middleton, 1977: 154). Nevertheless, despite the preponderant position of the Foreign Secretary himself, the role of the officials and clerks was not much less. British foreign policy before 1914 was not formulated exclusively by the Foreign Secretary and his cabinet colleagues; it was strongly influenced by the FO officials (Watt, 1965; Steiner, 1969).

In practice, both under-secretaries reported to the secretary of state and their duties were to carry out his orders, prepare draft letters and other special instruments as needed, to handle confidential matters, and to manage and generally supervise the work in the office (Jones, 1971: 15). Upon assuming Castlereagh, the FO Secretary of State in 1812, "One Under Secretary took the Northern Department, and one the Southern Department, the old distribution having to this extent survived" (Tilley and Gaselee, 1933: 42). Jones-Parry (1934: 314) argues that the ways in which Castlereagh and Canning organized the FO tasks cannot be clearly differentiated, and that if during Castlereagh's tenure the greatest burden of responsibility fell on one of the two under-secretaries, Edward Cooke over William Hamilton, this was not due to a bureaucratic division but because Cooke was more fully in the confidence of the secretary of state. Similarly, when Canning took over, Joseph Planta's skills and judgment would have brought him closer to the minister, who gave him the vast majority of the work. In other words, the distribution of tasks in the 1820s was not so much linked to bureaucratically established responsibilities, but to the degree of trust the secretary of state had in a particular member of staff.

In addition, the secretary of state was assisted by two officers, whose appointment were left to him, and who did not necessarily have to formally belong to the office: the précis writer, dedicated to summarizing incoming official dispatches and copying all outgoing for the private use of the minister; and the private secretary, who handled his private correspondence. Both positions were for young men in their 20s and were rarely held for more than two years, sometimes only for a few months. Although they earned the same salary (£300 a year), and although the précis writer was originally listed as the senior position, the private secretary soon assumed greater status and was considered a posting of real privilege (Bindoff, 1935: 153). Even if the private secretaries did not constitute an independent department, they were given a prominent role in the administration of the Diplomatic Service, and when the secretary of state ceased to be interested in minor appointments, the private secretary assumed that responsibility too. This included general management of the junior diplomats and their promotion, subject to the control of the under-secretary, if necessary (Tilley and Gaselee, 1933: 206). For Steiner (1981: 183), "the private secretary's office became an imperium in empire for it was the private secretary who, acting in the foreign secretary's name, recommended candidates for examinations, and arranged promotions, transfers and postings". In short, both positions were springboards to a diplomatic career and formed an important part of a small circle of staff devoted primarily to the political affairs of the FO (Bindoff, 1935: 153).

No less important was the role played by the so-called clerks. The chief clerk's department was the oldest in the FO, devoted mainly to the internal economy, the layout of the building, and the messenger service abroad and at home. He also shared with the private secretaries (and later with the head of the Consular Department), the management of the diplomatic and consular services. At the same time, the chief clerk was the expert in rules and regulations, as well as the authority in all matters of finance, making decisions which previously were considered almost indisputable, about what could and could not be done (Tilley and Gaselee, 1933: 201). According to Steiner, this was "a prestigious position [...] but was not involved in its political business"; the clerks

> "copied despatches, recorded correspondence in registers, made fair drafts and copies of important papers and cyphered and deciphered despatches. They worked from eleven to four but by the end of the eighteenth century the workload had become a heavy one though pay remained poor. The growth in the size of the establishment during the nineteenth century did not match the increasing amount of daily correspondence. In 1822, in addition to the two under-secretaries, the establishment consisted of one chief clerk, four first class or senior clerks, six second class clerks, six third class or junior clerks, three assistant junior clerks, a supplementary clerk in the chief clerk's department, a private secretary and a précis writer, a librarian and sub-librarian, a translator, two office keepers, a door porter and a printer."
>
> (Steiner, 1981: 178)

Steiner concludes that, curiously, during the first half of the nineteenth century, the political departments that safeguarded the archives and provided the information required by the secretary of state were of less importance than the administrative departments headed up by senior clerks. Also, while the chief clerk continued to administer financial affairs, the senior clerks ran the departments which had emerged in the 1820s (such as the Treaty and Royal Letter Department, the Consular Department and the Slave Trade Department). Finally, the political divisions were administered by the chief clerk's assistant. Later, Palmerston expressed dissatisfaction with this system in which 'second class clerks' carried out tasks of sufficient importance and confidentiality to be handed over to senior staff in the department.

However, even in its lower echelons, the FO did not employ staff who were restricted to purely bureaucratic tasks. As Algernon Cecil points out, at that time "the doctrine that a public servant has no public opinions was not yet established" (Cecil, 1923: 554). In this sense, Jones (1971: 144) argues that the "division of labour between intellectual and mechanical work was more easily adopted by administrative departments than by the Foreign Office, where the political work, the formulation of foreign policy, was still the most important function of the Cabinet". In this way, the FO "employed established clerks because it was thought that state secrets should be known only to clerks whose family and social connexions were identical to those of their political masters". Similarly, Steiner (1981: 185) states that the FO "resisted the introduction of a class of copying clerks and refused to countenance any distinction between intellectual and mechanical work" because "the business [...] was considered far too confidential [...] to be given to copying clerks. Even the most mechanical work, since it involved matters of the highest importance, had to be done by the diplomatic establishment".

This included the lowest echelon of the diplomatic service: the attachés. According to Bindoff (1935: 150–151), "the typical attaché [had] his formal education behind him. The average age of entry of all attachés from 1812 to 1860 was 21 years". As we will see, the vast majority were recruited from the most exclusive schools in England, Eton and Harrow, and from a very young age joined the system referred to as 'unpaid attacheship'. This was an imperfect mechanism as it led to a high level of desertion, due to various factors but mainly due to not receiving any pay for their work. The basic agreement involved an exchange in which the young attaché received, in exchange for his services, house, food and the experience necessary for the development of his future career (Bindoff, 1935: 145).

Castlereagh in 1816 and Canning in 1823 sought to remedy this weak point in the system by offering a salary to all FO attachés, which ensured greater stability for the newcomers and was considered the first step in a diplomatic career (the next step would be to obtain a secretary's posting in one of the world's legations). For this reason, the 'FO route' to a diplomatic career was the most advantageous and demonstrates the importance of earning a salary. But the salaries were so low that a certain degree of financial independence was required, which brings us to the debate about the "governmental business élite" (Jones, 1983a: 238) taking into account the social class of the staff employed by the FO and the diplomatic service.

c. The FO social class: recruitment, promotions and social background

Recent studies have focused on the formation of a "Foreign Office Mind" in the nineteenth century due to a restricted and elitist social base (Otte, 2011: 6). Also, Southern (2020) has rekindled the debate around social class and the FO, that is, the social classes that throughout its history directed its affairs and determined its structure. A key factor in this regard is the history of FO recruitment and promotion.

While the attachés were selected by the diplomats, all the FO clerks were appointed by the Foreign Secretary (Steiner, 1981: 178). Similarly, both the précis writer and the private secretary were under his personal patronage, and the Foreign Secretary "followed his own inclination as between giving them to clerks in the Office or to young men outside, though the precis writership, perhaps as the more 'public' of the two, was in practice more often held by a clerk" (Bindoff, 1935: 152–153). These two positions were filled by men chosen by the Foreign Secretary from among his relatives or friends. They were generally retained while he remained at the head of the FO or "until signs of an approaching change of government made it advisable to have [their] translation into diplomacy" (Bindoff, 1935: 155).

Furthermore, promotion was in the hands of the secretary of state and in those of his private secretaries who acted for him, dictating appointments for consulates and vice consulates:

> "The friendship of the Foreign Secretary was thus perhaps the most important single asset for an ambitious diplomatist. [...] It is noteworthy, too, that promotion among ex-private secretaries and precis writers, all proteges of Foreign Secretaries, was considerably more rapid than the general average. On the other hand, the death or resignation of a Foreign Secretary might spell disaster to his friends hopes of promotion."
>
> (Bindoff, 1935: 165)[3]

A large part of the staff employed at the FO and in the diplomatic and consular services were in post thanks to the Foreign Secretary's family, friend and business ties and networks (Otte, 2011: 9). However, this patronage was not simply that of one individual but embedded in a process of political and social selection. In this sense, Bindoff (1935: 165) shows that, in the first half of the nineteenth century, 'social convenience' prevailed over learning or intelligence when appointing personnel in the diplomatic service, and influence and patronage were more important than seniority and merit. According to Steiner (1981: 182–183):

> "The typical candidate then came from a good family, attended a prestig-ious public school, and, in the Victorian period, went abroad to France,

---

3 While most civil servants aspired to a position in Europe, those willing to cross the Atlantic were generally promoted earlier than those who chose to wait for a better option (Bindoff, 1935: 167).

Germany or both for a year to live with a family already known for improving the linguistic capabilities of aspiring diplomats [...] Once in the Office, men joined a circle of relatives, friends, and acquaintances who shared similar backgrounds and experiences. These men joined the same clubs and moved in the same political and diplomatic circles."

The FO elite was restricted to these circles and showed a marked bias against merchants until the first decade of the twentieth century. Similarly, Strang states that the systems of selection for the diplomatic service were mainly governed in this earlier phase by social prejudice, when foreign affairs remained the preserve of social oligarchies (Strang, 1955: 72). In Jones' view, the FO was one of the most conservative and aristocratic departments of the British government and its staff were mostly members of the most powerful British families, which reduced the influence of, in his words, the 'middle-class intellectual elites' and the important administrative innovations incorporated into other areas of government throughout the nineteenth century (Jones, 1971: 41). Platt (1968b: xxvi) also concluded that "the Foreign Service from the ministers down to the junior clerks and attachés was traditionally aristocratic". Steiner (1984: 19–20) writes, "diplomacy in the pre-1914 period was in the hands of a tiny elite. Its forms and practices were very much the product of an aristocratic society that persisted even after that class lost its position of primacy"; its main leaders came from the "traditional landed class which had long served the state" and "those who served these foreign secretaries came from a similar social caste". She argues that in the nineteenth century Parliament and the FO evolved in different ways: while in the former there was a greater presence of the mercantile and manufacturing classes, the FO maintained its "aristocratic bias" due to an "absence of men from trading and manufacturing families", reinforced by the homogeneity acquired by their educational exclusivism when recruiting personnel. As Ray Jones (1981) has indicated, this widely held consensus that the FO and the diplomatic service "remained the preserve of the aristocracy" dates back to the mid-nineteenth century.

This view persists today. For example, Otte (2011: 7) argues that "Britain's foreign policy elite was a small and self-contained establishment. This made for social exclusivity, and it reinforced the principal tenets of the 'official mind'. Its tone and ethos reflected the section of society from which it was recruited. The Foreign Office was one of the smaller Whitehall departments". He adds: "Only men from a certain social background tended to apply for the still prerequisite nomination by the Foreign Secretary to become candidates for the entrance examination. As one observer noted in the 1880s, the Foreign Office and diplomatic service were in the hands of 'a fraternity of gentlemen clerks, born and brought up in the official purple'" (Otte, 2011: 9). The fact that the FO was exclusive and aristocratic was evidenced in its method of recruitment, based on the patronage of the minister, and that, as stated, most of its officials were recruited from

Eton and Harrow. This system prevailed until the middle of the nineteenth century, when standardized entry examinations were established for the civil service.

Notwithstanding the above, Ray Jones (1983) takes a different view. He shows that more than half the officials belonged to families of 'professionals', which suggests a wider social base. In the first place, he sets out the difficulties for studying personnel during the first half of the nineteenth century due to the lack of systematic documentation, which explains the reason why the vast majority of studies concentrate on the second half and the beginning of the twentieth century (Jones, 1981: 50–51). He overcomes this problem by compiling a collective biography and concludes that the diplomatic service, far from continuing to be an ally of the aristocracy, was transformed into what he refers to as an 'intellectual elite' in British public service. Nevertheless, the system of patronage and nominations, which encouraged candidates belonging to the same social world as those who were already in the FO, prevailed, so that "both the social background and schools of the clerks of that social class and not intellectual attainment was the basic career criterion for a prospective Foreign Office clerk" (Jones, 1971: 64). In this sense, the continuation of social exclusivity in the British diplomatic service should not be confused with a predominance of aristocratic interests within it.

Southern (2020: 8) also questions the extent to which "the accusation that the British Foreign Office is an elitist institution" is correct using social class analysis. He points out that, although the FO and the diplomatic service had independent recruitment processes and contracting systems, their members did belong to a similar social and educational background: as in the rest of Europe, the diplomat of the establishment tended to come from the landed classes. As Steiner (1981: 181) indicated, it was the children of the aristocracy and nobility, many of whom had already engaged in professional careers, who were drawn into a diplomatic career. But Southern points out that this cannot be said for all FO officials; those who held the lowest positions should be considered differently. His overall conclusion challenges the absolute dominance of the aristocracy and landowning nobility. He argues that the FO staffing and leadership expressed the evolution of British society in which the industrial bourgeoisie eroded the power of the aristocracy, while still excluding the working class (Southern, 2020: 16).

In short, the opening of British diplomacy to what Southern calls the "middle classes", that is, the industrial and commercial bourgeoisie, abandoning recruitment exclusively from the aristocracy, began in earnest when the Whig historian Thomas Macaulay argued in 1833 that recruitment for the Indian Civil Service had to be through competitive examinations. However, the influx of recruits representing the commercial and industrial classes is earlier, as demonstrated by the development of the consular service.

d. The relationship between the FO and the diplomatic and consular services in the nineteenth century

In the mid-twentieth century, Strang (1955) described the 'Foreign Service' as the union between the home country's ministry of foreign affairs and the diplomatic and consular establishments abroad. While the FO was the headquarters of British diplomatic activity, the overseas establishments represented the front through which it operated, though both performed equivalent functions. The consular establishments would deal, for the most part, with the local provincial and municipal authorities rather than with the central governments in the capital cities and would be less concerned with general political questions as they concentrated on promoting British trade and looking after the individual interests of British subjects and companies.

Historical studies have shown how the Ministry of Foreign Affairs evolved, indicating the differences between the 'Old Foreign Office', of the late eighteenth century and much of the nineteenth century, and the modern one, the result of the 1906 and 1943 reforms, which consolidated a process of merger ('Amalgamation') between the FO, the diplomatic service, the consular service, the commercial diplomatic service and the overseas information services (Larner, 1972). In other words, although British diplomatic and consular representatives abroad were appointed between the sixteenth and early nineteenth centuries, their appointment was not in the hands of a bureaucratically unified body.

In its origins, the FO home staff were matched by a correspondingly small network of diplomatic posts overseas, with 21 missions in 1785, only three of which (Paris, Madrid and Constantinople) were headed by ambassadors (Historians, 1991). There are different views on the development and links established between the FO and the rest of the diplomatic services in the first half of the nineteenth century. Strang (1955: 68) points out that diplomatic and consular officials were separated, as diplomatic relations would have been considered exclusively political issues (Strang, 1955: 110). Similarly, Steiner (1981: 180) claims that, in terms of organization, the FO remained separate from the diplomatic service and both were independent from the consular service, each having its own recruitment, examinations, and career system. Transfers between them were exceedingly rare, "consuls often graced an ambassador's table and their reports were rarely read either by the head of the mission or by anyone on the political side of the Foreign Office" (Steiner, 1981: 180). Even Steiner suggests not only a separation between the services, but even a degree of antagonism as FO officials dubbed their diplomatic colleagues "social butterflies", while the latter referred to the FO as "office 'drudges'" who ignored their advice and failed to keep them properly informed. Diplomatic positions were unattractive for FO staff because the cost of living abroad was high and there was no positive incentive in the form of payment or promotion to facilitate exchanges. Nevertheless, Steiner argues that members of the diplomatic service generally experienced, if only briefly, a period of employment at the FO.

On the other hand, Bindoff (1935: 157) argues that the careers in the different diplomatic corps were not independent, and that there was a permanent exchange, especially when the consular service was growing and improving its organization. This was the case with "the advent of a new type of mission, nominally diplomatic, but designed primarily for the protection and furtherance of British commercial interests. Such were the Central and South American missions established by Canning and Palmerston".

In fact, between 1820 and 1827, the three services were integrated. After Castlereagh's suicide, the economist Joseph Hume criticized the excessive salary received by the British consul in Rio de Janeiro and denounced the corrupt exercise of patronage in the selection of consuls which resulted in incompetent personnel. Canning therefore reorganized the service; in October 1822 he drew up a list of applicants for the consular and diplomatic positions with references from their respective patrons (Jones, 1983). The list named more than 70 candidates, among whom were James Henderson (who was interested in a post anywhere in South America and was sponsored by Lord Lowther and Thomas Wallace, vice president of the Board of Trade, and Canning's great friend), and Woodbine Parish (who applied for the post of consul in Buenos Aires, although, strikingly, without a sponsor—the space reserved for the patron's name is left blank).[4]

All the patrons were linked in some way to Canning, "personal friends, constituency affiliates, diplomatic or consular service professionals, political colleagues [...], representatives of the court" and "officials of government departments of one kind or another", constituting a kind of "professional elite" of "men of business [...] hard-working officials who behind the facade of brilliant oratory from the front benches carried on the real work of government" (Jones, 1983: 234). These professional 'men of business' sought to recruit civil servants who, like them, were efficient and hard-working thus forming a professional elite irrespective of the patronage claims of the aristocracy. At that time, these professionals performed "the functions of both the junior minister and the permanent secretaries of modern government" and included among them "'the professional experts of the city' whose services were constantly being utilized by government departments" (Jones, 1983: 235–236).

In line with this view, the most influential man on Canning's list was Joseph Planta, through whose office most of the correspondence relating to consular patronage appears to have passed. Planta joined the FO as a clerk in 1802, and thereafter rose to become under-secretary in 1817, remaining in office for a decade: "his family tree reveals the network of relationships that bound together these 'men of business'" (Jones, 1983: 236). It is this connection that explains why Parish did not need a patron for his application: his

---

4 "List of Applicants for Consulships", October 1822, Leeds Public Library, Archives Department, George Canning Papers, Bundle 136, transcript in Jones (1983a: 233).

family was directly related to Planta's, through his grandfather, John Parish (Superintendent of Ordnance in the Tower of London), who was married to Elizabeth Planta, daughter of the Rev. Andrew Planta (Chaplain to George III and Assistant Librarian at the British Museum), father of Joseph Planta (Chief Librarian at the British Museum) and grandfather of Joseph Planta (son), who went on to have an outstanding career at the FO and, as we shall see, became a close friend of Woodbine Parish.

A key chapter in this history is Canning's reorganization of the consular department in 1825 and his appointment of not only a superintendent but also of all the attachés, having relieved the diplomats of this responsibility (Tilley and Gaselee, 1933: 47, 252). Since then, as we will see in the case of Parish, the same individual could move quickly from a position in the FO (clerk and Castlereagh's private secretary until his death), to a consular position (consul in Buenos Aires in 1823), and to a diplomatic post (*chargé d'affaires* in Buenos Aires in 1825) in the course of three years.

In this sense, Bindoff (1935: 157) rejects the hypothesis that the FO did not employ specialized commercial personnel until the end of the nineteenth century, arguing that "Canning professed himself opposed to giving diplomatic appointments to consuls, but the evident advantage of having men with commercial experience and local knowledge at these posts led his successors, though neither of set rule nor invariably, to promote consuls of proved ability". In other words, the case of Parish was not an exception, and

> "In the Central and South American missions, which accounted for 10 of the 12 appointments, the consul was usually made into a diplomat by easy stages. First given the diplomatic label 'and *charge' d' affaires*' as a suffix to his consular rank, he reached the second stage when the '*charge' d' affaires*' stood first in his title, to become finally, if he were fortunate, a full minister plenipotentiary."
>
> (Bindoff, 1935: 158)

II. The Parish family

To understand the social position of the author of the 1822 report commissioned by Castlereagh, we must refer to Parish's family and, in particular, to his father, also named Woodbine, an important London merchant whose business linked the United Kingdom with the Netherlands and Italy.

a. Woodbine Parish (father)

Woodbine Parish (father) was born on 17 August 1768, just before his parents moved to Ireland.[5] He was five years old when his father died, and

---

5 For both brief biographical sketches, see "Death of Sir Woodbine Parish, K. C. H."
   (21 August 1882); "Obituary" (October 1882); Ehrenberg (1925); Busaniche (1958);

he was adopted by his uncle, the merchant William Woodbine, of Yarmouth, England. In 1777 he was sent to study at the English College of Liege and, in 1780, he was invited to visit his uncle, John Parish, the Superintendent of Ordnance at the Tower of London, where he lived. There he met Joseph Planta, Chief Librarian of the British Museum and his son (the future prominent FO official), and they developed a close friendship.

After a short stay in London in 1783, he was sent to Livorno to live with an agent connected to his uncle's company. By the age of 21, when he returned to London to assist his uncle in the company, like many young men of his class, he had already visited China, the West Indies, Spain, Italy and most of the Mediterranean ports. Thanks to his experience and his command of French and Italian, he was sent as a commercial agent to Paris, the Netherlands and present-day Germany. The death of his uncle, in 1793, left him in charge of the company when he was still only 25 years old. In 1794, he joined the regiment of the Light Horse Volunteers, where he made important political connections, with Spencer Perceval (future British Prime Minister), Colonel Charles Herries (father of John Charles Herries, Chancellor of the Exchequer in 1827 and President of the Board of Trade in 1830) and Nicholas Vansittart (Chancellor of the Exchequer, 1812–1822). Two years later, in 1796, his son Woodbine was born.

At the beginning of the nineteenth century, Parish (father) was a partner in Lloyd's Coffee House[6] and was on the whole successful in his commercial enterprises, which lasted from 1792 till 1814. The following year, 1815, Nicholas Vansittart (then Chancellor of the Exchequer) offered him the post of Chairman of the Board of Excise in Scotland. Parish moved with his family to Edinburgh and held that position until 1823. In this year, an Act of Parliament was passed for the consolidation of the Revenue Boards of Scotland and Ireland with the Board in London. Parish accepted the reform and was given the post of Customs Commissioner for the United Kingdom.[7] In late 1830, having been recommended by Lord Bexley (Nicholas Vansittart), he was knighted with the Military Order of the Bath, presented by King George IV.[8] The following year, Parish and the 'scions of nobility' of the Board of Excise were criticized publicly for

Cutolo (1978); Fast (2001); Parish (2004); Hanon (2005) and Howat (2019). The principal source is the complete biography written by Woodbine Parish's granddaughter, Nina Kay Shuttleworth (1910), the greatest advantage of which is to have taken into account private correspondence and Parish's personal diary. Since then, no other historian has managed to consult these documents, as indicated in the correspondence between H. S. Ferns and Liborio Justo (1968: 545–547).

6 *Caledonian Mercury*, 30 April 1801.

7 "From the London Gazette of Saturday, Sept. 27", *Morning Chronicle*, 29 September 1823.

8 *Morning Post*, 2 December 1830.

having business interests while holding public office.[9] He therefore retired with a government life pension of £1,000 a year.

Some historians state that Woodbine Parish (son) had close family connections with the merchant from Bath, John Parish (whose company was one of the most powerful in Hamburg), and with the brothers John and William Parish Robertson.[10] However, these men did not share a common family tree, though possibly some distant ancestor.[11]

b. Woodbine Parish (son)

Woodbine Parish (son) was born in London on 14 September 1796 and, after attending school in Essex, went on to study at Eton College (facilitated by his father's social and political position). He took up his first government post at the age of 16 in the office of John Charles Herries.[12] In 1814, he was sent to Sicily to supervise the evacuation of the island by the British troops fighting Napoleon. The following year, he accompanied the expedition to Naples that restored the Bourbon dynasty after the defeat of Murat and, on his return journey, crossed the field of Waterloo a month after the battle. In 1815 Parish was appointed attaché to the Foreign Secretary Lord Castlereagh, and joined the British delegation travelling to Paris as Castlereagh's junior secretary (Middleton, 1977: 300). This post led to Parish developing a close relationship with Castlereagh and directly involved him in the most important political events in Europe leading to the establishment of a new post-Napoleonic order. In fact, it was Parish who wrote, in his own handwriting, the final text of the Treaty of Paris, on 20 November 1815.

---

9 *The Times*, 18 April 1831, p. 4 (The Times Digital Archive, accessed 24 November 2019).

10 José María Rosa (1964: 23) writes "Woodbine Parish (...) was another relative of the Parish of Bath and the Parish Robertson and Planta, who formed a dynasty devoted in the *Foreign* [Office] to the speciality of *el Plata* affairs". Likewise, Rock (2019: 54) states that Parish "was related to the Parishes of Hamburg and Bath and therefore to the Robertson brothers".

11 According to Kay Shuttleworth, the Parish family lived in Axholm in Lincolnshire, "where they had a respectable landed estate" before the revolution of 1666, but devotion to the royalists lost them their lands during the civil war. Woodbine Parish's direct ancestors date back to the early eighteenth century. Josiah Parish had four children, one of whom, David, married Mary Vanner of York; his son, Henry, born 19 December 1737, was Woodbine Parish's grandfather. For his part, the merchant, John Parish, was born on 5 March 1742, in Leith, Scotland, and moved from Edinburgh to Hamburg in 1755, accompanying his father, George Parish (Ehrenberg, 1925; Fast, 2001). The brothers Parish Robertson born in Kelso, Roxburgh, in Scotland, in 1792 and 1793 respectively, were the sons of a banker and, by the maternal line, were related to John Parish of Bath, who was their grandfather (Hanon, 2005: 705–706).

12 He was the son of Colonel Herries, the old friend of Woodbine Parish's father, and invited the young Woodbine to join his staff.

Figure 3.1: Sir Woodbine Parish (1796–1882)
National Portrait Gallery, London

On his return to London, Parish joined Joseph Planta (son) in Castlereagh's
private secretariat and was tasked with sorting out the vast amount of
post-1815 documentation. According to Middleton (1977: 300), he served
as clerk of the FO between January and June, 1816. In mid-1816, the staff
were reduced in number and Parish took up a position abroad, attached to a
special mission on the island of Corfu (present-day Greece), alongside Lord

Thomas Maitland, High Commissioner for the Ionian Islands.[13] He was appointed with Thomas Cartwright (later consul general in Constantinople and minister in Sweden) to arrange with Ali Pasha de Yanina in Albania the cession of Parga and indemnities for the Parganots.

When Parish returned to England in 1817 he rejoined Castlereagh's secretariat and was appointed clerk at the FO.[14] His concerns, like those of British diplomacy generally, were focused on the restoration of the 'European system' for peacetime, particularly to ensure the stability of the Bourbon dynasty to reign in France without the support of the troops of the Holy Alliance (Austria, Russia and Prussia). In 1818, the FO entrusted Parish with another important task at the heart of European politics: to accompany Castlereagh in the British delegation to a new congress of the Holy Alliance to be held in Aix-la-Chapelle.

During preparations for the congress, Parish's connections meant he was the official chosen to meet the financier Nathan Meyer Rothschild (with whom he had been in daily contact in 1814 and 1815) to obtain funds to subsidize the expensive British entourage. In a letter to his father, he described both the success of his meeting, in which he obtained a credit of £10,000 sterling, and his surprise at the financier's detailed knowledge of the members of the delegation travelling to Paris, even before this had been decided by the FO itself.

In November 1819 the diplomatic career of Woodbine's younger brother, Henry Headley Parish, began as FO clerk (Middleton, 1977: 300). Two years later, in October 1821, Woodbine Parish formed part of the retinue accompanying the recently crowned George IV on his journey to Hanover. Castlereagh (who by then had succeeded his father as Marquis of Londonderry) was ill for a time and his reliance on Parish strengthened the relationship between Parish and his political mentor. Parish became the person closest to the minister, working with him side by side from the early hours of the morning until the early hours of the next day, preparing documents, taking notes from dictation and carrying out his instructions. In a letter to his father, Parish described the strength of the bond between them: "a more kind-hearted and considerate master never breathed; it has been an immense gratification to me to have been so much with him" (Kay Shuttleworth, 1910: 224).

Castlereagh compensated his young secretary's dedication by sending him home as soon as possible, and Parish arrived in London on 20 November 1821. Also, in early 1822, Castlereagh entrusted him with a task of great political responsibility: as part of the preparations for the next congress of

13 In Argentina, Maitland is known for his *Plan to capture Buenos Aires and Chile, and then emancipate Peru and Quito* (1800) which probably showed San Martín how to cross the Andes. See Terragno (1998).

14 "STATEMENT, containing the Ranks, Dates of Appointments, and further remarks respecting those Persons now living who have served or are now serving under the Foreign Office (at home or abroad)", in *The Foreign Office List* (1857: 71).

the Holy Alliance, to be held in Vienna, he was to write of a report on the state of the revolutions in South America.[15] According to Kay Shuttleworth (1910: 232):

> "The events that led to South American emancipation were very little known in England, or indeed in Europe with the exception of Spain in the early part of the nineteenth century, and previous to the Congress of Verona Lord Londonderry wished for such information as was then available to be collected for his use. This was done by Parish, who was at that time in the Foreign Office, and his account, compiled from Admiralty papers and other sources, gives a clear idea of the early history of the South American States, which is still unfamiliar to many persons in this country."

Instead of examining this report, Shuttleworth moves on to discuss Parish's analysis of the history of Rio de la Plata, published almost two decades later in his book *Buenos Ayres and the Provinces of the Rio de la Plata* (Parish, 1839). The report on the South American revolutions of 1822 is not mentioned in any of the biographies or studies dedicated to Woodbine Parish.

The handwritten report confirms the context in which it was produced, starting with Parish's initial clarification: "Memorandum: These papers were prepared for Lord Londonderry [Castlereagh] to take to the Congress of Verona, to which I was preparing to accompany them—when in consequence of his Death—The Duke of Wellington went in his place. W. P.".[16] Between the end of July and the beginning of August 1822, Parish brought the documents to Castlereagh, as reported in a letter he sent to his father on 12 August after learning of the Foreign Secretary's shocking suicide six days earlier: "You may imagine my grief at the loss of my much loved and honoured master, a loss heavy enough for me, but for the nation quite irreparable. [...] I saw him a few days before his death, when I went to town with some papers I had to prepare for him to take to Verona" (Kay Shuttleworth, 1910: 225–226).[17] In the same letter, Parish reported that,

> "He was in the Under-Secretary's Office, and showed (at what I don't know) an impatience and irritation so unusual in him, that I was greatly struck by it [...] I had observed such a strange difference from his usual manner, that it had left upon me an undefinable impression that something

---

15 Castlereagh and the FO worked on the agenda of the Vienna Congress, held finally in Verona, from the beginning of 1822, according to Kaufmann (1951: 133).

16 Sir Woodbine Parish, South America. Volume containing printed and manuscript reports prepared for the Congress of Verona, 1822, The Royal Geographical Society (TRGS), SWP/3.

17 The author does not give the date of Parish's letter to his father, although she states it was written in Reigate, a week after Castlereagh's suicide, which suggests 19 August 1822.

had gone very wrong with him; it was perhaps the beginning of the malady, which showed itself so unmistakably afterwards, in his interview with the King, the Duke of Wellington, and others."

(Kay Shuttleworth, 1910: 226)

This last statement indicates that the meeting between Parish and Castlereagh was before the minister met with the king and Wellington, on 9 August, to obtain their approval of the policy to be announced in Verona, in which "he showed clear signs of insanity" (Bartlett, 1966: 262). In other words, Castlereagh drew up his famous Memorandum and Instructions for the Verona Congress having received Parish's report, or, at least, being aware of its content. A detailed study of this document will clearly indicate the link between Castlereagh's policy towards Spain and South America and his secretary's analysis of the South American revolutions. However, due to his master's suicide, Parish was unable to go to Verona himself.[18]

18 The letter to his father ends: "There is an end now of my going to Verona; under any circumstances I had no particular wish to be of the party, and now of course other arrangements must be made, but for this Lord Londonderry's successor must be named, it will probably be either the Duke of Wellington or Canning, if he will give up the Governor-Generalship [of India]. I was in Downing Street yesterday, the whole office is in a state of dismay and grief, which I cannot describe; never had they a kinder chief, or one of whom they had more cause to be proud" (Kay Shuttleworth, 1910: 226).

CHAPTER 4

The Woodbine Parish Report on the Revolutions in South America (1822)

This chapter will closely analyse the Parish report, focusing on its structure, sources, content and main conclusions, in order to assess its significance in the history of British diplomacy and intelligence vis-à-vis Latin America.

The title of the report's index is 'South America', and five chapters are listed: No. 1. Events in Buenos Aires since 1816 (23 pages); No. 2. Events in Chile since 1810 (32 pages); No. 3. Events in Mexico during 1821 (19 pages); No. 4. Appendix of Sundry Public Documents (26 pages); and No. 5. Actual state of the Different Governments (27 pages).[1] All five chapters were written by Woodbine Parish.

For some reason (probably because they were incorporated later), the index does not include three further chapters dedicated to Colombia, Chile and Mexico: 'A commercial Sketch of the Columbian Republic, with a few observations upon the expediency of the British Government acknowledging the independence of the new States of Spanish America' (17 pages); 'A Commercial and Statistical Sketch of the Republic of Chili' (17 pages), both written by James Henderson; and 'Memorandum on the late occurrences in the Kingdom of Mexico' (6 pages), by C. Parker. As we will see, these chapters do not focus on the historical process but rather describe the geographical, social and economic conditions of each state, and provide a complementary appendix to the Parish report. The differences in the three authors' handwriting suggests that each one wrote, in his own handwriting, his own chapter.

I. Sources of information

In presenting his report, Parish describes his sources of information. He has referred to information in the British press, checked whenever possible, and to the Admiralty reports received by the FO. He expressly notes the shortcomings

---

1 Sir Woodbine Parish, South America. Volume containing printed and manuscript reports prepared for the Congress of Verona, 1822, The Royal Geographical Society (TRGS), SWP/3. All quotations follow the original spelling and punctuation.

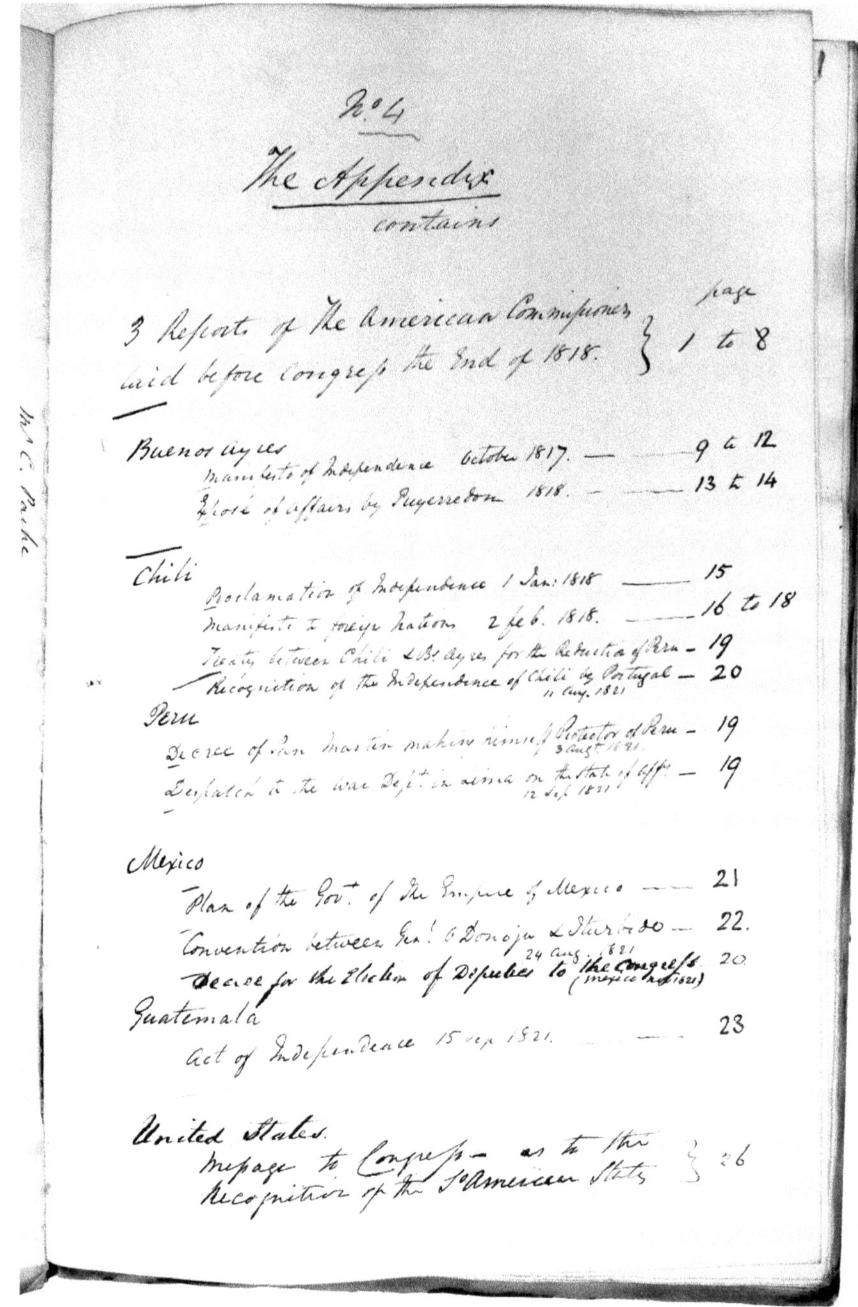

Nº 4

The Appendix
contains

3 Reports of the American Commissioners
laid before Congress the End of 1818. — page 1 to 8

Buenos Ayres
Manifesto of Independence October 1817. — 9 to 12
Exposé of affairs by Puyerredon 1818. — 13 to 14

Chili
Proclamation of Independence 1 Jan: 1818 — 15
Manifesto to foreign nations 2 feb. 1818. — 16 to 18
Treaty between Chili & Bs Ayres for the Reduction of Peru — 19
Recognition of the Independence of Chili by Portugal — 20
11 Aug. 1821

Peru
Decree of San Martin making himself Protector of Peru — 19
3 Aug 1821
Despatch to the War Dept in America on the State of Affrs — 19
12 Sep 1821

Mexico
Plan of the Govt. of the Empire of Mexico — 21
Convention between Genl. O Donoju & Iturbido — 22.
24 Aug 1821
Decree for the Election of Deputies to the Congress — 20.
(Mexico 7 Nov 1821)

Guatemala
Act of Independence 15 Sep 1821. — 23

United States.
Message to Congress — as to the
Recognition of the S American States — 26

Figure 4.1: "Appendix of Sundry Public Documents", in Sir Woodbine Parish, "South America. Volume containing printed and manuscript reports prepared for the Congress of Verona, 1822"
TRGS, SWP/3.

of this methodology and describes his report, in a letter to Joseph Planta, as no more than "a slight sketch": "As I have had a great deal of difficulty in tracing out the Events in the Southern Provinces, I fear after all you will find it but a slight sketch, compiled very much from newspapers, those in some degree checked by the Admiralty Reports in the Office which however are extremely partial and deficient".[2] The report includes a documentary appendix, consisting of a set of manifestos, declarations and official treaties made by the South American governments published in British newspapers, which Parish has selected, cut out, ordered and pasted in his report. From the United States, this appendix includes "three reports of the American Commissioners laid before Congress at the end of 1818" and "Mr. Page to Congress as to the Recognition of the South American States". From Rio de la Plata, "Buenos Ayres: Manifesto of Independence (October 1817)" and "Exposé of Affairs, by Pueyrredon (1818)". From Chile, "Proclamation of Independence (1 Jan. 1818)", "Manifesto to Foreign Nations (2 Feb. 1818)" and the "Treaty between Chili and Buenos Ayres for the Reduction of Peru and Recognition of the Independence of Chili by Portugal (11 Aug. 1821)". From Peru, the "Decree of San Martin making himself Protector of Peru (3 Aug. 1821)" and the "Dispatch to the War Department in Lima on the state of affairs (12 Sep. 1821)". For Mexico, the "Plan of the Government of the Empire of Mexico, Convention between General O'Donojú and Iturbide" and the "Decree for the Election of Deputies to the Congress (Mexico, Nov. 1821)". Finally, he included a document from a region which is not discussed: the "Act of Independence" of Guatemala (15 September 1821).

Parish does not cite the exact sources from which he took these documents. To find the origin of each and, at the same time, the newspapers to which he referred, we have compared the typography of each of the clippings in the report with those published in the British press at the time. The two newspapers Parish used most were *The Times* and *The Morning Chronicle* (seven documents each).[3] In other words, he used newspapers which supported both the Tory government (*The Times*) and the Whig (reformist) opposition (*The Morning Chronicle*).

Other authorities used by Parish (which he references in notes in the margin, as indicated in the following transcript) include authors who disagreed with Castlereagh and the Tories: William Walton (1810; 1814), a Whig merchant, writer and militant supporter of the South American revolutionary cause, and the North American commissioners sent to South America (Graham and Rodney, 1819). Referring to the latter, Parish writes in a letter to Planta "the best accounts [...] of a certain period are the Reports of the American Commissioners laid before Congress, and which contain a variety and abundance of information, especially on the Resources of the Country".[4]

2 W. Parish to J. Planta, London, 28 October 1822, RGH, SWP/3.
3 We have not been able to locate the exact source of four documents.
4 W. Parish to J. Planta, London, 28 October 1822, RGH, SWP/3.

Despite the limited number of references in the text, it is likely Parish had access to a greater number of works. Among his personal papers, included with the 1822 report in the Royal Geographical Society, is a copy of the *Catalog of Authors* (London: Ballantine & Law, 1807) compiled by Alexander Dalrymple, of authors who had written on Rio de la Plata, Paraguay and Chaco.[5] This is an invaluable document which offers insight into the knowledge available to Parish at the time, though it should be complemented with the handwritten notes, newspaper clippings and relevant books published after 1807 and therefore not cited by Dalrymple.[6] The papers include a note written by Parish entitled "Addenda to Mr. Dalrymple's Catalog of Works on the Rio de la Plata, Parish". Among the titles cited by Dalrymple are the following general descriptions of the River Plate and its history, many focusing on the British invasion of Buenos Aires in 1806 (Davie, 1805; Wilcocke, 1807; *An Authentic and Interesting*, 1806; *An Authentic Narrative*, 1808 and Gillespie, 1818).

As Parish points out, the most informative studies of the revolutions were those written by the American agents sent to South America in 1818 (Rodney and Graham, 1819; Brackenridge, 1820). The addenda also refers to Southey's *History of Brazil* (1810), the letters of Vicente Pazos (1819), Emeric Essex Vidal's illustrations (1820) and John Luccock's (1820) notes. It highlights in particular that "in 1816, an historical work was published of great merit entitled *Ensayo de la historia civil del Paraguay, Buenos Aires and Tucuman*, written by Doctor Don Gregorio Funes, Dean de Cordova, 3 volumes, 8, Buenos Aires, 1816, which is perhaps the best history of those hitherto writers of the Country".[7]

5 "Dalrymple's catalogue of authors who have written on the Rio de la Plata, Paraguay and Chaco, published in London in 1807, with manuscript annotations by Parish from 1807–37", TRGS, SWP/1.

6 Parish inserts in the margin of the catalogue a series of handwritten citations and small clippings of titles of printed books in order to either note the books and newspapers missing from the catalogue, or to comment on particular aspects of the items included. For example, in the margin of the reference to the *Mercurio Peruano*, he writes that it was "the most important work on South America during the rule of Spain", and points out that "a selection of articles from the *Mercurio Peruano*, chiefly on the geography of Peru, were translated and published in London under the title of Skinner's Peru, 4th., 180". A clipping next to it completes the quote: Skinner (J), *Present State of Peru; drawn from original and authentic documents, chiefly written and compiled in the Peruvian capital*, 1805. He also adds *An account of the European settlements in America* (1808), "by the celebrated Edmund Burke (though his name is not affixed to it), printed by Dodsley, London", "Dalrymple's catalogue of authors...", TRGS, SWP/1. The margin notes are indicated on the transcript of the documents

7 "Among [...] the periodical Works the *Registro Estadístico*, published by author [...] and the *Abeja Argentina* by a Society of literary individuals in 1823–1825... are the best". Parish adds "various publications have also appeared from the press at Buenos Ayres since the Independence of the Country, and some of the Periodical Publications

The catalogue continues with books published after 1822 and was evidently compiled by Parish throughout his diplomatic career and, most likely, completed in Rio de la Plata after his arrival as British consul in 1823. Nevertheless, Parish's 'addendum' is incomplete, as it does not cite several works already published in Britain: Depons (1807); Helms (1807); *A Full and Correct Report* (1807); Tucker (1807); Burke (1807; 1808); Antepara (1810); Mawe (1812); Palacio Fajardo (1817); Bonnycastle (1818); Howell (1819) and Henderson (1821) do not appear in the catalogue. Parish was probably familiar with some of these books: for example, although the report cites Walton (1810; 1814), these works do not appear in Rio de la Plata catalogue. As previously noted, Parish had close personal contacts with the British Museum through Planta, so we can assume, sooner or later, he became acquainted with most of the published books on the subject, although perhaps not all at the time of writing his report in 1822. To sum up, although we cannot be certain that Parish possessed this catalogue at the time of writing his report, we can neither rule this out.

The paucity of 'scholarly apparatus' of the Parish report and its considerable 'absences', can be explained by the specificity required of an intelligence report, the main objective of which is to provide a brief and concise answer to a political question. Parish had to compile his report in a short time, so a comprehensive, more exhaustive, account was not possible and was probably not required. His intelligence report, drawn up in the heat of the moment when pressed for time by events, was an important document for diplomacy and, in due course, following the publication of his book on the history of Rio de la Plata in 1839, was to become a major contribution to knowledge and historiography.

II. The content: a political analysis of the South American revolutions in real time

In addition to the problem of finding reliable sources, Parish faced the difficulty of describing and evaluating events that were still unfolding, this being one of the most challenging tasks of intelligence (Warner, 2007: 19). In this sense his report is a detailed analysis of what was known in Britain about the complex events in South America at that point in time, mid-1822, and it was on the basis of Parish's evaluation that Castlereagh drew up his Memorandum.

a. Buenos Aires

The report is structured chronologically and presents the most important facts relating to the revolutionary process between 1816 and 1822. It begins

in the years 1823 to 1826 contain much interesting information on the History and Statistics of the Country", *Dalrymple's catalogue of authors...*, TRGS, SWP/1.

with the Declaration of Independence of the "United Provinces of South America" (wrongly dated 6 July 1816, instead of 9 July). In presenting a document which at first sight would appear to corroborate the success of the revolutionaries, Parish adds that "the situation of these was however extremely critical", due to the military defeats in Peru, the threat of a Spanish reconquest, and the civil war between Artigas and Alvear which indicated a state of disorder and lack of discipline in the revolutionary forces.[8]

These critical circumstances might have persuaded the Buenos Aires government, aware of its material weakness and unable after successive attempts to obtain a "reconciliation" with Spain, to take a more conciliatory attitude than in its previous policy. It could have initiated negotiations with the Portuguese Court in Rio de Janeiro and offered territorial concessions, leading to a confrontation between Spain and Portugal if successful. However, due to Rio de la Plata's aversion towards the Portuguese, Parish argues that "It is therefore probable that all the proposals and temptations said to have been held out by the former [the Portuguese] have been illusory and that a secret [Portuguese] determination has always existed to recover the whole of the Eastern Territory upon the first favorable opportunity". The fate of the Banda Oriental is therefore one of the key underlying problems explaining the political tensions in the region. In this sense, the Portuguese invasion of Montevideo

> "May be considered as a most important advantage to the Government of Buenos Ayres at the time it occurred [...] by its weakening and distracting the attention of its most powerful Enemy and rival Artigas, the Government of the Provinces of Entre Rios; and secondly, by [occupying] Montevideo against any attempt which Spain might meditate for its Reconquest, an attempt which at that period could hardly have failed success."

According to Parish, the confrontation between Artigas and the Buenos Aires directory was due to Buenos Aires attempting to impose itself over all the other United Provinces, declaring its right to exercise sovereignty over the rest and to locate a central authority in the city of Buenos Aires, prospective capital of the new political order. The "tyrannical usurpations of Buenos Ayres" were denounced by Artigas who "insisted on a Federal Government, in which all the Provinces were to have equal Rights and Privileges". The conflict gave rise to counter accusations; Artigas denounced Buenos Aires for handing over territory under their control to the Portuguese, while Buenos Aires accused Artigas of colluding with Spain.

Parish emphasizes that Artigas "gallantly defended his Province against the Portuguese". He succeeded in attracting various leaders to his party and limiting the operations of the invaders who, by the end of 1819, had been

---

8 Woodbine Parish, "Events in Buenos Ayres since 1816", in "South America", TRGS, SWP/3. All the following references are from this chapter unless otherwise indicated.

confined to Montevideo, Colonia, and the Rincón de Gallinas—the point at the confluence of the Uruguay and Negro rivers. He also points out the important role played by the inhabitants of the Eastern region in the struggle against the Portuguese: "the hostility of the country people to them was so great that they had little communication with the Interior".

Parish describes the situation at the end of 1819 as follows: an alliance between Santa Fe, under Ramírez, and Entre Ríos, under Artigas, openly resisted any pretension by Buenos Aires to exert supreme authority over them; although Córdoba and Santiago del Estero probably agreed, they had been contained by a superior military force gathered in Tucumán; Salta and Jujuy also favoured a federal form of government; while the provinces of Cuyo, under the government of San Martín, supported the Buenos Aires policy; finally, Paraguay, under the authority of Francia, refused to participate in any conflict that might "disturb its own tranquility".

Faced with this opposition, the government of Buenos Aires established a secret correspondence with the French court to place the young prince of Lucca (married to a Brazilian princess) on the throne of the United Provinces. However, according to Parish, in 1820 "this scheme was defeated by an entire change in the Party at the head of the Government". Since then, the success of Artigas' party led to the demise of the Puyerredonists (sic) and brought to power Sarratea, a leader in the Federalist Party. Following this change in the Buenos Aires revolutionary government a Treaty or League was signed between the provinces of Santa Fe, Entre Ríos and Buenos Ayres, with the later addition of the rest of the provinces, agreeing to a form of federal government.

However, a new source of instability was the "party struggles amongst the federalist chiefs for the Chief command", leading to successive changes in leadership in the Buenos Aires government (Sarratea, Balcarce, Mexia, Soler and Rodríguez). Despite their differences, Parish points out, they all agreed on two points: to reject any type of agreement with Spain, which had sent commissioners to Buenos Aires in November 1820 who were unable to enter into any negotiation; and to attack the Portuguese invaders and expel them from Montevideo and the entire Banda Oriental. Meanwhile, foreign states presented new challenges. Artigas was defeated by the Portuguese and had to go into exile in Paraguay. In October 1820, a French squadron once again proposed the crowning of a foreign monarch, and an American agent, Mr. Forbes was officially established in Buenos Aires.

In March 1821, long-standing federal party differences finally erupted into open war between Buenos Aires and Entre Ríos under Ramírez, who seemed to have succeeded Artigas and proposed the formation of a new alliance. Once again, military confrontation created a "rhetorical" war: Rodríguez, governor and captain general of Buenos Aires, published a proclamation accusing Ramírez, governor of Entre Ríos, of conspiring to hand over that province to the Portuguese on the condition that they jointly attack Buenos Aires, and summoned the Buenos Aires people to take up arms to defend the city. Ramírez, meanwhile, prepared to invade Buenos Aires, and Carrera, who, since his expulsion from Chile, was now a follower of the "Artigas faction", assembled a "Body of Indians in the South to assist Him".

Although Parish acknowledges that "there is a great deficiency of information as to the events immediately growing out of this dissention", he assumes that around September 1821 the displacement of Ramírez and Carrera (the former, dead; the latter captured and sent to Mendoza) would have determined that "Buenos Ayres was in a tolerably settled state under the Government of Rodriguez and peace with the Interior was almost entirely restored".

At the same time, the Portuguese had taken control of the Banda Oriental and the inhabitants of Montevideo, occupied by Portuguese troops, had placed themselves under Portuguese rule in a "public act"; "the whole of the Country called the Banda Oriental of the River Plata was annexed to the Crown of Portugal under the name of the Cisplatine Province".

b. Chile

The report on Chile, though not as detailed, begins in 1810, noting that the revolutionary movement started in Santiago, on 18 July 1810, when Captain General Carrasco was deposed. This resulted in "a provisional form of Government on the same principles with those set up in other parts of South America to govern for the time being <u>in the name of the King</u>" (underlined in the original).[9]

Parish describes the political conflicts facing the Chilean leaders since the congress of 1811, which were caused essentially, in his view, by the mutual antagonism of two families, the Larrain and the Carrera. The latter prevailed and placed themselves at the head of the government. Despite recognition by the regency in Spain, these disputes led the viceroy in Lima "to attempt the execution of a Plan for extinguishing at once the flame of the Revolution".

According to Parish, this led to lengthy confrontation between royalists and those in favour of independence which extended across the whole of Chilean territory, primarily in Santiago, Concepción, Talca, Chillan and Valparaíso, between 1812 and 1814. The vicissitudes of the war led to Carrera's departure and the assumption of command by Bernardo O'Higgins at the end of 1813. The following year, the royalist advance on the capital and the taking of Talca led to the dissolution of the junta and the rise to power of Lastra, governor of Valparaíso, as supreme director. A convention, in May 1814, sought the agreement of the parties in dispute. It was agreed that the royalists should evacuate Chilean territory within two months, the Spanish regency should be recognized, and that deputies should be sent to the Spanish Cortes. The deposition of Lastra by Carrera, the reconstitution of the junta in August 1814, and Carrera's confrontation with O'Higgins at the Battle of Maipú,

9 Woodbine Parish, "Events in Chile since 1810", in "South America", TRGS, SWP/3. All the following references are from this chapter unless otherwise indicated.

gave some indication of the serious rifts within the revolutionaries' party, dividing it, in Parish's terms, into two factions which nonetheless agreed on independence. The royalist threat posed by the viceroy in Lima brought them together again, with O'Higgins at the head of the army and Carrera in Santiago. However, a crushing defeat of the revolutionary forces by the royalists caused the entire captaincy of Chile to fall back into the hands of the royalists in October 1814.

With Spanish power re-established in Chile, and after describing the ensuing proscriptions, expulsions, arrests and punishments against subversives, Parish moves his focus to the United Provinces of Rio de la Plata, specifically to Cuyo, whose governor, General José de San Martín, had begun to organize a military force to recover Chile. Parish points out the substantial work required to forge an army of 4,000 men who needed to be strictly disciplined and prepared for the extremely difficult task of crossing the Andes to attack the royalist armies. It was, in Parish's analysis, a task so brilliantly carried out that it achieved its objective sooner than planned when the royalist forces were defeated at Chacabuco and the kingdom of Chile liberated in 1817. At the same time the revolutionary army defeated an attempt by royalist General La Serna to penetrate the north of the United Provinces.

c. Peru

There is no separate chapter on Peru, which is instead analyzed as part of the Rio de la Plata and Chilean process. According to Parish, "in Peru, the war was principally defensive during 1818, and to nearly the close of 1819. The country miserably exhausted, and neither Party feeling strong enough to make any decisive effort against the other". The conflict was left undecided. The royalists occupied territory along the Humahuaca River, between Tarija and Suipacha, establishing their headquarters in Cotagayta and counting on an important, although dispersed, force of 8,000 men. For their part, the revolutionaries continued in possession of the neighbouring provinces of Jujuy and Salta, due largely to the strong defence mounted by the inhabitants whenever the Spanish tried to invade them. Parish, who considers the revolutionary governments of Buenos Aires and Chile as two distinct parties, refers to their mutual agreement to collaborate to achieve independence in Peru: "The possession of Chili determined the Independents to combine in a general attack upon the Vice Royalty of Peru, and a Treaty was signed between the Buenos Ayrean, and Chilian Government [...] on the 5th February 1819, for the express purpose of expelling the Royal forces from that territory". However, Parish notes a "a natural antipathy" between the Peruvians and Chileans, and believes the Peruvian "better classes" aspired to a monarchy under a European prince (not a Bourbon), of which he supposed both San Martín and O'Higgins were aware. However, he points out that this would contradict the "Declaration of the Government of Chile to the inhabitants of Peru", which openly stated the objective of establishing a general confederation and a representative government.

After describing the preparations for the attack on Lima, which were largely in the hands of San Martín (and noting the successive defeats suffered by Lord Cochranes's naval forces at the end of 1819), Parish indicates that the assault was planned for early 1820: "San Martin, after the Battle of Maypo, returned to Chili for the avowed purpose of personally attending to the preparations for the reduction of Lima, which he hoped to be ready to attack by the beginning of 1820 provided the threatened Armament from Spain should not arrive in the Rio de la Plata". The last political event of 1820 mentioned in the report is the arrival in Buenos Aires of the French frigate bringing news, supposedly, of new proposals regarding the coronation of the prince of Lucca, the Portuguese government having been in communication with the main independence leaders (Carrera, San Martín and O'Higgins) and offering them arrangements regarding the future captaincy general of Chile, were they to collaborate with said policy.

In 1820 San Martín launched his expedition from Chile to Peru, achieving his first successes against the royalist forces commanded by General O'Reilly. While the land advance on Lima was being prepared, Cochrane having completely blockaded the Peruvian coast, San Martín issued a proclamation stating he would not negotiate with the viceroy until he recognized Chilean independence.

In the midst of these events, in 1821 the province of Guayaquil (later incorporated into the government of Venezuela) declared independence due to the success of "the patriots" on the western coast. This encouraged expectations that Lima, on which the fate of the entire viceroyalty of Peru depended, would soon fall to the revolutionaries. As the independence forces advanced, so too did British trade. The sea blockade was loosened and the passage of friendly and neutral ships was allowed in exchange for payment of duties. In Parish's words:

> "The blockade produced strong remonstrances on the part of the British Commodore [Cochrane], but was subsequently gradually removed from those parts of the Coast which fell into the hands of the independents, with which neutral and friendly vessels were allowed to trade, upon the payment of a fixed tariff of Duties. Valparaiso was made nearly a free Port, and upon the whole British commerce received considerable encouragement from the independent Government, although the detention of several vessels by the blockading squadron, had given rise to some complaints and remonstrances on the part of the British Commodore."

The account of the final assault on Peru highlights the contributions of Lord Cochrane, San Martín and the Chilean army, as well as the dissension and confrontations within the royalist forces that led to successive defeats and the deposal of viceroy Pezuela who was replaced by General José de la Serna while awaiting European aid. In July 1821, La Serna was forced to sign a 20-day armistice with San Martín, the objective of which was to negotiate the end the war. The information that Parish had to hand allowed him to report that on 5 July La Serna had evacuated Lima and San Martín had taken the city on 8 July, and, shortly after, had taken the title of Protector of Peru as head of an interim government (the corresponding decree is attached in the appendix). As an epilogue, Parish reports that, according to the latest news in April 1822, there was still a small royalist force in the interior of Peru, despite the fact that Callao had been taken by the liberation armies.

d. Mexico

The Mexican Revolution is the least analyzed by Parish, who briefly refers only to the year 1821. He reports that, despite the wave of insurrections across the kingdom of Mexico, the Spanish cause had still been strong until April 1821 when Colonel Iturbide was ordered to march against the insurgents in Acapulco. However, Iturbide "entered into negotiations with them, and placed himself at their head",[10] proposing to Viceroy Apodaca that he should adopt the Spanish constitution, and that the king of Spain, or one of his successors, be invited to Mexico and recognized as emperor. In the meantime, the viceroy would continue in post under certain restrictions.

The rejection of this proposal resulted in confrontation and led to Iturbide gaining the upper hand so that "by June the whole Kingdom of Mexico was in a State of Insurrection". Parish then describes the political situation at the time in which "Ferdinand was styled Emperor in all Public Decrees. The Inquisition which had been abolished by the Regency in Spain was re-established and the suppressed Monasteries restored. The Clergy everywhere favored the Independents", and it was believed that the viceroy himself would not resist, so he was deposed by the royalists and succeeded by General Novella. Added to this was the reduction of the garrison in Veracruz, due to desertion, and, in July, the capitulation of Puebla to the independentists.

The report then goes on to describe the events that, according to Parish, surprised even the royalists in New Spain. Shortly after arriving from (constitutional) Spain to assume the position of viceroy, General O'Donojú met with Iturbide in Córdoba where a convention was signed on 24 August 1821. Parish summarized the principal articles of the agreement.

In his correspondence with General Dávila (the governor of Veracruz), O'Donojú explained his reasons for signing a convention with Iturbide, among which were "the liberality of Spain, the enlightened state of the age, and the state of public opinion in New Spain". He also ordered the convention to be published and for troops from Havana to re-embark if they landed in Veracruz. However, royalist General Dávila firmly opposed this plan: he rejected the convention and maintained the Veracruz garrison. Parish concludes that "The conduct of General O'Donojú throughout

---

10 Woodbine Parish, "Events in Mexico during 1821", in "South America", TRGS, SWP/3. All the following references are from this chapter unless otherwise indicated.

this transaction is generally disapproved by the Royalists, in having made such important sacrifices on the part of Spain, without authority, without a struggle, and without giving himself time to ascertain the true state of the Country". Nevertheless, "the Revolution was effected at the Capital, Merida, without difficulty in the most formal manner, by almost all the constituted authorities on the 15th September". General Novella, elected by the royalists to succeed Viceroy Apodaca, initially refused to recognize the Cordoba Convention. But O'Donojú, accompanied by Iturbide, managed to convince him to sign a brief six-day armistice on 7 September. Subsequently, Viceroy O'Donojú assumed the position of captain general and proclaimed, on 17 September, the Cordoba Convention in Mexico.

With only 3,000 men in the royalist forces, a governing junta of 12 representatives was created, including O'Donojú, Admiral Apodaca and General Novella. A regency was agreed and O'Donojú was appointed captain general and political head or prefect of the province of Mexico. In November 1821, the regency of the imperial government of Mexico was established, composed of five individuals: Iturbide, as president; O'Donojú; Bárcenas, archdeacon of Valladolid; Yáñez, member of the Supreme Court of Justice; and Velázquez de León, former secretary of the deputy prime government. Iturbide continued as head of the imperial army of the three guarantees and generalissimo of the land and marine forces. The bishop of Puebla was to be president of the Supreme Board, made up of 37 representatives, and Almanza was appointed vice president. An independent government seemed to have been established in all New Spain, with the exception of the fort of Veracruz, where the royalist troops (under General Novella), reduced by desertion, numbered only 500 men.

Parish reports the rumour that, during the Cordoba conferences, O'Donojú believed none of the infantes (the King of Spain's brothers) would accept the imperial crown, and had tried to convince Iturbide to bypass the Braganza family (of Portugal) and offer the throne to Don Carlos, son of the grand duchess of Lucca, as the future sovereign of New Spain.

Meanwhile, the province of Guatemala declared itself independent in October. The Spanish Cortes met soon after to decide on its future form of government and whether Guatemala should remain separate or join New Spain. General Liñán, who still had a force of about 10,000 men and, though inactive, had remained faithful to the cause of Spain, was imprisoned in December but regularly supplied with payments and provisions. Parish concludes that "It was expected that matters would remain in a state of tranquility until the decision of the Spanish Government upon the Convention of Cordova could be received".

e. The socioeconomic reports: Colombia, Chile and Mexico

As stated, Parish's report includes three socioeconomic reports on Colombia, Chile and Mexico as complementary appendices. The first two were written by James Henderson and the third by C. Parker.

James Henderson was born in Whitehaven, Cumberland, between 1782 and 1783, exact date unknown (Goodwin, 1891: 399; Brown, 2009). He was involved in diverse activities whose central objective was the development of British capital and commerce in South America following state intervention. In this sense, he represented Britain in Colombia unofficially from 1818 (Armstrong, 1960: 18). In 1819, in search of fortune or to obtain a consular post, he embarked for Rio de Janeiro (Henderson, 1821: 1). Despite his contacts (he was received at the home of a merchant, taking with him a letter of recommendation from a nobleman, possibly Viscount Lowther), his application to the British consul-general, Henry Chamberlain, was unsuccessful, and he returned to London in 1821 (Henderson, 1821: 606).

Shortly after his return to Britain, he published *A history of the Brazil* (Henderson, 1821) describing the commercial prospects for Great Britain based on an economic, social and geographical description of Brazil.[11] In addition, probably continuing in his role as an informal agent in Colombia, he represented the British Whig MP Sir James Mackintosh when the Colombian government ignored a trade agreement between Mackintosh and Luis López Méndez (special envoy and plenipotentiary minister of Venezuela in London), signed on 27 February 1821.[12]

Mackintosh, a professor and doctor, and an important figure in the Whig Party, argued in parliament against the Tory government, urging it to immediately recognize the new South American states, though his interest in supporting the "American cause" was not only political.[13] Henderson began a campaign of political propaganda arguing that immediate recognition of the new states would obtain for Britain commercial privileges which were vital in its ongoing rivalry with the European powers and the United States for commercial hegemony.

To this end, he published two influential pamphlets in 1822, addressed to the two most important "parties" favouring recognition: the "South Americans" and the Board of Trade. In the first, he urged the new states to link up politically and economically with Great Britain which would pledge its financial and political support (Henderson, 1822a). In the second, he addressed the British government department in charge of overseeing foreign trade and set out his views on the benefits of trade between South America and the United Kingdom (Henderson, 1822b). The following year, he continued his campaign and published *Observations on the Great Commercial Benefits that will result from the Warehousing-Bill* (Henderson, 1823).

---

11 In his introduction, Henderson stated that the book communicated "new information respecting a portion of South America, now more than ever interesting to the commercial, political, and scientific worlds" (Henderson, 1821: iii).

12 López Méndez had been appointed to the position in November 1817, with the mission of obtaining arms, ammunition, and clothing for the revolutionary army, the object of the contract signed with Mackintosh (Martínez Garnica, 2019: 392).

13 On Mackintosh's business in Colombia, see *Gobierno de la Nueva Granada* (1852).

In this context, due to the fact that by 1822 he had published three studies on South America and had made his name as one of the main supporters of the recognition of the new South American states, as well as an ally of the principal Whig who argued the case in parliament, Parish decided to attach Henderson's two analyses of the situations in Colombia and Chile to his own report.

We know very little about C. Parker, not even his full name.[14] According to his own statements in the report, he lived in Mexico for some years from 1811, "with the special permission of His Catholic Majesty's Government, being employed part of my time by the Lords Commissioners of His Britannic Majesty's Treasury".[15] In Mexico, he forged a close friendship with some members of the government, such as Mariano Almansa. Along with his residence in Jamaica, his experience would have offered him detailed knowledge of Central American trade and its connection with Cadiz, the heart of the Spanish Empire.

Republic of Columbia

Henderson presents a detailed geographical, social and economic description of "the Republic of Columbia", which he also refers to interchangeably as the "Columbian Empire".[16] The first aspect highlighted in the report is the territorial extension of the so-called provinces of "Caracas or Venezuela" and Nueva Granada, as well as the size of their populations, concluding that "the Columbian Empire embraces a territory of 130,000 square leagues and two million and a half population". This data is important when considering "the commercial capabilities and facilities of this important Republic", and for this reason Henderson states, "I will confine myself principally in this sketch, to such productions and places as are mainly essential for the purposes of British trade".

The report begins with a detailed description of the political divisions of Venezuela, the location and distances between their respective districts and the main productive and commercial features of each. It points out the importance of the state making advances among the indigenous populations in Guiana, leading to further commercial opportunities, although the land is of little use. Describing the capital, St. Thome or Angostura, Henderson

---

14 His name is not mentioned in Mackie (2014) or in "The Personnel of the Foreign Office, 1782–1846" (Middleton, 1977: 260–320).

15 C. Parker, "Memorandum on the late occurrences in the Kingdom of Mexico", London, 4 February 1822, in Parish, Woodbine, "South America", TRGS, SWP/3. All the following references are from this chapter unless otherwise indicated.

16 James Henderson, "A commercial Sketch of the Columbian Republic, with a few observations upon the expediency of the British Government acknowledging the independence of the new States of Spanish America", in Woodbine Parish, "South America", TRGS, SWP/3. All the following references are from this chapter unless otherwise indicated.

states that, for the moment, "the whole of this district presents a prodigious field for commercial pursuits, but the only returns it offers at present for our manufactures, are hides and a trifling supply of indigo and cotton, notwithstanding its capabilities of production are not surpassed by any other part of the world". He highlights exports from Cumaná of cotton, cocoa, sugar, indigo, tobacco and salt, adding thar the 13,000 inhabitants of Barcelona "have such a taste for dealing in live and dead cattle that the cultivation of the soil has been neglected", but notes nevertheless the export of hides, tallow, salted beef, oxen and mules, mainly to the West Indies and Cuba. Regarding Caracas, the most important feature is the fertility of its soil, offering "in profusion not only all the productions of the West Indies", but also cocoa ("of a highly esteemed quality"), vanilla, tobacco, sugar, coffee, indigo, cotton, cochineal, sarsaparilla, balsams, tinctures, drugs, gums, shearing, aloes and cassia. Similarly, "the widely extending plains of the interior are peopled with herds of cattle horses and mules; the mountains with sheep and deer, which will likewise contribute to the commercial importance of this empire". Henderson goes on to list the advantages of Puerto Cabello, Coro, Maracaibo, Trujillo, Varinas and the main cities of the Venezuelan interior.

In the same way, Henderson describes the 16 districts of the extensive province of Nueva Granada and of Quito. Santa Marta follows Maracaibo as the capital of gold mining, though there is still no systematic exploitation. He points out the importance of the Magdalena River, which divides Cartagena, flowing from the southern regions of the province, and suggests that when it is further explored it could "form a grand commercial communication from hence, almost with the Pacific, through the heart of the Empire". Its margins are rich in cocoa, Magdalena chocolate being highly esteemed, and "cotton, tobacco, palm-wine, sugar, Brazil wood, Vanilla, etc., with which the capital, Santa Marta, carries on a trade to Carthagena and other ports on the main". The city's "large and commodious harbor" is noteworthy, as well as other products of the region: hides, cattle and pearl fishing, as well as the "highly productive" Cartagena savannas, mountains and forests. When referring to the port, Henderson warns that it is "exceedingly unhealthy", although it is protected from the winds and its waters are calm, which makes it possible to send goods by sea from Santa Fe and the southern districts. In summary, "if it was not so intensely hot and the air so unwholesome, this city would become a very desirable situation for commerce", concluding that "its exports in indigo, sugar, cotton, cinchona, ipecacuanha [*sic*], cocou, etc., is said to have amounted to £200,000 annually, and the imports to half a million sterling".

Henderson writes that Panama lost some of its importance when the Lima galleons stopped calling there, so that its trade was limited to Veracruz and the southern ports down to Peru. Porto Bello, "St. Jago de Nata", Veragua and Tacames lead to the extensive district of Popayán, which enjoys considerable trade, receiving European products from Cartagena and supplying Quito, and exporting cattle, mules, tobacco, dried beef, salted pork, butter, rum, cotton, etc., to Chocó and other places in exchange for precious metals. The interior districts are also described: Mérida, San Juan de los Llanos, Santa Fe de Bogotá, Antioquia (famous for its gold, silver and quicksilver mines), Jaén de Bracamoros (for its tobacco), Maynas and Quixos. The report concludes describing Quito's internal trade, receiving European articles from Guayaquil and exporting wheat in return, and exporting some of its products to Guatemala, in return for indigo, iron and steel. The city of Guayaquil, the main port on this coast, is noted for its cocoa exports.

Republic of Chili

Henderson classifies Chile into three parts, "Chili-proper" (which he considers the most important), comprising the districts of Copiapo, Coquimbo, Quillota, Aconcagua, Melipilla, Santiago, Rancagua, Colchagua, Maule, Itata, Chillan, Puchacay, and Huilquilemu; "Indian-Chili or Araucania" (occupied by the indigenous "nations", Araucanians, Puelches, Pehuenches, Chiquillanes, Cunches, Huilliches); and "Insular-Chili" ("the islands spread along the shores of this Republic").[17]

The geography, climate and produces of each are then described. Referring to Chile as a whole, he considers the population of 850,000 insufficient for the further expansion of territory. He is critical of the people's general attitude and of certain features of the cities, which in his view are not conducive to trade and production. The increase in (poorly exploited) mines, for example, has curtailed the development of agriculture. However, he is sure that the political and commercial freedoms encouraged by the new government will reverse this situation. And he is also confident that the development of "civilization" will successfully incorporate the indigenous peoples into production, trade and, most importantly, consumption, noting that "the Indian will be withdrawn from his solitary and apathized [*sic*] way of life, and by discovering the comforts of a new and preferable mode of existence, will throw much into the scale of active agricultural and commercial traffic".

Referring to the Araucanians, the most powerful nation of the so-called "Indian-Chili", he writes "It is very probable, however, that by conciliatory measures, these people may be induced to enter into permanently pacific arrangements with the Spaniards; when their demand on commerce would, no doubt, become very considerable, and possessing a fertile and auriferous territory, their means of payment are abundant".

Although he highlights the importance of mining (copper and gold primarily, plus silver, lead and iron) in Coquimbo, Copiapó, Curico, Uspallata, Huilquilemu and Aconcagua, Henderson points out that production is not straightforward though present deficiencies could be resolved with the introduction of steam engines, as was the case in Peru, which would

---

17 James Henderson, "A Commercial and Statistical Sketch of the Republic of Chili", in Woodbine Parish, "South America", TRGS, SWP/3. All the following references are from this chapter unless otherwise indicated.

guarantee a return in metals for British imports. His calculations regarding ore production, and merchandise traded in return, are not hopeful:

> "the quantity of gold and silver, exclusive of smuggling, that is collected annually in Chili, may be said to average near £400,000 sterling, of which, the best calculation States, one fourth to be gold, and the remainder silver [...] The only return which this Republic at present offers for British importations, consists of metals, hides, vicuna wool, and cocoa, the latter being received from Guayaquil, and other places, in return for grain, wine and some other vegetable productions, and it is, at least what has hitherto appeared in British ports, very inferior; although there is no doubt an excellent quality of this article is grown in the districts north of Peru."

Some important cities, such as Guasco and "all the other towns of Copiapo", and Valparaiso, are classified as "a miserable place". He points out, however, that rumours of the opening of the Chilean ports (before this actually happened) led to a large number of British merchants sending their goods there, not only from Britain but also from Rio de Janeiro and Buenos Aires, which created a significant depreciation in their value but nevertheless allowed them to penetrate the market. The imported goods were acquired by large sectors of the population which led to further interest in consuming British products:

> "The expectation, for a considerable period, of the opening of the ports or Peru, previously to the actual occurrence of that event, produced shipments to Chili by British merchants, not only direct from Great Britain, but from the surplus stocks in Brazil and Buenos Ayres, to such an amount that the sales have, almost without exception, been at depressed and losing price; and although this overflowing supply is attended with immediate misfortune, and great disappointment of expectation, yet the result will be found to be beneficial in our future commercial intercourse with those countries. The diffusion of British manufactures at such a low value, amongst an uncivilized population, having enabled them to become purchasers, generally, of luxuries which they did not previously possess, and having thus contracted a taste for those articles, they will not (I have had an opportunity of observing) relinquish them, on any sacrifice."

This led to Valparaiso becoming "for some time, the grand emporium of Chillian as well as Peruvian commerce" with between twelve and fifteen English establishments. But many of them have recently moved from Chile to Lima, because "the English complain of the disagreeable huts [...] and particularly of the bigotry [...] and jealousy which pervades the minds of the people, generally, against foreigners".
Henderson also notes the unfavourable state taxes:

> "the duties on British imports, are levied with great inequality, being collected at the rate of 34 ½ per Cent on certain fixed valuations, which

are by no means fairly applicable to the various gradations of value, in many articles of our manufactures [...] Goods coming from Buenos Ayres, having there paid the full imports duty of 30 per Cent, are chargeable with an additional 14 ½ per Cent if introduced into Chile by land, and 17 ½ per Cent, of by sea."

Another negative point about Chile is that the Spanish are still in possession of part of the country, both on the mainland (Valdivia) and on the island of Chiloe, while much of the country is under indigenous (Araucania) control. The report abruptly concludes with the description of the Chilean islands, without noting any particular practical consideration.

Kingdom of Mexico

Parker's report is shorter than the others and demonstrates how difficult it was for Britain to ascertain recent political developments in Mexico. Nevertheless, it keeps to the main objectives as set by Henderson with respect to Colombia. The report covers the years from 1817 and explains that, despite discontent with the Spanish government and a general desire for independence in both creoles and Europeans, an organized independence movement did not develop and, by 1819, most of the provinces in Mexico remained at peace. However, in December 1821, the situation changed when "all the American Deputies of Cortes going to Madrid, in arriving at Vera Cruz openly affirmed that their first efforts should be devoted toward the independence of New Spain. The principal events of the late revolution which has insured and confirmed the liberation of Mexico almost without the effusion of blood took place in January 1821".[18] Iturbide's intervention strengthened a particular form of independence which involved inviting the Spanish monarchy to establish itself in America, and "No sooner were the principles on which Iturbide had proclaimed independence known in the different Provinces, than the spirit of liberty and independence immediately manifested itself in all classes and ranks, with the exception only, of a few Europeans".

The independence movement expanded rapidly and, by July 1821, when the new Viceroy, O'Donojú, arrived, the entire kingdom of Mexico, with the exception of the capital and Veracruz, was in Iturbide's power. Parker briefly refers to the Cordoba convention, pointing out that "O'Donojú then proceeded to Mexico, where he received Iturbide as head of the Mexican government. O'Donojú is since dead, report says by poison". In short, the current government consists of a council and a regency, under the presidency of Iturbide, who is surrounded by "men of property and talent". According to his information, Iturbide's intention was to remain in government, and

18 C. Parker, "Memorandum on the late occurrences in the Kingdom of Mexico", London, 4 February 1822, in Woodbine Parish, "South America", TRGS, SWP/3. All the following references are from this chapter unless otherwise indicated.

even to crown himself king: "The present opinion seems (and I think
not unfounded) that Iturbide's views are of a more ambitious nature than
promised in the first instance, and little doubt is entertained but that he will
continue at the head of Government; at the Theatre, and in public he has
been frequently greeted with the title of 'King'".

III. The conclusions of the report: overview and proposal

I

In his final chapter, Parish reiterates the main objective of his report, that
is, to address the key question he was asked by Castlereagh and the FO: to
determine the "actual State of the Governments in South America".[19] This
involved explaining the specific political organization of the different governments and the existence (or otherwise) of political ties with Spain.

He firstly outlines the form and essential characteristics of each government, concentrating on their political and legal aspects, focusing primarily
on Buenos Aires and Chile, though also referring to Paraguay, Venezuela
and Mexico. Parish explains the particular significance of Buenos Aires:
"with respect of the form of Government established by the Independents
in the different revolutionized Provinces of South America, it would appear,
that Buenos Ayres had at first assumed a controlling influence over all the
other Provinces of La Plata" (underlining in the original). The Tucumán
Congress brought together deputies from all the provinces in the viceroyalty of the River Plate (wrongly called "Vice Royalty of Buenos Ayres")
and concluded with an agreed constitution. In his words, "This Congress
assumed at once the Sovereign Power of the Country, declared its absolute
Independence of old Spain, and adopted a Provisional form of Government.
Being afterwards adjourned to Buenos Ayres it occupied itself in drawing up
a Constitution which was subsequently completed and received the assent
of the People".

Parish describes the constitution of 1819, in particular the three powers
established in the constitution: the legislative, executive and judicial.
The legislative body is a bicameral national congress ("two Houses")
of representatives and senators. There are certain requirements for a
citizen to be eligible and certain privileges are granted to its members or
deputies. Parish explains "The Deputy [...] must possess 4,000 Dollars of
Property, or some equivalent which is not well defined in the Article", and
he includes the periods of duration of the offices as well as the features
and mechanisms of both legislative chambers for their operation, renewal
and approval of laws. Regarding the executive branch of government, the

---

19 Woodbine Parish, "Actual State of the Governments in South America", in "South
   America", TRGS, SWP/3. All the following references are from this chapter unless
   otherwise indicated.

supreme director of the state, he describes the political and legal aspects, as well as the director's relationship with the national congress and election of ministers. Finally, regarding the judicial, he refers mainly to the Supreme Court of Justice, highlighting an element that, as we will see, recommends the dispatch of consuls to South America: "This Court shall, exclusively, take cognizance of all causes relating to Envoys and Consuls from Foreign Nations, all causes in which a Province may be a party, all those concerning public functionaries, all those relating to crimes committed against the Law of Nations".

Parish then briefly describes the situation of the South American states which are independent of the government of Buenos Aires: Entre Ríos, Santa Fe, Paraguay and Chile (although Artigas' leadership is mentioned, there is no explicit reference to the Banda Oriental which, as stated, was at the time debated between the United Provinces of the River Plate and the Portuguese Empire). Parish explains that Entre Ríos and Santa Fe, provinces which had previously belonged to the "Vice Royalty of Buenos Ayres", no longer recognize its government. They now formed an independent league "under the exclusive, and arbitrary command of Artigas", who despite declaring in favour of independence, "had separated himself from the general interests of the *Buenos Ayreans*".

Likewise, Paraguay is "under the control of a single Individual, Francia, styling himself Dictator of Paraguay". In other words, Parish clearly differentiates the constitutional government established by Buenos Aires from the individual, dictatorial and authoritarian domination, in his terms, of the federal league and Paraguay. He points out, however, a key difference between the two: while Artigas promotes open conflict with Buenos Aires, Francia maintains good relations and does not seek to make political alliances with neighbouring provinces; he aims to retain autonomy, which enables him to consolidate his power.

Parish indicates that the government of Chile "is distinct from that of the United Provinces of La Plata, although the closest intimacy exists between them". When describing its key aspects, he quotes verbatim the proclamation of independence of 1 January 1818: "Chili and her adjacent Islands, are stated to form, in fact, and right, a free, independent, and Sovereign State, to be forever separated from the Monarchy of Spain, and to be fully qualified to adopt the form of Government most convenient to their own interests". The difference with respect to Buenos Aires is that the supreme director, O'Higgins, will establish, again cited verbatim, "a federal form of Government to be established by a General Congress, whenever the circumstances of the War will permit the actual Government to turn their attention to the Subject". The close relationship with the government of Buenos Aires is explained by the crucial role the provinces of Cuyo, under the direction of San Martín (referred to as 'Buenos Airean') played in making possible a Chilean government. A treaty of cooperation was signed between Chile and Buenos Aires on 5 February 1819, "by which they bound themselves, to cooperate for the liberation of Peru, and mutually guaranteed the independence of the State, to be formed out of that Vice Royalty".

With reference to the government of Venezuela, organized under the name of the republic of Columbia and including the provinces of Caracas, Nueva Granada and Quito, Parish describes it as "very similar" to the government of Buenos Aires. However, his description is brief. He notes that Venezuela has a federal constitution, sanctioned by a national congress on 21 December 1811. The national congress "occasionally meets" and "Bolivar as chief Magistrate has the principal Direction of Affairs". Unlike the United Provinces of the Rio de la Plata, parts of Colombia are still controlled by the Spanish: Puerto Cabello, Panama and the capital Quito.

Finally, the situation of Mexico differs from the others in that the government should be in the hands of a junta and regency representing King Fernando, or a prince of his family. However, recent events prevent Parish from giving a definitive assessment of the future form of government in Mexico, pending the Spanish king's response to the proposals made by those favouring Mexican independence.

The report concludes with the second key element determining "the present state then of the Revolutionized Provinces", that is, the "state of relations [with] the Mother Country". For reasons that he does not explain, Parish focuses mainly on Buenos Aires and Chile. His conclusion is blunt: "With respect to the relations of the South American Provinces under the Government of Buenos Ayres and Chili with the Mother Country, they seem to be irrevocably at an end".

The basis for this assertion is the declarations of independence that both states published, respectively, in 1816 and 1818, which "solemnly, and definitively, pronounced their absolute, and Entire independence of Spain". This was a political decision recently confirmed, when the offers of the Spanish commissioners sent to Rio de la Plata in 1820 were rejected, because the "reconciliation" they offered did not imply, in any way, the recognition of independence. Finally, the definitive break between Spain and the governments of Buenos Aires and Chile was their strenuous (although, for the moment, failed) attempts to obtain political recognition from the major foreign powers: "The Provinces have hitherto however, in vain appealed to Foreign Powers for any acknowledgment of their political character".

Parish then presents the final conclusions of his report, which we quote extensively given their significance:

"The present state then of the Revolutionized Provinces may be said to be as follows:

Buenos Ayres and the Provinces of La Plata entirely freed from the Mother Country.

<u>Chili</u> and <u>Peru</u> the same, with the exception of Callao [Callao has since been reduced][20] into which place the greater part of the Royal Forces (about 4.000) have been thrown, but with little expectation of being able to maintain themselves. La Serna wars also with a small force in the interior of Venezuela.

<u>Venezuela</u> and the Provinces of Quito, the Caraccas and New Granada free, with the exception of Porto Cabello, the Province of Panama and the Capital of Quito by the last account still in possession of the Royal Forces.

In <u>Mexico</u> affairs must be considered as still undecided. The Royal Forces in that Country are supposed to be about 10.000 men considerable, and although tranquil at present, may be still influenced by the Decision of the Mother Country upon the Proposals lately made to her by the Independents. The fortress of Vera Cruz is in the possession of a small garrison of the Royalists."

To further elucidate the Mexican question, Parish presents a brief summary of the situation in constitutional Spain around 1821, arguing that the Cortes' attention was focused on the South American provinces. The Cortes formed a secret committee that proposed a plan for the future government of the Americas, which would be presented to the Americans. The Spanish and American provinces would be divided into three governments or sections of the Cortes: Costa Firme, Nueva Granada and Quito, in Santa Fé (de Bogotá); New Spain, Cuba, Santo Domingo and Puerto Rico, in Mexico; and Peru, Chile and Buenos Aires, in Lima. Although each government would have its own Cortes, which would send three delegates to the General Cortes in Spain, the whole would be under the power of a royal infante who would have the powers of a viceroy.

But Parish warns there is little consensus in the Spanish government on how to achieve its strategic objectives. He points out that "the Spanish Ministry appear to have been averse to the immediate consideration of the subject", and that "Bardaxi seems to have been inclined to wait until the next year", while "his opinion however was decidedly against sending out an Infant", because "in that case, the Colonies would be forever lost to Spain". On the contrary, "He wished for the mediation of Great Britain" and had disapproved of General O'Donojú's conduct in Mexico, "whose Convention with Iturbide would never be ratified", and that his action constituted that of "a Traitor to his Country".

Finally, Parish offers one last piece of information that seems to confirm, along with the previous, that a new agreement between Mexico and Spain is unlikely to be achieved. In the discussions on the report of the secret committee on South American affairs, "No less than forty-Eight deputies

---

20 A note in the margin, probably included by Parish after the report had been completed.

from the South American Provinces appear to have been present as Members of the Cortes. These Deputies presented a petition for the immediate Consideration of the Report, which was rejected".

II

Based on these political conclusions, and the accompanying economic, social and geographical analyses of South America provided by Henderson and Parker, the Parish report includes a set of "recommendations" for political action which constitute a truly tactical programme to overcome the impasse that British diplomacy was facing due to the counterrevolutionary policy of the Holy Alliance.

At the end of his description of Colombia, Henderson celebrates the existence of a republican government that, in its quest to overcome the old barriers to trade and production imposed by Spain, sought to link up with the main markets of the world. For Henderson, proof of the "sincere disposition" of the Colombian government to achieve this objective is the promulgation of the list of tariffs that will be paid to the state for the circulation of merchandise, sanctioned on 22 September 1821.

Three articles, in particular (article 5, tariffs on manufactured fabrics; 11, which opened the door to a trade agreement; and 12, a discount for foreign ships travelling directly from Europe), indicated, according to Henderson, that Britain should urgently sign a trade agreement with Colombia, thus enabling Britain to obtain conditions equivalent to those enjoyed in Brazil, the main British port in South America.[21]However, Henderson does not limit said policy to Colombia. He includes all the emancipated states of South America. To substantiate his argument, he refers to the size of the market of the five South American republics, with a population of not be less than 14 million, to which a million or so indigenous people should be added. Taking into consideration the population numbers, Henderson calculates the average consumption of imported British merchandise, transferring the statistics he manages for Brazil to the whole of Latin America. He concludes that it would represent a commercial volume of £12 million a year.

But given that "this trade is not ostensibly recognized by the British Government", a significant part of that volume would be lost in the payment of taxes that could be avoided. Henderson's conclusion was simple: recognition of the new states would make possible the signing of trade agreements that would alleviate the tax burden on trade. He recommends that the British government should put pressure Spain to carry out such a measure and, taking into account the North American example, at the same time consuls

---

21 James Henderson, "A commercial Sketch of the Columbian Republic, with a few observations upon the expediency of the British Government acknowledging the independence of the new States of Spanish America". All the following references are from this chapter unless otherwise indicated.

should be sent to the main South American ports to obtain preferential trade agreements. Due to the importance of this argument, we quote at length:

> "In this state of the case how much weightier are the considerations presented to the British Government, than to any other power for using its immediate influence with the Mother Country to induce it to acknowledge the independence of the transatlantic colonies.
>
> And if any existing political relations, render this preliminary arrangement absolutely requisite, before our Government can enter into any commercial regulations with the new States, the sooner so desirable an object is accomplished the better, and those members of the British Senate who are distinguished for their enlightened and liberal consideration of commercial affairs, will largely promote the prosperity of trade by hastening this question to an early conclusion.
>
> The Government of the United States has already avowed its determination of pressing the Court of Madrid to an arrangements with the Republics of Spanish America; but that Government does not regard the non-completion of the measure it is about to recommend to Old Spain, as any restraint upon its policy of dispatching consuls, in the meantime, to the principal ports of the new Republican States, anticipating, doubtless, by such a concession some commercial preference."

Henderson's programmatic proposals are not simply his own opinion, as they appear again in Parker's report, which concludes with the question of foreign trade and notes that (as in Colombia), "a commission has been appointed to regulate and settle the conditions on which foreign trade is to be conducted". Along the same lines as Henderson, Parker offers an approximation of the country's commercial power, assuring that during the last war (the Peninsular War), a Spanish government licence allowed the regular trade of $100,000 per week, almost entirely of British goods, between Kingston and Veracruz.

Parker states that a licence obtained by the Parish commercial house (from Hamburg, not connected to Woodbine Parish's family), granted by the North American government, allowed him to promote trade worth $20 million with Mexico (no time measure is specified, but we suspect that it is an annual volume), which would amount to between 10 and 12 million dollars annually for British manufactures.

He also points out that four years previously the United States had sent an agent to make contact with the 'Independents', though without success.[22] Since then, Parker had acquired all the documentation in this regard and had sent it to Home Popham, at the Jamaica station.

The intention of this reference to North American policy was, as with

---

22 C. Parker, "Memorandum on the late occurrences in the Kingdom of Mexico", London, 4 February 1822. All the following references are from this chapter unless otherwise indicated.

Henderson, to convince the British government that the dispatch of a British agent would be well received in Mexico, and would confer significant commercial advantages to Great Britain:

> "If I might venture an opinion, I should say that an Agent from this country would be very favorably received, and the advantages likely to accrue in commercial point of view most important. The Mexicans have hitherto been unaccustomed to communicate or hold intercourse with foreigners and at such an important crisis might feel flattered and gratified at being noticed by His Britannic Majesty's Government, and induced to hold out that preference to our commercial relations which other powers will in all probability soon feel anxious to insure. We have hitherto (through clandestinely) enjoyed a large proportion of the trade of that vast Empire, but there is no doubt that under the present state of affairs the advantages to this country might be very considerably increased."

Parker's report concludes with a stark warning: if urgent trade relations are not established with Mexico, American competition could gain a decisive advantage in the country:

> "The Americans are the principal rivals we have to dread, their fine fast sailing vessels, enterprise, and as I before stated, contiguity, give them decided advantage, and no time should be lost in supplying the wants of Mexico, which must be done from some Quarter, and which they are probable at this moment on the alert to accomplish, by endeavouring to establish commercial relations between the two countries."

III

After Castlereagh's death in early August 1822, Parish wrote to his father from the FO, assuring him that the Duke of Wellington "goes to Verona in the place of Lord Londonderry, and Mr. Canning comes to the Foreign Office; he wishes Planta to continue as Under-Secretary. Lord Clanwilliam will go with the Duke to Verona, and will I suppose get some Mission abroad" (Kay Shuttleworth, 1910: 228). George Canning took over as Foreign Secretary on 16 September and one of the main issues he had urgently to address was "the state of our own relations with Spain, connected as they were with those between Spain and her revolted Colonies; and, 4th, the language to be held by the Representative of this country at the Congress at Vienna, which was subsequently adjourned to Verona" (Stapleton, vol. 1, 1831: 131, 141).

At that time, without Castlereagh at the helm, the FO was struggling to prepare the papers for Verona. Parish therefore came into direct contact with Canning and, at the end of October 1822, presented him his report, through Joseph Planta, accompanied by a letter. In the letter Parish points out that his work was only to offer "an outline of the Revolutions of Buenos Ayres, Chili and Peru", anticipating that they "have been entirely distinct from those which [...] have taken place in the Northern Provinces of New Granada, the

Caracas and Mexico".[23] With reference to the latter, he warns that "I have no materials here to work", which is why he points out the inconclusive nature of the report on Mexico, because "the occurrences which have there led to Iturbide to be chosen Emperor, are so very recent that it is [...] necessary to recapitulate them". Likewise, he points out the difficulties faced "in tracing out the Events in the Southern Provinces", and laments, as stated, that "I fear after all you will find it but a slight sketch, compiled very much from newspapers [...] in some degree checked by the Admiralty Reports in the Office which however are extremely partial and deficient". His letter also explains the original idea for the report and its political purpose, advising that it should be sent to the Duke of Wellington, the highest authority in the British delegation at the Verona congress.

These facts allow us to read in a different light the well-known Canning (Stapleton, 1887, vol. II: 48–63) and Wellington (*Despatches*, 1867: 386–388) Memorandums on the Latin American question, produced in November 1822: as was the case with the Castlereagh Memorandum of July 1822, these later memoranda result directly from the intelligence presented by Parish in his 1822 report.

23 W. Parish to J. Planta, London, 28 October 1822, TRGH, SWP/3.

Conclusions

Parish's report, enriched by Henderson's and Parker's contributions, presents a snapshot of the main events in the South American revolutions, especially in Buenos Aires, Chile, Peru, Colombia (Venezuela, Nueva Granada and Quito) and Mexico, at that point in time (early 1822). It also describes the structure and organization of the newly established governments, primarily their political and constitutional characteristics, and the geography, society and economies of Colombia and Chile.

Despite its limitations, which the author acknowledges, Parish's report is based on documentation similar to that employed by intelligence agencies in the modern era, combining mainly 'open sources' with fewer, though qualitatively more important, secret sources provided by the Admiralty (Herman, 1996: 50; Warner, 2020: 2). As Nicolson (1939: 97) noted in his classic study, the "use of the printing press as an ally to diplomacy is as old as Swift and the Treaty of Utrecht". In this case, it was undoubtedly a first-rate source of information.

The Parish report was to be used for assessing the political situation in the regions which had fought for independence and, in particular, their relationship with Spain. Secondarily, the report considers the economic advantages of the subcontinent for British commercial, financial and industrial capital, and recommends policies based on the information provided.

With respect to the revolutionary processes, the leading role played by Buenos Aires across the vast region of the former viceroyalty of Rio de la Plata is clearly significant. Without failing to point out the lack of definitive intelligence, the report details the struggles within the Federal Party which, at the time of writing, had resulted in Buenos Aires being a "tolerably settled state" and peace with the governments of the interior provinces "almost entirely restored".

The report ends with the annexation of the Banda Oriental to the crown of Portugal, newly named the Cisplatine Province (Provincia Cisplatina) and insists that although the Chilean government is independent from Spain and closely allied to that of Buenos Aires, unlike Buenos Aires, the areas to the west of the Andes remained under the control of the royalists, as in Peru and Mexico.

With respect to the organization of the new governments, the report differentiates between governments with division of powers and republican constitutions (Buenos Aires, Chile and Colombia) and those sustained by dictatorial and arbitrary forms of government based on personality (the Federal League and Artigas; Francia's Paraguay). As far as the republican governments are concerned, the report indicates certain nuances which differentiate the political systems. Chilean federalism is contrasted with the unitary system of Buenos Aires, and elements of authoritarianism in Colombia are mentioned. The report also differentiates these three governments which, despite their differences, had already declared independence and would be able to establish a definitive form of government in the short term, from the case of Mexico, governed by a junta and regency representing the Spanish monarchy. In other words, as events in Mexico were unfolding and Spain's response to the Mexican proposal still forthcoming, a definitive evaluation of Mexico's future form of governance could not be ascertained.

Finally, in a section entitled "Present state of the revolutionary provinces", the report provides a general assessment of the current political and military relations between the new states and Spain. Parish divides the geography of the revolutionary regions into three categories, based on the results of the wars and the effective control, or otherwise, of territory. In this sense, he insists that Buenos Aires and Chile are completely liberated from Spain. This is also the case for Peru, Quito, Caracas and New Granada, though with the proviso that within their territories certain areas were still in the hands of royalist forces. In Mexico, however, the course of events is still uncertain, not only because of the pending official Spanish response but also because a royalist force of considerable strength was still in control of the fort at Veracruz.

After a brief review of the situation in Spain, Parish suggests (correctly, as it turns out) that the proposal presented by the Cordoba Convention will be rejected and war renewed. O'Donojú had been accused of treason and there existed diverging opinions within the Spanish Cortes on how to address the situation in South America.

The geographical, economic and social analysis was provided by James Henderson. As well as presenting the regional geographies and products in some detail, Henderson's principal aim is to focus particularly on what might be considered "essential for the purposes of British trade". In this sense, his population and per capita consumption calculations for the whole of Spanish America are compared with those he obtained himself during his residence in Brazil, concluding that the commercial volume of trade would reach a figure in the millions. He argues that the collection of import duties and the consumption of British manufactures will be greater than in "any other Empire or State in the world". He is also certain that revolutionary governments are willing to reduce trade tariffs for nations that recognize them as independent and who sign trade agreements with them.

Considering these points, Henderson argues strongly that the British government should press Spain to recognize the independence of the South American states with some urgency. And taking North America as an example, at the same time Britain should send consuls to the main ports of the new South American states to sign bilateral treaties offering preferential trade with Great Britain.

As stated, these considerations were presented to Castlereagh at the end of July 1822. They coincide exactly with the memorandum that the Foreign Secretary drew up for his use in the Verona Congress: the classification of the states into three categories and the dispatch of consuls to sign commercial treaties that implied diplomatic recognition, pending official recognition by Spain.

After his death in early August 1822, Castlereagh was replaced by the Duke of Wellington at the Verona Congress, and by George Canning in the FO. By September, Wellington had received the Castlereagh Memorandum indicating the policy he should propose to the Holy Alliance, which is based on the Parish report. On 15 November, Canning drew up his famous memorandum on South America which he presented to the cabinet, supported only by the prime minister. His position was that the South American states should be immediately recognized as independent and that both he and the prime minister would resign if their policy was not accepted (Cecil, 1923: 556). The text stated that "Important as the interests may be which are now in discussion at Verona, yet, in the present state of the world, no questions relating to continental Europe can be more immediately and vitally important to Great Britain than those which relate to America" (Stapleton, vol. II, 1887: 48). Canning's memorandum, like Castlereagh's, is based on the facts presented in the Parish report, the descriptions of the political situations in the revolutionary states and the recommendation that commercial consuls should be dispatched immediately. The basis for the recognition was:

"The degree of recognition must of course be proportioned to the degree of force and stability which the several States may have respectively acquired, and to the absence of struggle for ascendency on the part either of the mother country or of parties into which each State may be divided. Neither in Buenos Ayres nor in Chili is there a vestige of Spanish force. [...] Nor is there in either of these three States such a contest for power as either to endanger its independence or to disqualify it for maintaining external relations."

(Stapleton, vol. II, 1887: 58–59)

The aim was, of course, to defend trade and protect British capital in South America. Wellington expressed it openly at the Congress of Verona when he stated:

"From a period commencing during the late war with France his Majesty's subjects have had commercial relations with those provinces, with the consent of the government and of the court of Spain; and those relations, as well as the various and complicated relations which exist between his Majesty's subjects and all parts of the world, have long rendered it necessary that his Majesty should so far recognise the existence *de facto* of the governments formed in those several provinces."

(Despatches, 1867: 386)

Like Canning, the political grounds for British recognition were to be found in "the utter relaxation of the authority of Spain over the whole of this part of the world".

As we can see, the Parish report is further evidence that FO policy towards Latin America cannot be attributed simply to the personal qualities and talents of Castlereagh or Canning. It complements the view in the historiography of late nineteenth-century Britain that British policies were not dictated by any one personality but were the result of broader considerations that had their main nerve-centre in the FO (Otte, 2011: 4). Clerks should no longer be considered as mere assistants to the minister, or their work as "'largely mechanical', docketing, indexing, ciphering and deciphering" (Otte, 2004: 35). On the contrary, the high academic standards required of them, as well as an excellent command of foreign languages, shows, at least in the case of Parish, that they could be required to carry out more high-powered tasks. Obviously, the writing of the report and its qualitative importance, as expressed in the policies it gave rise to, was not a "mechanical" job. In this way, the report supports the thesis that the FO was a knowledge-based organization in which "efficient information management procedures, guaranteeing a controlled information flow, had to be devised, properly maintained and constantly revised, geared towards the needs of informed policy-making and decisive action" (Otte, 2004: 36).

But, just as we should not consider British foreign policy to be solely the result of individual decisions, neither can it be fully understood without taking into account the social class of FO officials and their relationship with the British ruling classes.

Although different in their approaches (Castlereagh preferring to work with the Holy Alliance through the congress system, and Canning withdrawing from this old alliance), the two foreign secretaries sought the most efficient way of reconciling the interests of the rising commercial and industrial bourgeoisie with the old aristocratic and land-owning classes, without endangering the order and governability of the country which was increasingly threatened by working-class conflict.[1] As far as Parish is concerned, his career in the FO

---

1 See the relevant comments in the classic studies published by Archibald Alison (1861: 171–172) and Algernon Cecil (1923: 555–556). The former argues "Mr Canning, therefore, was sailing under borrowed colours when he made his famous boast of

proves that the purported absence of clerks from families of the mercantile classes is incorrect. In this sense, we argue that Parish's activity in the FO in general, and the report on the revolutions in South America in particular, were a channel for the strategic development of mercantile and manufacturing capital within the British state.

It could be argued therefore that the 'intermediate' officials of the FO were a conduit by means of which the social class that most sought to influence the British government and its foreign policy at the time could put forward a particular strategy which would be to their advantage. In this sense, Parish and, in particular, Henderson, both closely linked in their different ways to British commercial capital, acted as a nexus between the interests of this class and the political direction of the British state by means of reasoned, fact-based argument and historical analysis, leading to a political recommendation that resolved the South American question. Although his report was required to describe as factually correct as possible the political events and socioeconomic realities in South America, Parish may have selected Henderson to express what he, as an 'impartial' official, could not.

In other words, the tactic of sending commercial agents with consular powers to the new Latin American states should not be attributed solely to individuals (Castlereagh, Canning), or even to the British Tory government. It had already been employed by the United States and had also been proposed by some of the South American official envoys. It was a conjunctural solution promoted by the Hanseatic mercantile bourgeoisie and the British commercial and industrial classes, and it was the policy recommended by the Parish and Henderson reports. It was a tactic that, in 1822, made it possible to overcome the contradiction between the development of British industrial and commercial capital (in the throes of the industrial revolution) and the preservation of legitimist monarchical governments, both absolutist and constitutional.

In other words, analysis of the report and the lives of its authors in the context of the economic transformations experienced in Britain at the beginning of the nineteenth century indicates that the specific interests of the

'calling a new world into existence to redress, the balance of the old' (because) the credit or the discredit of calling it into being belongs to Lord Castlereagh rather than Mr Canning"; and the latter suggests "No two Ministers, perhaps, have, at any time since Cabinet Government begun, exhibited greater differences of character and temperament than Castlereagh and Canning; yet it was in their day that the doctrine of continuity in the conduct of Foreign Affairs may plausibly be said to have been brought to birth [...] in practice, there was no vital difference between them; and the Instructions which Castlereagh gave, a little before he died, to Wellington as prospective British Envoy at the Congress of Verona, might have been penned by Canning [...] The recognition of the independence of the republics of Spanish America, which was Canning's proudest boast, had entailed a struggle between the Crown and the Foreign Secretary".

social classes underpinning Britain's so-called "Policy-Making Elite" (Watt, 1965; Steiner, 1984) must be taken into consideration to fully understand British foreign policy. In this sense, the concept of an 'elite' does not clarify the nature of the process as it unhelpfully merges different social realities. The same applies to terms such as 'networks' of influence (ranging from politicians, diplomats and intellectuals to businessmen and the press) and to the category 'actors'. None of these can develop autonomously outside social relations (Kennedy, 1981; Fisher and Best, 2011; Dittmer, 2017).

The report also helps explain why, the following year, the FO chose Parish and Henderson for the posts of consul in the two main capitals of South America, Buenos Aires and Bogotá (Humphreys, 1940: XVIII–XIX). In addition, they had contacts and, in the case of Parish, knew Spanish. Similarly, Parish's warning in the report about the scarcity of reliable information explains why Canning instructed consuls and commissioners to send in regular political and economic reports on the ports where they were posted, justifying this decision with reference to the FO's lack of information (Humphreys, 1940: XII).

Finally, the Parish report allows us to evaluate the changes in British foreign policy towards Latin America from another perspective. Having pulled back from any form of territorial conquest (1806–1808), and having not met with success in mediation between Spain and its colonies, or with the idea of establishing constitutional monarchies, the British recognition of the independent republican states of South America was a necessary fourth strategy made possible by circumstances which, a few years previously, had been unthinkable, and which responded to the joint efforts and the shared interests of those who governed the political and economic destinies of both the United Kingdom and the newly formed South American states.

Part II

Documents

I

The Woodbine Parish Report on the Revolutions in South America (1822)[1]

1 [TRGS, Sir Woodbine Parish, South America. Volume containing printed and manuscript reports prepared for the Congress of Verona, 1822 (SWP/3)]. In the following transcripts, the author's comments are enclosed in square brackets.

<h1 style="text-align:center">Index[2]</h1>

I. Letter of Presentation

II. Events in Buenos Ayres since 1816

III. Events in Chili since 1810

IV. Events in Mexico during 1821

V. The Republic of Columbia, by James Henderson

VI. The Republic of Chili, by James Henderson

VII. The Kingdom of Mexico, by C. Parker

VIII. Actual State of the different governments in South America

IX. Appendix of Sundry Public Documents[3]

2 [The original index in Parish's manuscript is as follows: "South America: No. 1. Events in Buenos Ayres since 1816; No. 2. "Ditto in Chile since 1810"; No. 3. "Ditto in Mexico during 1821"; No. 4. "Appendix of Sundry Public Documents"; No. 5. "Actual state of the different Governments". We have expanded it to include the three annexes (which form part of the report but were not listed in the original index) as well as an extended description of the contents of the documents included in the appendices].

3 [The original index of appendices is as follows: "No. 4. The Appendix contains: 3 Reports of the American Commissioners laid before Congress the end of 1818, pages 1 to 8. Buenos Ayres: Manifesto of Independence, October 1817, pages 9 to 12; Exposé of Affairs, by Puyerredon [sic] (1818), pages 13 to 14; Chili: Proclamation of Independence, 1 January 1818, page 15; Manifesto to Foreign Nations, 2 Feb. 1818, pages 16 to 18; Treaty between Chili and Buenos Ayres for the Reduction of Peru, page 19; Recognition of the Independence of Chili by Portugal, 11 August 1821, page 20; Peru: Decree of San Martin making himself Protector of Peru, 3 August 1821, page 19; Dispatch to the War Department in Lima on the state of affairs, 12 September 1821, page 19; Mexico: Plan of the Government of the Empire of Mexico, page 21; Convention between General O'Donojú and Iturbide, 24 August 1821, page 22; Decree for the Election of Deputies to the Congress (Mexico, November 1821), page 20; Guatemala: Act of Independence, 15 September 1821, page 23; United States: Message to Congress as to the Recognition of the South American States, page 26". We have reordered the documents chronologically and completed the title references to assist the reader and to provide a coherent account of the development of the South American revolutions as recorded in these key documents. We have retained the original spelling throughout].

I. Letter of Presentation

Mem. These papers were prepared for Lord Londonderry[4] to take to the Congress of Verona, to which I was preparing to accompany them – when is consequence of his Death – The Duke of Wellington went in his place. W. P.

My Dear Planta

I send you the Result of my labours in the Country: you will observe it is confined to an Outline of the Revolutions of Buenos Ayres, Chili and Peru: These have been entirely distinct from those which have taken place in the Northern Provinces of New Granada, the Carraccas and Mexico, and upon which I have no materials here to work. But it is of little consequence, as with respect to the former there are several published accounts; and as to Mexico, the occurrences which have there led to Iturbide to being chosen Emperor, are so very recent that it is hardly necessary to recapitulate them.

Although I have had a great deal of difficulty in tracing out the Events in the Southern Provinces, I fear after all you will find it but a slight sketch, compiled very much from newspapers, tho' in some degree checked by the Admiralty Reports in the Office which however are extremely partial and deficient.

The best accounts down to a certain period are the Reports of the American Commissioners laid before Congress, and which contain a variety and abundance of information, especially on the Resources of the Country.

I have nothing here later than the middle of 1821, at which time however matters may be said to have been finally decided.

Ever Yours,

W. Parish

28th October 1822. Riegate[5]

To Joseph Planta, Esq. Foreign Office.

---

4 [Robert Stewart, Viscount Castlereagh].
5 [Reigate, Surrey, England].

II. Events in Buenos Ayres since 1816

N° 1. Buenos Ayres, 1816

On the 6th of July 1816, the Solemn Declaration of Independence was pronounced by "the Representatives of the United Provinces of South America assembled in General Congress ["] at Tucuman.[6]

The situation of these Provinces was however at this time extremely critical. Their forces in Peru had been totally defeated and dispersed by the Royal Army; and on the other hand they were anxiously fearing the arrival of a formidable Expedition from Cadiz in the Rio de la Plata, where the Civil War between Artigas and Alvear (which about that time terminated in the overthrow of the Latter) had left the Revolutionary forces in a state of total disorder and indiscipline.[7]

Under these very critical circumstances the Government of Buenos Ayres conscious of its own want of physical strength and having failed in all its attempts to effect a Reconciliation with The Mother Country, acted with more prudence and foresight than have usually distinguished it, in commencing a negotiation the object of which was by offers of large territorial cessions, to lure the Court of Rio de Janeiro into Measures which (as the event soon proved) would scarcely fail to produce a serious misunderstanding if not an actual rupture between Spain and Portugal.

1816

It is much to be doubted whether any of the gigantic schemes of Conquest and Aggrandizement of which the Brazilian Government was at that time suspected, had any solid foundation, and still more whether they could ever have been carried into effect.

The Portuguese are regarded with a feeling of jealously and aversion which it would have been impossible to overcome, and which the Government of Buenos Ayres has found the utmost difficulty in restraining on many occasions when a rupture with Brazil would have seen the height of folly

---

6 Declaration of Independence of the Provinces of La Plata, 6 July 1816 [Margin note].
7 Com^{der} Bowles to Lt. Thos. Hardy [Margin note].

and Impolicy. It is therefore probable that all the proposals and temptations said to have been held out by the former have been illusory and that a secret determination has always existed to recover the whole of the Eastern Territory upon the first favorable opportunity".[8]

The Portuguese however marched an Army into the Banda Oriental and forcibly took possession of Montevideo and nearly the whole country on the left bank of La Plata. The military possession of this territory by the Portuguese may be considered as a most important advantage to the Government of Buenos Ayres at the time it occurred.

1st, by its weakening and distracting the attention of its most powerful Enemy and rival Artigas, the Governor of the Provinces of Entre Rios; and secondly by securing Montevideo against any attempt which Spain might meditate for its Reconquest, an attempt which at that period could hardly have failed success.

The disputes between Artigas and the Government of Buenos Ayres had originated in his opposition to the claim advanced by the Director who declared his Right to exercise Sovereignty in every part of the United Provinces, and that the city of Buenos Ayres was to be considered as the great central point from which all authority should emanate.

Artigas on the contrary insisted on a federal Government, in which all the Provinces were to have equal Rights and Privileges, and in his Proclamations, he continually protested against the tyrannical usurpations of Buenos Ayres, charging the Director and the Congress with a Plan for delivering up the whole Country to the court of Brazil. On the other hand, this Party were accused by their opponents of intriguing with Spain.

Artigas however gallantly defended his Province against the Portuguese, and succeeded in drawing several chiefs to his Party.

<u>1819</u>
Their constant attacks confined the operations of the Portuguese Invaders, and to the end of 1819 their possessions had extended no further than Montevideo, Colonia, and a position in the Rincon de Gallinas, a point formed by the confluence of the Rivers Uruguay and Negro, whilst the hostility of the country people to them was so great that they had little communication with the Interior.

At the close of 1819
The Province of Santa Fe under Ramirez joined with that of Entre Rios under Artigas, in openly resisting the assumption of all supreme authority over them by Buenos Ayres. Córdoba and Santiago del Estero perhaps at that

---

8 Com.[der] Bowles to Com.[der] Hardy [Margin note].

time had the same feeling, but were overawed by a superior force assembled at Tucuman. The Provinces of Salta and Jujuy were likewise believed to favor a federal form of Government.

The Provinces of Cuyo under San Martin strenuously supported Buenos Ayres. Whilst that of Paraguay under Francia refused to communicate with any of its neighbours or to take any part in any contest, likely to disturb its own tranquility.

The Government of Buenos Ayres had however entered into a secret correspondence with the Court of France to place the young Prince of Lucca (who was to be married to a Princess of Brazil) upon the throne of the Provinces, an overture which appears to have originated with the French Government, and with the secret and conditional acceptance of which by the Government existing at Buenos Ayres in Jan. 1820 a French frigate actually sailed from the Rio de la Plata.

This scheme was defeated by an entire change in the Party at the head of the Government.

1820

The success of Artigas Party drove out the Puyerredonists [*sic*] who had hitherto ruled the Provinces, and Sarratea, a strenuous supporter of the <u>Federalist</u> Party, so called, being chosen Cap. General. The whole correspondence with the Court of France was published.

The first consequence of this change of Party was an immediate Treaty or League between the Provinces of Santa Fe, Entre Rios and Buenos Ayres and the other Provinces of La Plata, agreeing upon a Federal form of Government. But the whole summer was spent in party struggles amongst the federalist chiefs for the Chief command. Sarratea, Balcarce, Mexia, Soler and Rodriguez were by turns at the head of the Government.

They all however seemed to agree upon two points. 1st Upon the Rejection of the offers made to them by the Mother Country, which had sent out Commissioners who arrived off Buenos Ayres in November 1820 endeavoured to treat with them, and who not being prepared to acknowledged the Independence of the Provinces as a preliminary to any negotiation whatever, were obliged to depart without even being suffered to land. And secondly, in a resolution to attack the Portuguese invaders and to drive them out of Montevideo and from the Banda Oriental.

But Artigas, who was the main spring of this feeling against the Portuguese, was continually defeated by them in the Entre Rios, and his principal officers being gradually destroyed by the Portuguese, he himself was at length obliged to seek safety in Paraguay where He was imprisoned by Dr. Francia, the independent chief of that Province.

Carrera on his return to Santiago was taken prisoner and conducted to Chillan.

1814

The year 1814 was opened by a rapid attempt of the Royalists forces to get possession of the capital; Talca was taken and the Junta precipitately retreating occasioned a Commotion at Santiago in which the Junta was declared dissolved, and Lastra, the Governor of Valparaiso being nominated Supreme Director, a Convention was signed on the 5th May 1814, between the contending parties.

By this act, it was agreed that the Royalists should evacuate the territory of Chili in 2 months, that the Spanish Regency should be acknowledged, and that Deputies should be sent to the Spanish Cortes.

In the mean time, Carrera escaped from Chillan, and raising a party in Santiago deposed Lastra on the 23^{d} August 1814, and reestablished the Junta, placing himself at his head. Upon of hearing of these events O'Higgins immediately marched against Carrera, and a bloody battle took place between the two factions at Maipo which ended in favour of the latter (this place afterwards became the scene of a much greater action between the Royalists and Federalists). Shortly after this event, intelligence was received that the Vice Roy of Lima had refused to ratify the Convention signed at Santiago on the 5th of May, and that General Osorio was marching with a large force against the Independents of Chili. This news united all Parties in their own defence. O'Higgins was placed at the head of the army, and Carrera returned to Santiago. But Osorio completely defeated the Patriots under O'Higgins, and the whole Captain Generalship fell into the hands of the Royalists in October 1814.

Numerous proscriptions, arrests and punishments followed: and

1814–1815

the father of the Carreras was banished with many others to the Island of Juan Fernandez. In this state of things General San Martin who had been appointed Governor of the Province of Cuyo, by the Government of Buenos Ayres to which it belonged prepared to organize an Army for the purpose of attempting the Recovery of Chili.

This however was a work of time.

1817

It was not till the beginning of 1817, more than two years after the conquest that He found himself fully prepared to cross the Andes with an Army of 4000 men... Having trained and disciplined his forces with incredible pains He executed his march across the mountains so suddenly that he descended into Chili before it was known that he was even on his way.

Defeating in a decisive Battle the Royal forces at Chacabuco, he recovered at once possession of almost the whole Kingdom of Chili. On the other side, the Army of the Independents of Peru, which had been again gradually augmented and organized, repulsed an attempt made by the Royalist General La Serna, to penetrate from the North into the Province of Tucuman.

1818

These Successes on the part of the Patriots led to the solemn Declaration of the Independence of Chili, on the 1st of January 1818.[10]

Signed by O'Higgins, elected Supreme Director of the Government, upon the refusal of San Martin (to whom it had been first offered) to accept it.

The campaign of 1818 was opened by the Royalists with a vigorous attempt made by the Vice Roy of Peru to reconquer Chili. General Osorio was detached from Lima on this service with a force of 4,000 men, who disembarking at Talcahuano in January, gained a considerable advantage over San Martin, in an action near Talca. The latter retreated in disorder to Santiago, but gaining time to reassemble his Army, on the 5th of April was enabled in his turn to attack Osorio, whom he completely defeated in a decisive Battle at Maypo[11], the consequence of which was, the almost total abandonment of Chili by the Royal forces, Valdivia, and the Isle of Chiloe, being the only Posts remaining in their hand.

In Peru, the war was principally defensive during 1818, and to nearly the close of 1819. The country miserably exhausted, and neither Party feeling strong enough to make any decisive effort against the other.

1819

At the close of the latter year, the Royal Army under General La Serna, occupied a line on the River Humaguaca, extending its left to Tarija, and the right to Suipacha, the Head Quarters being at Cotagayta. They were supposed to be about 8.000 strong, but much dispersed amongst the different Provinces in its rear, where revolutionary movements caused them frequent alarms.

The neighboring Provinces of Jujuy and Salta were in possession of the Independents, the Inhabitants of which rose, en masse, whenever the Spaniards attempted to invade them.

The possession of Chili determined the Independents to combine in a general attack upon the Vice Royalty of Peru, and a Treaty was signed between the Buenos Ayrean, and Chilian Government[12] on the 5th February 1819, for the express purpose of expelling the Royal forces from that territory.

10 1 January 1818 Declaration of Independence of Chili [Margin note].
11 Battle of Maipo, 5 April 1818 [Margin note].
12 Treaty between Buenos Ayres and Chili, 5 Feb. 1819 [Margin note].

The two Parties mutually guaranteeing the Independence of the Government to be established in the Capital, whenever the Liberation of the Country should be effectuated.[13] "The Peruvians were believed to have a natural antipathy to the Chilians, which might render them averse to any subsequent proposition for placing them under the Government of Chili. Among the better classes, a general wish was believed to prevail for a Monarchical form of Government, under any Prince from Europe, not of the Bourbon Line (to which their hatred was daily increasing), and in this feeling, it was thought, that both General San Martin and O'Higgins the Supreme Director of Chili, secretly acquiesced".

The public declarations however of O'Higgins and the Chilian Government hold uniformly no other language than the strongest desire for a <u>General Confederation</u>, and a <u>Representative Government</u> as the first step to the formation of which[14], a general census had been already ordered in 1818 of the whole population.

San Martin, after the Battle of Maypo, returned to Chili for the avowed purpose of personally attending to the preparations for the reduction of Lima, which he hoped to be ready to attack by the beginning of 1820 provided the threatened Armament from Spain should not arrive in the Rio de la Plata.

Lord Cochrane, in the meantime, collected a naval force of 9 ships of war, which acting under the denomination of the Chili Squadron, sailed from Valparaiso in September 1819 for Callao upon which place however His Lordship failed in two direct attacks, and was obliged for a time to abandon the Enterprise.

It was shortly after this, that the French Frigate, supposed to be the bearer of some further proposals respecting the Prince of Lucca, arrived in the Rio de la Plata, and connected with the Affairs of the Western Provinces, it is worthy of remark[15] "that Carrera one of the followers of Artiga's Party (which had recently obtained the direction of the Government of Buenos Ayres) and whose family at the commencement of the Revolution had held the Government of Chili told the English Commodore, that the Portuguese Government had once made an offer to Him, of the future Captain Generalship of Chili, if he would cooperate in the Plan for placing that Prince upon the Throne of the United Provinces of the Rio de la Plata. Carrera stated at the same time his belief that overtures of a similar nature had been made to San Martin and O'Higgins".

---

13 Capt. Sheriff to Com.[der] Hardy [Margin note].).
14 vide Declaration of the Chili Government to the Inhabitants of Peru [Margin note].
15 Com.[der] Hardy [Margin note].

1820

It was not till near the close of 1820 that San Martin had completed his preparations for His intended attack upon Peru, and that the Expedition sailed from Chili. The Buenos Aires Government shortly afterwards received from him an official account of his having effected a landing at Pisco, and having defeated, in a decisive action, the Royal forces under General O'Reilly who had been made prisoner.

The Army was expected to march immediately upon Chancay and the vicinity of Lima. In his proclamations to the People of Peru, General San Martin uniformly declared his determination never to negociate [sic] with the Vice Roy till he should acknowledge the Independence of Chili.

Whilst San Martin was thus successful by land, Lord Cochrane declared the whole Coast of Peru in a state of Blockade.

1821

The Province of Guayaquil[16], to the north of Peru, about the same time declared itself independent of the Mother Country, consolidating its Government under Olmedo, formerly a Deputy to the Cortes and the general success of the Patriots upon the Western Coast, encouraged an expectation of their ultimately obtaining possession of Lima, upon which it was felt, the fate of the whole Vice Royalty of Peru depended.

The blockade produced strong remonstrances on the part of the British Commodore, but was subsequently gradually removed from those parts of the Coast which fell into the hands of the independents, with which neutral and friendly vessels were allowed to trade, upon the payment of a fixed tariff of Duties.

Valparaiso was made nearly a free Port, and upon the whole British commerce received considerable encouragement from the independent Government, although the detention of several vessels by the blockading squadron, had given rise to some complaints and remonstrances on the part of the British Commodore.

In June 1820, the blockade was taken off by Lord Cochrane except for two degrees of the Coast, including Callao and Lima, which were still defended by the Spaniards. The Chilian Army prepared for their reduction by a combined attack and took up a Position near Huacho Bay, at Huacero, about 60 miles to the north of Callao and here they were joined by a part of Lord Cochrane's force, which having been landed at Pisco, effected a junction with them by marching round the mountains at the back of Lima.

---

16 This Province afterwards incorporated Itself with the government of Venezuela [Margin note].

The Royal forces supposed to be from 7 to 10,000 men strong remained in their entrenched camp about 2 leagues from that place. In this state of affairs, the Vice Roy Pezuela was suddenly deposed by the Army upon the pretext that all their recent misfortunes had originated in his personal mismanagement ('misconduct' crossed out). He was replaced by Don Jose de la Serna who was elected by the Army to hold protempore the Government till a reference could be made to Europe.

In July however, General La Serna being reduced to great extremities by the Independents, was induced to sign an Armistice for 20 days with San Martin with a view to endeavour by negotiation to put an end to the war.

Subsequently on the 5th of July La Serna evacuated Lima, and San Martin took possession of it on the 8th. A garrison of 400 men was left in Callao and the Royalists afterwards succeeded in September in throwing a large force about 4.000 men, into that place with a view to protract the termination of the war.[17] The Fortress however was ill supplied with provisions and San Martin had determined to reduce it by cutting off all supplies and assistance.

San Martin had taken the Title of Protector of Peru and assumed the Government ad interim.[18]

<u>April</u>
P.S. Callao has since been taken by the Independents. There still however by the last accounts existed a small Royalist Force in the interior.

17 Vide appendix, page 19 [Margin note].
18 vide Decree in the Appendix, page 19 [Margin note].

IV. Events in Mexico during 1821

N° 3. Mexico

<u>1821</u>

Though partial Insurrections had taken place in the Kingdom of <u>Mexico</u>, yet, upon the whole the cause of the Mother Country retained there its preponderance, until in April 1821 a Colonel Iturbide who had been ordered to march against the Insurgents at Acapulco entered into negotiations with them, and placed himself at their head. He then wrote to the Vice Roy Apodaca proposing to him to adopt the Spanish Constitution, and that either the King of Spain or one of his Brothers should be invited to repair to Mexico, where he should be acknowledged as Emperor. The Vice Roy in the interim to continue his functions under certain Restrictions.

A large force was however immediately ordered by the Vice Roy to march against Him. Iturbide nevertheless obtained considerable success, and by June the whole Kingdom of Mexico was in a State of Insurrection.

Ferdinand was styled Emperor in all Public Decrees. The Inquisition which had been abolished by the Regency in Spain was re-established and the suppressed Monasteries restored. The Clergy everywhere favored the Independents and the Vice Roy himself being believed not to exert himself to the utmost against them, was deposed by the Royalists and succeeded by Novella who was appointed to hold the Government.

The garrison at Veracruz was reduced by desertion to less than 800 men and at the close of July the City of Puebla capitulated to the Independents.

About the same time, General O'Donohu [*sic*] arrived from Spain to take upon himself the Government of the Vice Royalty of Mexico. His arrival was shortly followed by a personal meeting with Iturbide at Cordova, where to the astonishment of the Royalists the new Vice Roy was induced to conclude a Convention with the Independents chief on the 24th of August.[19] The principal articles of this agreement, were an acknowledgement of the Independence of the Mexican Empire; an Invitation to Ferdinand to proceed to Mexico to take upon himself the Imperial Crown, and in his default, to his heirs and

---

19 Convention of Cordova, August 24 1821 [Margin note].

Successors; the appointment of a Junta of Government, and the election by it of a Regency of three persons, to hold the reins of Government till the arrival of the Monarch, and the assembly of a Cortes which was fixed for the 1ˢᵗ of January 1822. General O'Donojú to be a member of the Junta, which, however would have little or no power after the election of a Regency. All individuals to be allowed to depart with their Property or remain in the Country as they should think proper, with the exception of some official and military persons who being notoriously inimical to the independents cause, were to quit the Country with their Property. General O'Donojú lastly engaged to employ his authority in order that the Royal Army might evacuate Mexico.

Iturbide assumed the title of Chief of the Imperial Army of the Three Guarantees. These Guarantees are for the preservation of Religion, of Independence and of union between Spaniards and Americans, although their respective Countries should be independent of each other.

In his correspondence with General Davila, the Governor of Veracruz, O'Donojú endeavoured to explain the motives which induced him to conclude this Convention. He stated as his chief reasons, the liberality of Spain, the enlightened state of the age, and the state of public opinion in New Spain. Ordering at the same time the Governor of Veracruz to publish the Convention, and immediately to reembark the troops from the Havannah, should they have landed at Veracruz.

In reply, General Davila objected strongly to the Convention, which he declined publishing. He excused himself also from sending back any Reinforcements from the Havannah, which he considered absolutely necessary for the garrison of Veracruz.

The conduct of General O'Donojú throughout this transaction is generally disapproved of by the Royalists, in having made such important sacrifices on the part of Spain, without authority, without a struggle, and without giving himself time to ascertain the true state of the Country.

In September the Province of Yucatan declared itself in favor of Mexican Independence. The Revolution was effected at the Capital, Merida, without difficulty and in the most formal manner, by almost all the constituted authorities on the 15ᵗʰ September. The Governor Escheverri [*sic*] consenting to continue in the command.

General Novella, who had been named by the Royalists to succeed the Vice Roy Apodaca in Mexico, at first positively refused to acknowledge the Convention of Cordova.

General O'Donojú, however accompanied by Iturbide, having proceeded to the neighbourhood of Mexico, succeeded in prevailing upon him to sign an armistice with them for 6 days on the 7ᵗʰ of September. The Vice Roy O'Donojú afterwards assumed the authority of Captain General, and proclaimed at Mexico on the 17th of the same month the Convention of Cordova.

There were only 3.000 men of the Royalists Forces left to defend the Kingdom of Mexico at that time. A Junta of Government consisting of 12 was subsequently formed, and General O'Donojú, Admiral Apodaca and General Novella were named members thereof. A Regency was elected and General O'Donojú was also named Captain General and Jefe Politico or Prefect of the Province of Mexico.

Iturbide continued for the present to be chief of the Imperial Army of the Three Guarantees, and the Independent Government appeared to be established throughout the whole of New Spain, with the exception of the Castle of Veracruz, in which the Troops (under General Novella) were reduced from desertion to 500 men.

It is said that during the Conferences of Cordova, O'Donojú under the belief that neither of the Infants, Brothers of The King of Spain, would accept the Imperial Crown, persuaded Iturbide to pass over the Family of Braganza and declare the Infant Don Carlos, son of the Grand Dutchy of Lucca, next in the order of succession, which Prince it was generally hoped would be the future Sovereign of New Spain.

The Province of Guatemala declared itself independent in October, and a Cortes was as soon as possible to be assembled there, to decide upon the future form of Government, and whether Guatemala should remain alone, or unite itself to New Spain.

In November last, the Regency of the Imperial Government of Mexico, was composed of 5 individuals: Viz. Iturbide as President; General O'Donojú; Barcenas, Archdeacon of Valladolid; Yañez, a member of the Supreme Court of Justice; and Velazquez de Leon, formerly Secretary of the Vice regal Government.

The Bishop of Puebla was to be President of the Supreme Junta, consisting of 37 persons, and Almanza was named Vice President. Iturbide continued to be Generalissimo of the Land and Sea Forces.

Shortly after General O'Donojú died at Mexico, the Bishop of Puebla was appointed to his seat in the Regency, and Don Alcocer a Priest succeeded to the Presidency of the Junta.

General Linan [*sic*] with a force of about 10.000 men still attached to the cause of Spain, though inactive was in December last encamped not far from Mexico and was regularly supplied with Pay and provisions. It was expected that matters would remain in a state of tranquility till the decision of the Spanish Government upon the Convention of Cordova could be received.

V. The Republic of Columbia

A commercial Sketch of the Columbian Republic, with a few observations upon the expediency of the British Government acknowledging the independence of the new States of Spanish America, by James Henderson (afterwards appointed Consul General in Columbia by G. Canning).[20]

The Empire now comprises the ci-devant Provinces of Caracas or Venezuela and New Granada, the first by an estimate (reputed authentic) about the year 1811, was stated to extend over a space of 50,000 Square leagues, and to contain 850,000 inhabitants, the latter to have 65,000 square leagues of territory, with a population of two million and a half, which however four or five years afterwards was computed at only two million.

A very recent statement by authority of the Spanish government represents the extent of the Caracas at 64,561 square leagues with 900,000 inhabitants, and New Granada at 80,433 square leagues with 1,600,000 inhabitants.

From this data, we may fairly infer that the Columbian Empire embraces a territory of 130,000 square leagues and two million and a half population, allowing for the loss of lives occasioned by the earthquake at Caracas in 1812, and by the sanguinary warfare that may now be regarded as finally terminated. Speaking of the commercial capabilities and facilities of this important Republic, I will confine myself principally in this sketch, to such productions and places as are mainly essential for the purposes of British trade.

The political division of Venezuela (little Venice) or Caracas are seven, namely Guiana, Cumana or Paria, Barcelona, Caracas-proper, Coro, Maracaybo and Varinas.

The district of Guiana, which extends over a circumference of 1000 leagues along the eastern and Southern banks of the Orinoco and its branches, although incalculably rich in soil hitherto remains almost in its pristine state, having only a scanty population of ten thousand creoles (without mentioning

---

20 [The words in parentheses are written in pencil].

the Indians, who, as civilization increases will add much to the commercial advancement of this fine district) dwelling upon the margins of the Orinoco.

The capital St. Thome or Angostura is situated upon the right bank of that river about 250 miles from the Atlantic, and the whole of this district presents a prodigious field for commercial pursuits, but the only returns it offers at present for our manufactures, are hides and a trifling supply of indigo and cotton, notwithstanding its capabilities of production are not surpassed by any other part of the world.

The districts of Cumana and Barcelona follow next along the coast in a north westerly direction from the Orinoco; the Chief town of Cumana, and one of the oldest of this continent, is the City of the same name, the fine river Manzanares flowing through it forms a commodious port and the entrance of the harbour is highly beautiful. The City rises out of the richly cultivated plain, with the horizon darkened by the elevated Andean chain that traverse these districts to the gulph of Paria. The only danger in the port is the Moro Roxo shoal near half a mile in breadth, but with abundance of depth all around.

The population of Cumana is 18,000, and its exports consist of a fine quality of cotton (grown principally in the vicinity of Cariaco, a town containing 6,000 inhabitants at the extremity of the gulph of the same name running eastward from Cumana), Cocoa, a small portion of sugar, indigo, and tobacco which is produced at Cumanacoa, one of the principal towns of the district about thirty miles from Cumana. The salt works of Araya upon the peninsula formed by the gulph of Cariaco, constitute a considerable branch of commerce.

Barcelona, the chief town of the district of its name, is about forty miles west of Cumana, upon the left margin of the Neveri, and had 13,000 inhabitants, who have such a taste for dealing in live and dead cattle that the cultivation of the soil has been neglected, although well adapted for cotton, cocoa, etc.: the principal articles of export are therefore, hides, tallow, salted beef, oxen and mules, which have been hitherto shipped for the West Indies and Cuba, and this port has been famous for receiving the contraband goods of Trinidad.

The districts of Cumana and Barcelona are estimated to contain 90,000 inhabitants. The district of Caracas-proper, and Coro, follow next upon the Coast and with the interior district of Varinas, bordering upon them to the southward, are said to include a population of 500,000 souls.

The soil of Caracas-proper is exceedingly fertile, and affords in profusion not only all the productions of the West Indies but numerous others; its cocoa is of a highly esteemed quality, and it presents for the return cargo, Vanilla, tobacco, sugar, coffee, indigo, cotton, cochineal, sarsaparilla, liquorice, balsams, dyewoods, drugs, gums, squills, storax, aloes, cassia, etc., and the widely extending plains of the interior are peopled with herds of cattle, horses and mules; the mountains with sheep and deer, which will likewise contribute to the commercial importance of this empire.

The City of Caracas is the capital of the Province, and at the period of the earthquake in 1812, which three of my friends had the misfortune to witness, it contained near 50,000 souls, but that fatal catastrophe and subsequent events have reduced them to 30,000. This city is situated upon the edge of a charming valley, some distance from the coast, and its port is the small town of La Guayra, where the sea is generally agitated creating some difficulty in the landing and discharging of vessels.

Port Cabello, is the next port of consequence in a North Western direction of 100 miles from La Guayra, having a fine harbour in the gulph of Triste, not far from the island of Curacoa, and although very unhealthy is reputed to be the entrepot of Western Venezuela.

Coro, the chief town of the district so called, is upwards of one hundred miles north west of Porto Cabello; its trade is with the West India islands in mules, hides, goats, cheese, coarse pottery ware, etc., all of which come from the interior; its population amounts to 10,000 souls, about the same as that of Porto Cabello.

Among the principal towns of the interior of Carracas-proper may be enumerated those of Casora, Tocuyo famous for its wheat, Guanara, Barquisimeta, Victoria, Tulmero having many indigo, tobacco, and cocao planters; Maracay, Valencia with a rich district and tobacco grounds on the eastern side of the lake of its name employing 12,000 persons; San Carlos, Arauca, Calaboso, San Juan del Pao, St. Felippe and many others; these towns possess a population of from 8 to 12,000 each, who contribute their share to the articles of export already mentioned and have a prevailing taste for British manufactures.

Maracaybo is an extensive district and its capital, situated upon the spacious lake of the same name, has a commercial population of 25,000 persons; the best schooners that navigate the Spanish main are built here. The lake has upon its margins several small towns, namely San Pedro, Parante, Las Barbacoas, Gibraltar, etc.

The inhabitants of the town of Truxillo, which is about sixty miles distant from the lake, convey their productions thither, and by it to the capital. The tobacco, sugar, cotton, coffee, etc., of Varinas the capital of the district so denominated, of San Jayme, St. Fernando de Apure, San Antonio, towns of the same district, are transmitted principally by the noble river Meta to the Orinoco.

New Granada, the other important Province of this infant Republic, comprises sixteen districts, namely Veragua, Panama and Darien whose shores are washed both by the Pacific and Atlantic oceans; Carthagena and Santa Marta bordering upon the latter sea, Choco, Popayan, Jacames, and

Quito upon the former; Merida, San Juan de los Llanos, Antioquia, Santa Fe, Quixos, Jaen de Bracamoros, and Maynas, are interior districts the two latter as well as Quito being bounded by Peru on the South.

Santa Marta follows next in order to Maracaybo on the Spanish main the whole district being interspersed with rugged mountains possessing gold, but hitherto the mines are not worked to any profitable purpose, and at the village of Ocana, 200 miles south of the Capital copper ore is found.

The great river Magdalena, which divides this district from Carthagena, flows from the Southern districts of the Province and when more fully explored, will be found to form a grand commercial communication from hence, almost with the Pacific, through the heart of the Empire. Its margins in this district, and the adjoining one, are celebrated for the production of fine cocao, and the Magdalena chocolate is everywhere in high estimation, to it may be added cotton, tobacco, palm-wine, sugar, Brazil wood, Vanilla, etc., with which the capital, Santa Marta, carries on a trade to Carthagena and other ports on the main.

This city has a large and commodious harbour, and the other towns of the district are Puebla-Cordova, Puebla-Nueva, Puebla de los Reyes, Tamalameque, Tenerife and Hacha. To the articles of commerce mentioned, we may add hides, cattle and the produce of the pearl fishery, which might be followed to much advantage on different parts of the coast.

The district of Carthagena is covered with elevated mountains, forests and savannahs, the latter are highly productive. The city of Carthagena is exceedingly unhealthy, but has one of the most commodious harbours on the coast and being secured from all winds the water is as tranquil as a river; the produce of Santa Fe ant the Southern districts are transmitted here, and if it was not so intensely hot and the air so unwholesome, this city would become a very desirable situation for commerce. Its exports in indigo, sugar, cotton, cinchona, ipecacuanha, cocoa, etc., is said to have amounted to £200,000 annually, and the imports to half a million sterling.

The principal towns in the district are Turbaco, Mompox, Tolu, St. Sebastian de Buenavista, Barances, Santa Maria, Guamoca, Zamba and Zinu, the two latter being ports in the gulph of Darien. The district of Darien which embraces a territory of two hundred miles long, and only eighty wide between the two oceans, is principally in the possession of native tribes, being so unhealthy and the forests so impervious that few Europeans have settled in it. Its produce is cotton and tobacco, and the capital St. Cruz de Cana, upon the frontiers of Choco, has gold mines.

The district of Panama is at the present of more importance than the preceding, containing three cities and many other villages. The city of Panama, situated at the extremity of a bay of the same name in the Pacific, is the capital which has lost some of its consequence since the galleons from

Lima discontinued to visit it. The trade is with the district of Veracruz and the ports southward to Peru, from whence it derives supplies of maise, poultry, wheat, cattle, etc.; its European goods are received from Carthagena, being conveyed up the Chagre (the principal river in the district) and by land from Cruses, the point to which the river is navigable. The gold and silver mines of Panama as well as the pearl fishery might be rendered with proper management of much commercial importance; Cedar, Mahoganhy, balsams and gums, are the main articles it hitherto affords in exchange for imports.

The city next in consequence is Porto-Bello, having as its name denotes a fine port on the Atlantic Ocean, but being surrounded with high lands is particularly unhealthy and its productions and trade inconsiderable. The other city is St. Jago de Nata situated in a bay on the Pacific about sixty miles south west of Panama; there are many villages and farms in this district but it is upon the whole thinly inhabited.

The district of Veragua, although considered to be situated in North-America, forms a part of this Republic, it derived its name from the denomination of 'Verdes Aguas' (green waters) given by Columbus to the river, and it is celebrated only for being the country where the first European colony in America was attempted to be settled by that navigator. The continued opposition of the Natives has up to this time prevented many settlements; the principal are the cities of Veragua (the capital), Puebla-Nueva and Santiago el Angel.

The gold and silver mines of Veragua are very abundant, but the working of them is rendered almost impracticable from the rugged nature of the country and the intricate and only means which they possess of conveying the produce over the mountains on the backs of the natives.

The district of Choco, extending southward, from Darien, on the Pacific, is little explored being overspread with boundless forests and having none of the agreeable aspect of cultivation or pasturage. The sources of the Atrato, that enters the gulph of Darien and of the San Juan, which flows into the South Sea approximate so near in the interior of this district that a monk of the village of Zitara, it is said, caused a canal to be dug which united them and that since 1788 Canoes, laden with cocoa, have proceeded by those rivers from the Atlantic to the Pacific.

No doubt can exist of this district being rich in gold; the washings of Novita, Litara and Taddo produce about 10,000 marks of that precious metal annually. Platina is chiefly found in this and the adjoining district of Antioquia.

The district of Popayan is very extensive and a branch of the Andes traverses its northern part. It carries on a considerable trade in receiving European goods from Carthagena for the supply of Quito, and in exporting cattle, mules, tobacco, dried-beef, salted pork, lard, rum, cotton, etc., which are sent to Choco and other places in barter for precious metals. A great branch of traffic also is in the exchange of gold for silver; for as gold is abundant and silver scarce, the latter is much sought after. Popayan, the capital, is situated in the fine valley of Cauca, and has upwards of 20,000 inhabitants. The remaining towns are Carthago, Ibague, Cali, Timana, Neyva, Sebastian del Oro, Mercaderes, St. Juan de Pasto, etc. The district of Tacames is bounded on the north by the preceding district, and on the south by Quito.

Vanilla, achiote, indigo and sarsaparilla are found or cultivated in abundance, and the forests produce lofty and valuable trees; great quantities of wax are exported, likewise cocoa, which is equal to that of Guayaquil.

Tacames, the capital, is situated in the bay of the same name on the Pacific, about 100 miles north west of Quito. A famous mine of Esmeraldes is not far distant from this city. The other towns (which are of little importance) on the coast, are Tumaco, Tola, San Mateo de Esmeraldes and La Canea; there are also upwards of fifteen small towns in the interior.

The district of Quito is very extensive, running for 600 miles along the Pacific in the confines of Peru, including the jurisdiction of Guayaquil, and extending far into the interior.

The city of Quito, the capital, is situated on the eastern slope of the western branch of the Andes, about one hundred miles from the coast, having a population of sixty thousand. The climate is healthy but the country is incessantly subject to earthquakes, as it encloses the highest volcanic mountains of the Andean chain, amongst which are Chimborazo,21,400 feet in height, and the burning Cotopaxi.

The commerce of Quito is chiefly internal; it receives European articles from Guayaquil for which wheat is returned and transmits some of its produce to Guatimala for which indigo, iron and steel are obtained.

The chief towns and sub-districts of Quito, proceeding from north to south, are San Miguel de Ibarra, Otabalo, Latacunga, Riobamba, Chimbo, Guayaquil, Cuenca and Loja; they contain from 10 to 15,000 inhabitants each, with the exception of Riobamba and Cuenca, which have upwards of 20,000 each. There are many other towns and villages in this district, which constitutes a highly important portion of the new Republic.

The city of Guayaquil is the principal port along this coast, situated at the mouth of the river and at the bottom of the bay of the same name and notwithstanding the exceeding unhealthiness of this city and district it is rising in importance being the emporium chiefly of the produce of the others towns. The exports consisting mainly of Cocoa, amount to £100,000 and the imports to £200,000 annually.

Many of the districts of Quito, if not the whole, contain gold, which with their fine timber and the advantage of situation will contribute to their commercial advancement.

Having partially described the districts bordering on the Atlantic and Pacific oceans, I will now proceed to give a very brief account of those situated in the interior of this Republic.

The district of Merida is bounded by Maracaybo on the North, Caracas proper on the east, Santa Marta on the west, and Santa Fe and Juan de los Llanos on the South.

A peculiar feature of its western portion, is the high mountains which entirely pervade it, covered with perpetual snow and rendering the climate variable.

Its commercial productions are sugar, cocoa and coffee; cattle are very numerous, and the principal plantations are situated near the city of Merida (the Capital) which contains 12,000 inhabitants, and is two hundred miles south of Maracaybo. The town of Pamplona, about 150 miles north east of St. Fe de Bogota, has gold in its vicinity; the other towns are St. Christoval and La Grita.

The district of San Juan de los Llanos is the most easterly one of the Province of New Granada, and is confined on the east by Varinas, on the south by Quixos, on the west by Santa Fe and Popayan, and on the north by Varinas and Merida.

The Capital of the same name is fifty miles south east of St. Fe de Bogota, and its other towns are small. The principal articles of exports are cocoa and dressed leather, the plains abounding with cattle and deer. The Rio Meta, the Vichada and the Cassanare flow through this district and supply the means of transmitting the goods of New Granada to Caracas and Guiana.

The district of Santa Fe or St. Fe de Bogota is confined on the north by Merida and Santa Marta, on the west by Antioquia, on the south by Popayan, and on the east by the elevated summits of the Andes. It is situated in the very Centre of the Province of New Granada.

The city of St. Fe de Bogota, the Capital of this extensive Province, stands in a rich and spacious plain on the east of the great chain of the Andes; its elevation of 8,700 feet above the level of the sea renders the climate rather cold, and the inhabitants of this city, amounting to thirty thousand, enjoy a perpetual spring.

The other towns of most importance are Mariquita, Villa de la Purificacion, Socorro, San Gil, Honda, Velez, Muzo, Tuna, and Leiva, all situated in the different jurisdictions into which the district is divided.

Mariquita, eighty miles south of Santa Fe, is rich in gold and silver mines which are at present imperfectly worked. The district of Antioquia has Carthagena and Darien on the north, Choco on the west, Santa Fe on the east, and Popayan on the south.

It is celebrated for its mines of gold, having the central ridge of the Andes within its precincts. Quicksilver, so valuable in a mining country is occasionally found here. Three thousand four hundred marks of gold are annually exported from hence to Mompox. The silver of New Granada is chiefly found in this district, at the mine of Vega de Supia which has been recently discovered.

The Capital of this district, which is imperfectly explored, is Santa Fe de Antioquia founded as far back as the year 1541.

The district of Jaen de Bracamoros is bounded on the south by Peru, on the east by Maynas, on the horth by Quixos, and on the west by Quito. The city of Jaen, with 5,000 inhabitants, is the Capital; there are three other small towns, namely Valladolid, Loyola and Santiago de las Montañas, and about ten villages peopled by Indians. Its commerce consists in cotton, tobacco, and mules, and a brisk trade is carried on with Peru and Quito. Cocoa flourishes, but from the difficulty of carriage cannot be exported with profit; the tobacco is of a superior quality and the cigars of Jaen are universally sought after. Nearly the whole of this district however, is at present overspread with forests.

The district of Maynas consists mainly of immense forests; it is the most south eastern territory of the Province and extends to the Portuguese possessions on the Amazons. The City of St. Francisco de Borja is the Capital, containing few inhabitants mostly Creoles and Indians. The Spaniards have many missions in this district, besides others upon the Napo and the Rio Negro. The district of Quixos is bounded on the north by Popayan, on the west it is divided from Quito by the Cordilleras Cayambe Cotopaxi, etc., on the south its confines are Maynas and Bracamoros and on the east Portuguese Guiana. The southern part of Quixos is called Macas, and it is separated into a district under that appellation, of which the chief town is Macas and Seville de Oro.

The Capital is named Baeza, but it is a village of only ten houses, the Governor residing at Archidona, a small town of 600 inhabitants of all castes, there are many missionary villages in Quixos, but this district is mainly in a primeval state and in the possession of the aborigines, many of this tribes being of a warlike disposition.

From the preceding description some idea may probably be formed of the productions, and immense territorial capabilities of these districts, now constituting many federal states of the Republic; which will soon feel its progressive commercial advancement in the open navigation of the Meta, a river that had been little explored till one of General Bolivar's Officers proceeded by it, nearly from its source, through the centre of the Empire to the Orinoco, thus connecting the commerce of the Atlantic by water conveyance, with the districts of the Pacific.

The Spanish Government had long prohibited the navigation of the Meta (and it was consequently little known) in order that the productions of New Granada might be carried to Carthagena, thereby almost totally putting a stop to the cultivation of the rich countries bordering upon this river, which have hitherto chiefly remained in the possession of the Indians.

The sincere disposition on the part of the Columbian Congress to give a stimulus to the commercial powers, so long dormant and so largely enjoyed by the Republic, and to encourage foreign trade to those Dominions is manifested by the recent promulgation of the following tariff.

General Congress of Columbia

List of duties payable on importations

Art. 2 – 5 per Cent on bar iron, plate, tin and copper; also paper, medicines, instruments of surgery, tackle, pitch, tar, cables, cordage and Anchors.

Art. 4 – 20 per Cent on beaver, woollen or silk hats; wax or spermaceti, either manufactured or in paste; wine, vinegar and acid of every kind, gold and silver, watches, lace, riding sadles, earthenware of Europe and Asia, glass and crystal.

Art. 5 – 22 ½ per Cent on silk of Europe and Asia, precious stones, jewels, thread and silk lace, print handkerchiefs, artificial flowers, feathers, looking glasses, perfumes, essences, and scented waters, spiceries from India or elsewhere, dried fruits or the expressed juice, capers, etc.

Art. 6 – 25 per Cent on shoes and boots, household furniture, utensils in copper, bronze, iron steel and tin; tallow in the lump or manufactured; flour, salted meat and all eatables.

Art. 7 – 35 per Cent on spirits or foreign liquors, from the grape, sugar cane or other material.

Art. 8 – Other kinds of merchandise, liquors and commercial articles not specified in the preceding articles shall pay 20 per Cent.

Art. 9 – The above stated duties shall be deducted from the value fixed by the tariff approved at Carthagena on April 22° 1817 and its supplements until the necessary alterations be made.

Art. 10 – The rate of duties imposed by the preceding articles shall be applicable solely to the cargoes of National Vessels.

Art. 11 – Merchandise imported by vessels of neutral or friendly states shall pay 5 per Cent over and above the preceding duties unless it shall be otherwise stipulated by particular treaties of commerce.

Art. 12 – An abatement of 7 ½ per Cent shall be allowed from the above duties on the cargoes of national vessels, and 5 per Cent on those of foreign vessels, provided they proceed directly from European ports to Columbia.

All decrees, regulations and laws in opposition to the present are revoked and annulled.

This law shall begin to operate in the 1st of January 1822

(signed by the President of the Congress)

J. M. Del Castillo

22 September 1821 / Vice President of the Republic

A subsequent decree excepts from the above duties, books, maps, charts, philosophical apparatus, paintings, sculptur, engravings, implements of agriculture, and all instruments useful in navigation, or in the arts and sciences.

A law has also passed for establishing a college in each Province and primary schools for teaching the Spanish and Latin grammars, the principles of rhetoric and philosophy, and the useful branches of mathematics.

As the decree now stands the principal part of British imports into Columbia, being Cotton manufactures, will pay a duty of 17 ½ per Cent, provided they proceed direct from Europe, and from the hint thrown out in Article 11 a treaty of commerce on the part of the British Government with this Republic would no doubt reduce the duty to 12 ½ per Cent, which would be 2 ½ per Cent lower than the Brazilian duties on British imports of cotton goods, and nearly 20 per cent lower than those at present levied in other parts of Spanish America open to our commerce.

The highly beneficial consequences to British commerce, in procuring speedily and officially, a distinct and clear understanding with the emancipated States of Spanish America, relative to the collection of import duties, may be estimated by the probable extent of the consumption of our manufactures by those countries, largely surpassing in amount, as it ultimately must do, that of any other Empire or State in the world.

The known population of the five Republics, into which Spanish America may be now said to have politically resolved itself, is by the most authentic computation not less than 14 Millions, to that may fairly be added one million of unnumbered Indians (who will at no distant time become equally available in a commercial estimate) making a total of 15 millions souls.

I calculate upon an average that this mixed species of population will consume one pound sterling each, of British imports annually; and this argument may be supported by an incontrovertible fact, that a similarly mixed total population of three million and a half comprised in the Brazilian territory, half a million of which may be considered as unchristianized and Aborigines and creating no demand upon trade, actually consume about three million sterling of British manufactures.

We will however, to be on the right side of the question, contemplate an opening trade that will quickly grow up into a demand of 12 millions a year upon the manufactures of Great Britain, and as long as this trade is not ostensibly recognized by the British Government, and the collection of duties is left to the caprice of the custom house officers at many of the ports, three fourths of the whole amount of imports will be necessarily subjected to the payment of one half more than would otherwise be required.

Assuming that three fourths of those imports, hitherto, are not more than three million annually, by an overrated duty of 15 per Cent this portion of them is burthened with an excess of impost amounting to four hundred and fifty thousand pounds sterling.

In this state of the case how much more weighty are the considerations presented to the British Government, than to any other power for using its immediate influence with the Mother Country to induce it to acknowledge the independence of the transatlantic colonies.

And if any existing political relations render this preliminary arrangement absolutely requisite before our Government can enter into any commercial regulations with the new States, the sooner so desirable an object is accomplished the better, and those members of the British Senate who are distinguished for their enlightened and liberal consideration of commercial affairs, will largely promote the prosperity of trade by hastening this question to an early conclusion.

The Government of the United States has already avowed its determination of pressing the Court of Madrid to an arrangement with the Republics of Spanish America; but that Government does not regard the non-completion of the measure it is about to recommend to Old Spain, as any restraint upon its policy of dispatching consuls, in the meantime, to the principal ports of the new Republican States, anticipating, doubtless, by such a concession some commercial preference.

VI. The Republic of Chili

A Commercial and Statistical Sketch of the Republic of Chili, by James Henderson.[21]

This Empire may be regarded as a tripartite, comprising Chili-proper, Indian-Chili, and Insular-Chili; and stretching along the Pacific Ocean from 23° to 45° So. Lat. Whilst its greatest width does not exceed 280 miles.

The territorial extent of Chili has been variously estimated, it may, however, be taken at about 35,000 square leagues, although a statement recently published in Spain carries it much higher, but that account, most probably includes the desert of Atacama, that separates this Republic from Peru on the north.

It is confined on the east by the Buenos Ayrean districts of Cuyo, and Tucuman, and the wilds of Patagonia; on the south by the same desert country; and the West by the Pacific.

The known chilian population does not exceed 850,000 persons, who are totally inadequate to a very partial cultivation of so considerable an extent of territory, even if their habits were agricultural and industrious; but a reliance hitherto, upon the produce of the imperfectly worked mines, has engendered a general listlessness and apathy, ill adapted to afford any promise of the rapid agricultural amelioration of this country, notwithstanding a peculiarly fertile soil presents every inducement to engage in so desirable an undertaking. Some idea may be formed of its powers of production by the crops usually affording from eighty to one hundred, for one, in the valleys and places removed from the coast. The general profusion of wild and luxuriant vegetation is as remarkable, as it is encouraging to those disposed to convert the soil into the growth of such commercial productions, as the new stimulus given to trade will require, by the introduction of commercial and political freedom into this Republic. The spread of civilization, which will succeed this improved condition of Chili, will show itself, it is to be hoped, in the establishment of roads, the most essential medium of diffusing knowledge and improvement in new countries; by such means the Indian will be withdrawn

21 [Document not included in the manuscript's index].

from his solitary and apathized [*sic*] way of life, and by discovering the comforts of a new and preferable mode of existence, will throw much into the scale of active agricultural and commercial traffic.

The metallic productions of Chili, are not less abundant than the vegetable, although equally neglected; the contemplated introduction of steam engines, as is the case already in Peru, will, however, afford the certainty of an adequate supply of different metals for the return cargo, but it is to be apprehended, from the redundancy in which they will be brought to market before many years have elapsed, that they will cease to be a desirable exchange for European importations.

Copper mines abound over the whole country, the ore commonly containing gold; the copper already imported into Great Britain is from Coquimbo, in which district and that of Copiapo, mines of this metal have long been celebrated, and are not fewer in number than from eight to nine hundred; the mine of Curico recently discovered, with the exception of Payen, is by far the richest in the country, its ore containing gold and copper in nearly equal portions, and exhibiting a very brilliant appearance. The richest silver mines are generally met with in the most elevated and frigid parts of the Andean mountains which has been a sufficient reason, with a people of little energy, to abandon many of them. In the less elevated country, the most noted are those of Santiago, Copiapo, Coquimbo, and Aconcagua.

The silver mine of Uspallata, about 30 Miles north west of Mendoza (a town in the Buenos Ayrean district of Cuyo) yields on an average fifty marks per quintal. Gold is found in the silver, copper and lead ores, likewise in the plains and beds of rivers, and there is scarcely mountain in the Andean chain that does not contain their precious metal. Lead is common to all the silver mines, and in some instances, it is worked for its own value.

In the district of Coquimbo, Copiapo, Huilquilemu and Aconcagua, iron mines are met with, and the sands of rivers and the sea, afford this metal in profusion; tin is likewise common in sandy mountains.

The quantity of gold and silver, exclusive of smuggling, that is collected annually in Chili, may be said to average near £400,000 sterling, of which, the best calculation States, one fourth to be gold, and the remainder silver.

The Chillian Andes consist of three parallel ridges, the central one having an elevation of 20,000 feet above the level of the sea, the less elevated ridges are connected with the main chain by transversal branches, being themselves upwards of 20 miles distant from it, the one constituting the eastern, and the other the western confines of this mountain phenomenon which produces a great variety in the Chillian climate, being, however, almost in every gradation of it, with the exception of the perpetually snowy regions, eminently congenial to health and life. Highly blessed as the inhabitants of this Republic are, in this particular, they are subjected, by the contiguous volcanic Andes, to frequent earthquakes, but not of that overwhelming and horrific nature, which occasionally marks the convulsions of the earth in Peru and the Carracas.

Chili cannot boast of any very fine rivers, in consequence of the short distance between the sea and the Andean Cordillera from whence they emanate; there are however upwards of one hundred and thirty, the chief of which are the Rio Bueno, Sinfondo, Chaivin, Valdivia, Jotten, and the Maule, and such as they are, with the diffusion of agriculture and commerce, they will become of the highest importance to the country.

The only return which this Republic at present offers for British importations, consists of metals, hides, vicuna wool, and cocoa, the latter being received from Guayaquil, and other places, in return for grain, wine and some other vegetable productions, and it is, at least what has hitherto appeared in British ports, very inferior; although there is no doubt an excellent quality of this article is grown in the districts north of Peru.

In the northern districts of Chili, sugar, cotton, jalap, indigo, tobacco, sarsaparilla, and some other articles adapted for the return cargo, are scantily produced. The expectation, for a considerable period, of the opening of the ports of Peru, previously to the actual occurrence of that event, produced shipments to Chili by British merchants, not only direct from Great Britain, but from the surplus stocks in Brazil and Buenos Ayres, to such an amount that the sales have, almost without exception, been at depressed and losing price; and although this overflowing supply is attended with immediate misfortune, and great disappointment of expectation, yet the result will be found to be beneficial in our future commercial intercourse with those countries. The diffusion of British manufactures at such a low value, amongst an uncivilized population, having enabled them to become purchasers, generally, of luxuries which they did not previously possess, and having thus contracted a taste for those articles, they will not (I have had an opportunity of observing) relinquish them, on any sacrifice.

We will now proceed to the description of the three territorial divisions of this Republic; and Chili-proper being by far the most important, it will come first under consideration.

Chili-proper contains the main part of the Spanish population, and extends over a country 700 miles in length, from the northern confines of the Empire. It is divided into thirteen districts which, proceeding from North to South are Copiapo, Coquimbo, Quillota, Aconcagua, Melipilla, Santiago, Rancagua, Colchagua, Maule, Itata, Chillan, Puchacay, and Huilquilemu.

The district of Copiapo has the deserts of Atacama on the north, the Andes on the east, Coquimbo on the South, and the Pacific on the West, and is nearly 300 miles in length. It is celebrated for mines of gold and copper, and no part of Chili is richer in minerals; it affords fossil salt and Sulphur, likewise turquoise and other gems. The rivers which irrigate it are the Copiapo, Guasco, Salado, Castagno, Totoral, Quebradaponda, and the Chollai. Copiapo, the capital, is situated above thirty miles from the sea, on the river of the same name, which has, at its mouth, the best port on the coast; the city is regularly built and contains about 4000 inhabitants.

Guasco is a port at the mouth of the river of its name, and has already been visited, as well as the preceding place, by British ships, to take in copper. It is a miserable place, as are all the other towns of Copiapo.

The district of Coquimbo is bounded on the north by Copiapo, on the east by the Andes, South east by Aconcagua, South west by Quillota, and on the west by the Pacific. It is 130 Miles in length and upwards of 100 in breadth; and contains rich gold, copper and iron mines. The rivers are the Chuapa, Limari, Tongoi, and Coquimbo. The great copper mine of Coquimbo, is situated on a mountain of a conical Shape, rising from the plain and serving as a land mark to vessels visiting the port.

The capital, La Serena or Coquimbo, situated near the sea in 30° S. Lat: upon the river of the same name, is described as a most picturesque and beautiful situation; the SW surrounding country presenting a landscape of a very animating appearance.

It was the second city built by Valdivia in the years 1544, and although large has only about 5000 inhabitants; the streets run in straight lines, are wide, and cross each other at right angles, forming squares and leaving room for gardens. There are three convents, an ancient Jesuits college, a town house and a church. The bay of Coquimbo is the only good one on its coast, and is well sheltered by several islands contiguous to it. Tongoi is a small harbor about twenty miles farther to the south, where vessels are laden with copper, hides, tallow, etc.

The district of Quillota is confined on the north by Coquimbo, northeast by the Andes, South east by Santiago, and west by the ocean. It is 70 miles in length from north to South, and sixty in width, has numerous herds of cattle, and abounds in gold and copper mines. This district has about 15,000 inhabitants, and is irrigated by the rivers Limache, Aconcagua, Longotoma, Chuapa, and Ligua. The harbours are Valparaiso, La Ligua, Concon, La Herradura, Quintero and El Papudo. The capital Quillota, or St. Martin de la Concha, is situated in a charming valley on the banks of the river Aconcagua in 32° 50' S. lat: but is a place of little note.

Valparaiso, situated in 33° S. lat: although a miserable place has still very recently been, for some time, the grand emporium of Chillian as well as Peruvian commerce, being about sixty miles from Santiago (an internal city and the capital of the Republic).

Twelve to fifteen English establishments were formed here, having also stores in Santiago, but many of them have lately removed to Lima. The English complain of the disagreeable huts, they are compelled to occupy in Valparaiso, and particularly of the bigotry, profound ignorance and jealousy which pervades the minds of the people, generally, against foreigners. The duties on British imports, are levied with great inequality, being collected at the rate of 34 ½ per Cent on certain fixed valuations, which are by no means fairly applicable to the various gradations of value, in many articles of our manufactures.

Goods coming from Buenos Ayres, having there paid the full imports duty of 30 per Cent, are chargeable with an additional 14 ½ per Cent if introduced into Chile by land, and 17 ½ per Cent, of by sea.

The harbour of Valparaiso is free from rocks and shoals, except to the north east, where there is a rock within a cables' length of the shore, and as it never appears above the water, is dangerous; the port is exposed to the north winds. Three miles from Valparaiso, there is a pleasant and flourishing little town called Almendral. The next town of importance in this district is Petorca, situated near the Andes, being very populous in consequence of the great number of miners who resort thither to work the mines in its vicinity. The other towns of Quillota are Plaza, Plazilla, Ingenio and Caza-Blanca.

The district of Aconcagua, has Quillota on the north and west, the Andes on the east, and Santiago on the South. It is a level and well irrigated district, about the same extent as Quillota, producing a considerable quantity of grain. In the mountains which bound it, are several copper mines, with the famous silver mine of Uspallata.

The principal rivers are the Aconcagua, Chile, Ligua, and Longotoma, the former flowing through the great valleys of the district, and those of Quillota, Curimon and Concon. Aconcagua is traversed by the high road leading to St. Juan de la Frontera, by which treasure, and articles of traffic are transmitted to Buenos Ayres. The inhabitants of their district do not exceed 9,000, and its capital, San Felipe, is situated on the Aconcagua. The village of Curimon, nearer to the Andres, has a convent of rigid Franciscans.

The district of Melipilla, is confined on the north by Quillota, east by Santiago, South by the river Maypo, which separates it from Rancagua, and west by the ocean. Its sea coast is of little extent, and its breadth is about 70 miles; the principal productions are wine and grain. The largest rivers, that flow across it are Maypo, Maypocha, and Poanque. The chief town of the district is Melipilla or St. Josef de Logrono, situated in a charming and fertile country, near the Rio Maypo, thinly inhabited, owing perhaps to its contiguity to the Metropolis. St. Francisco de Monte and St. Antonio at the embouchure of the Maypo, although very inconsiderable, are the only other towns of note.

The district of Santiago has Aconcagua on the north, the Andes on the east, the Rio Maypo on the South, and Melipilla on the West. It is between sixty and seventy miles square, and the gold mines amounting to 234, are in the mountains, and only worked during the summer. There are many silver, several copper and tin, and one lead mine; those of Lampa are the most famous of the first. Jaspar has been recently found in the settlement of Monte Negro, of which vases, jars, etc., are made. This district is irrigated by many beautiful rivulets, besides the rivers Mapocho, Colina, and Lampa, and no part of Chili surpasses it in richness of soil; the quantities of corn, wine, fruits, etc., produced are very considerable; and the whole mountain range on its eastern confines is rich in metallic substances, the streams emanating from their summits and sides, bringing considerable portions, and gold in particular is commonly found amongst the sand of their beds.

The City of Santiago, founded by Valdivia in 1541, is the capital of this district, and the metropolis of Chili. It is delightfully situated in an extensive valley, inclosed on the east by the grand Cordillera, on the west by the hills of Prado and Poanque, on the north by the river Colina, and on the south by the Mapocho. It is near 60 miles from its port of Valparaiso and the population is about 40,000, some portions of which are Indians, but the main part are Creoles. The streets are very wide and paved, running in straight lines, with small squares at intervals, each house having a garden, that is irrigated by canals brought from the river, which also furnishes the grand fountain in the chief square with water. The cathedral, 390 feet in length was planned and commenced by two English artists, and finished by Indians whom they had taught, besides it, there are four churches, nine monasteries, four colleges, an university, seven chapels, seven nunneries, an orphan house, an hospital, and the mint, which is a fine stone building erected by an artist from Rome. Here all the mummery of the catholic religion prevails to its full extent. The road from hence to Valparaiso is very excellent having been made by several English prisoners, who were compelled to work upon it.

The district of Rancagua is bounded on the north by the Maypo, which divides it from Santiago and Melipilla, on the east by the Andes, on the south by the Chachapoal, which river separates it from Colchagua, and on the west by the ocean. Its length is about 120 miles and its breadth forty embracing a fertile country and containing about 13,000 inhabitants of different complexions, dispersed in small settlements over the district. The capital is Rancagua or St. Cruz de Triana, a small place situated in 34 18' S. lat. And 70° 42' West long; on the right margin of the Chachapoal and fifty miles south of Santiago. The small town of Algue has been recently founded, about twenty miles from the capital towards the sea coast, in consequence of a rich gold mine discovered in its vicinity. The Maypo, Codagua, Cochalan, and Chachapoal flow through the district.

The district of Colchagua lies between the Chachapoal on the north, the Andes on the east, the Rio Jeno on the south, and the Pacific on the west. Near the Andes its breadth is 70 miles, but contiguous to the coast it is not more than 40, while its length from west to east is 130 miles. The capital is St. Fernando, in 34° 20' s. lat., near Rio Tinguirica, was founded in 1742, and contains 12,000 inhabitants. Topocalma is a port at the mouth of the river so called, which flows past the city of Santiago. Rapel is a small place near the lake so called, and is noted for having a hill, in its vicinity, with a singular cavern, consisting of a single vault fifteen yards long and about four in width, having a natural door way two yards high. The other towns although very inconsiderable, are Rio Clarillo, Roma, Malloa, and Navidad.

The district of Maule has Colchagua on the north, the Andes on the east, Chillan on the southeast, Itata on the southwest, and the Pacific on the west. It is 130 miles in length, and 120 in breadth, and abounds in grain, cattle, salt and gold; the cheese made here is esteemed the best in Chili. The inhabitants of this fine district are chiefly Araucanian Indians, who are subject to the Spaniards, and dwell in villages governed by their Caciques. The great Volcano of Peteroa is on its eastern confines, amid the towering Andes, and is the most dreadful of all Chillian Volcanoes. It is 100 miles So. So. east of Santiago. The capital is Talca or St. Augustin, 100 miles south of Santiago, situated on the river Maule; to the north east of it is a small hill that furnishes abundance of Amethysts, and another of a singular cement sand called talca. Its population is considerable, on account of the rich gold mines in the mountains. Amongst several other towns and villages, Curico, Cauquenes, St. Saverio de Bella Isla, St. Antonio de la Florida, and Lora are the principal. It is watered by various rivers, the chief of which are the Maule, Ligua, Mataquito, Purapel, Loncamilla, Longavi, Achiguema, Putugan, Huenchullami, Lircay, Panque, Rio Clara and the Lantue.

The port of the district is Asterillo, a small bay, between the Maule and the Mataquito rivers. The district of Itata, is bordered by Maule on the north, Chillan on the east, Puchacay on the south, and the ocean on the west, its length from west to east is 60 miles, and its breadth thirty. The river Itata, from which its name is borrowed, intersects the district, and the only other stream of note is the Longuea. The fertility of Itata is very great, and it produces the best wine in Chili, which is called Concepcion, in consequence of its being made on estates of persons belonging to that city. The sands of the rivers contain gold. Coulemu, a small place in 36° S. lat., founded in 1743, is the capital.

The district of Chillan, is confined on the north by Maule, east by the Andes, south by Huilquilemu, and west by Itata. Its length towards the Andes is seventy miles, and its breadth forty; the whole district is a plain, peopled with immense flocks of sheep, whose fine wool is highly esteemed. The capital St. Bartolomes de Chillan, was founded in 1580, is seventy five miles north east of Concepcion, has a numerous population, one church, three convents, and a college founded by the Jesuits. The Cheif rivers are the Cato, Nuble, and Chillan.

The district of Puchacay, has Itata on the north, Huilquilemu on the east, the river Biobio on the south, and the sea on the west, being seventy miles in extent from west to east, and thirty five from north to south. It possesses a fertile soil and abundance of gold. Gualqui, built in 1754 upon the right of the Biobio in 36° 50 so. lat., is the capital. Concepcion or Penco is the most important town in the district and was founded by Valdivia in a valley on the sea coast. It has been several times destroyed by the Indians, and once by an earthquake in 1751, but was always rebuilt, on account of having the finest bay on this coast, and being a place of much consequence to the Spaniards from its contiguity to the Araucanian frontier. The inhabitants amount to nearly 14,000, and this city has a palace, a treasury, and a variety of religious establishments.

The district of Huilquilemu is bounded by Chillan on the north, the Andes on the east, the Biobio on the South, and Puchacay on the west. It is a country rich in gold, which is procured by washings in the numerous rivers flowing from the Andes. The Indians are of the same tribe with those of Itata, and having been a long accustomed to defend their country against the Araucanians, they are warlike and courageous.

The capital is Estancia del Rey or St. Luis de Gonzaga, recently built near the Biobio in 36'50 so. lat., the other places of this district are small villages, and it contains the four frontier forts of Yumbel, Tucapel, Santa Barbara, and Puren. The Spaniards are not in possession of any other part of Continental Chili, in proceeding southward, from the Rio Biobio till 40° so. lat., where they have the city of Valdivia and the country contiguous to it, but as their tenure is very precarious beyond the walls of the town, it cannot be called a district. The city is situated on the margin of the river so called, and was founded, in 1551, by Pedro de Valdivia, who gave it his own name, and accumulated much gold in its vicinity. It was attacked and destroyed by the Araucanian Indians, who carried the inhabitants into captivity, but was soon rebuilt, and much more strongly fortified, having ever since resisted the attacks of the Indians. All the rivers near Valdivia have much gold dust in their sands, and the plains abound with fine timber. The fortress is provisioned by sea, from the ports of Chili.

Indian-Chili or Araucania, in which the above city is situated, extends from the river Biobio to the south of Chiloe as far as 40° south lat., being 430 miles in breadth, in some places, and also including both the central and eastern ridges of the Andes from 33° to 45° lat. The nations who occupy this extensive region, consist of the Araucanians, who are masters of the country between the Biobio and Valdivia rivers, the Andes and the Pacific; the Puelches, who inhabit the western flank of the Cordillera and its central valleys; the

Pehuenches further north on the Andes; and the Chiquillanes, their territory stretching north to 33° so. lat., and indefinitely to the east. South of the Valdivia as far as 45°, is occupied on the sea coast by the Cunches, the plains near the Andes by the Huilliches, and the mountains by the Puelches.

The Araucanian is the most powerful and considerable nation amongst them, having their territory regularly divided into departments, governed by Toquis or Generals, to whom the Apo-Ulmens are subordinate, and on these latter are dependent the Ulmens, who are Chiefs of the minor territories' divisions. The whole are occasionally assembled in coyag and they usually meet on a plain. Their dress consists of clothes fitted close to the body, with ponchos or cloaks made of cotton, and so beautifully worked that they are, in some instances, worth upwards of one hundred dollars.

Their heads are bound with embroidered woollen, ornamented with plumes of emu-ostrich, and other beautiful feathers. The women wear a robe of woolen stuff descending to the feet, and bound round the waist with a girdle, over which is thrown a loose cloak. The hair is permitted to grow very long, and is formed in tresses ornamented with gems; necklaces, bracelets, and rings on every finger, complete the female adornments. A greenish blue is the national colour worn by both sexes.

Their wars are bloody, and as they are excellent horsemen, the cavalry is formidable, their arms being swords and lances, and those of the infantry clubs and pikes. Their onset, like that of most Indians, is furious, but conducted with peculiar order, and although their ranks are swept down by the cannon, they generally close with their Spanish opponents, and fighting hand to hand, are very frequently conquerors in spite of superior discipline and arms. Thus they have so far, disappointed all hopes entertained by the Spaniards, of reducing them to subjection, and being in alliance with the other nations (who are in a more savage state) they bid defiance to their antagonists. They have in like manner resisted all the attempts of other European nations to land upon their shores.

It is very probable, however, that by conciliatory measures, these people may be induced to enter into permanently pacific arrangements with the Spaniards; when their demand on commerce would, no doubt, become very considerable, and possessing a fertile and auriferous territory, their means of payment are abundant.

Insular-Chili, consists of the islands spread along the shores of this Republic. The three Coquimbanes, Mugillon, Totoral, and Pajaro, lie of [sic] the coast of Coquimbo, and are each near eight miles in circumference, but uninhabited. Quiriquina, at the entrance of the harbour of Concepcion and Talca to the south of it, are two islands of nearly four miles in length; in the latter there are many wild horses and hogs. Mocha lies off the coast of Araucania in 38° 40', and although exceedingly fertile, it is very extraordinary, that the Spaniards permit it to remain uninhabited, its extent not being less than sixty miles in circumference. It is generally frequented by the whalers, from England and the United States, who find wild hogs in abundance upon it. The most important group of the Chillian isles, are those denominated the Archipielago of Chiloe, being an assemblage of forty seven situated in a large bay, near the southern extremity of Chili, and extending from Cape Capitanes to Quillan or from 41° 50' to 44°, and from 73° to 74° 20' west long.

Of these, thirty two have been colonized by the Spaniards and Indians, and the rest remain in their pristine and wild state. Chiloe or Isla Grande, the largest of the inhabited islands, is situated at the entrance of the gulph of Chiloe or Ancud, between 41° and 44°, being 180 miles in length and sixty at its greatest breadth, giving name to the whole group. Grain is not so abundantly produced as on the continent, but horse and cattle are bred in considerable numbers, as are sheep and hogs; the two latter constituting the principal commerce of the Islands. The Chilotes are the best sailors in South America, and their Piraguas are numerous in the seas surrounding their island, being navigated with sails as well oars. The inhabitants of the Archipielago amount to twenty five thousand, about one half being Indians, dispersed in eighty settlements, and the remainder, of Spanish descent, occupying four towns, and various farms.

The commerce of these islands is carried on by a few vessels from Peru and Chili, which bring sugar, tobacco, brandy, matte, wine, salt, and European manufactures, and receive in return red cedar and other boards, timber of different kinds, cloaks manufactured by the Indians, hams, dried and salted fish, etc., but the trade will never be very considerable in consequence of the navigation of the Straits, formed by the Islands, being dangerous even for vessels of moderate burthen.

The capital is Castro, in 42° 40' upon an arm of the sea on the eastern side of the island of Chiloe, and was founded in 1566 by Gamboa; the houses, as is the case with all the rest in this Archipielago, are of wood. The other towns are Chaco, in the middle of the north coast of Chiloe; San Carlos, on the Bahia del Rey, and built on account of the difficulties attending the entrance to Chaco, it has 1200 inhabitants.

The other islands have each one settlement and a missionary church, excepting Quinchuan, which has six; Lemui and Llachi each four, and Calbuco three. South of the Islands of Chiloe, is the Archipielago of Guaytecas and Chonos, lying in a gulph between 44° 30' and 46° so. lat., and comprehended within the Province of Chiloe, but are uninhabited, being mere masses of granite rock covered with forests. Some of them, Teguchuan, Ayaupa and Yquilao are visited periodically by the Indians of Chiloe to put cows in them for the pasturage, which is very luxuriant.

In addition to what has been stated relative to the commerce of Chili, it carries on a traffic with Peru in wheat, tallow, copper, matte, etc., to the amount of £130,000 annually, and receives as part of the return, about £95,000 in sugar, native cloths, indigo, rice, etc., and has besides considerable dealings, by land, with La Plata, for matte or the Paraguay tea, through the medium of eight very indifferent roads or tracks, leading from Chili to Tucuman and Cuyo (the two nearest districts of Buenos Ayres) of which that already mentioned, as traversing Aconcagua, is the best; it is bordered on one side by the steep beds of the Chile and the Mendoza rivers, and on the other by frightful and impractical precipices, and is so narrow that, in many places, the rider is obliged to descend from his mule and proceed on foot, nor does a year pass without some of those animals being precipitated into the thundering streams below.

Here, indeed, is an awful pausing place for the traveller, who is nevertheless, if a civilized being seized with peculiar feelings of admiration and wonder at the grand picture presented to his view, consisting of uninterrupted piles of mountains constantly losing themselves in the snowy regions of the air, their sides interspersed with richly fruitful valleys and dreadful precipices, giving birth to rivers, and displaying the highly sublime, and most terrific feature of nature.

VII. The Kingdom of Mexico

Memorandum on the late occurrences in the Kingdom of Mexico,
London, 4th Feb., 1822, by C. Parker [...].

In May 1817 (after four years desultory warfare which at this period was nearly quelled by the King's Troops) Mina rekindled the flame and disembarked in the Bay of St. Bernardo with a small expedition formed in the U. States consisting of 300 men; the rapidity with which he commenced his operations, and the extraordinary success attending his attacks against very superior Bodies of the Kings troops caused it to be generally believed that there was a combination in his favor throughout the Kingdom; he had many wellwishers amongst the Europeans, and generally with the Creoles, but was at length overpowered, taken prisoner, treated in the most ignominious manner, and that by order of the Vice Roy. From this event, and the unpopular Government of the Mother Country arose a general desire for independence both amongst Europeans and Creoles, however, neither those of property or influence took the lead, from which circumstance the revolution assumed no organized form and in January 1819 most of the Provinces were in an apparently pacific state.

In September 1820 Dn. Juan de la Cruz, Captain General of Guadalajara, received a letter from a Creole of respectability, which informed him that private Juntas were held in Mexico, Puebla, and several other principal towns, conceived and attended by men of consequence and influence, the object of these meetings being to form a new and general plan of independence, this letter, and other important documents were forwarded to the Vice Roy Apodaca who was so far deceived or imposed upon by those around him, that he thought it unnecessary to notice this momentous information.

In December 1821 all the American Deputies of Cortes going to Madrid, in arriving at Vera Cruz openly affirmed that their first efforts should be devoted toward the independence of New Spain. The principal events of the late revolution which has insured and confirmed the liberation of Mexico almost without the effusion of blood took place in January 1821. A large sum of money was to be conveyed from Mexico to Acapulco, belonging to the merchants of Manilla, when great interest was made to obtain the command of the Govt for Col. Iturbide, a man, who for a length of time had not been employed in any confidential service owing to the Vice Roy's want of confidence in him, the point was however gained, and on his march to Acapulco he threw off the mask, seized the property confided to his charge, and his troops both Europeans and Creoles swore to the independence of Mexico; he immediately sent a messenger to the Vice Roy stating what had been done, and laid before him the terms in which the independence of the Kingdom had been proclaimed which are as follows.

1rst. The Crown of Mexico shall be offered to Ferdinand the 7th provided he resides in the Kingdom, otherwise to one of his royal Brothers.

2nd The Catholic Religion to be observed, and no other tolerated.

3rd The lives and property of all Europeans to be respected.

4th The Government to be a moderate Monarchy.

5 The Court of Madrid to be immediately informed to these events, and in the interim a Provisional governative Junta shall be formed in the Capital of Mexico composed of the principal People of the Country, one half Creoles, the other Europeans -the Vice Roy Apodaca to be President-.

To this communication the Vice Roy sent an undecided reply, but lost no time in concentrating all his forces at Mexico, and withdrawing those from the Country. No sooner were the principles on which Iturbide had proclaimed independence known in the different Provinces, than the spirit of liberty and independence immediately manifested itself in all classes and ranks, with the exception only, of a few Europeans. The Vice Roy Apodaca remained inactive in the Capital, and was at length deposed by the Troops, and Brig. General Novella appointed his successor; the Troops sent by the latter to oppose Iturbide declared in his favor, and joined him on their march; amongst the principal European officers were Col. Bustamante and his Division, Brig. Celestino Negrete gave up the whole Province and Capital of Guadalajara, and under Col. Lonasis, Valladolid shared the same fate, Puebla a town of the greatest importance next to the capital surrendered after a trifling resistance.

In July last the whole Kingdom of Mexico, with the exception of the Capital, and Vera Cruz were in possession of the Independents, at this moment, the new Vice Roy O'Donojú arrived. Vera Cruz was then bombarded and closely beseiged, but a suspension of arms was effected thro' a proclamation issued by him, and he sent his commissioners to Iturbide then at Cordova, following himself shortly after when he assented to and confirmed the conditions on which the independence had been declared, with the exception, that he, O'Donojú should not hold the high office of President formerly offered to Apodaca. O'Donojú then proceeded to Mexico, where he received Iturbide as head of the Mexican Government. O'Donojú is since dead, report says by poison.

The present government consists of a Junta and Regency, Iturbide is President of the latter, and has been voted a perpetual annuity of 120,000 dollars, all the members have been appointed by him, and are composed of men of property and talent, never before the case in this Kingdom, nor do I believe in any other Spanish settlement during the late revolutions.

A commission has been appointed to regulate and settle the conditions on which foreign trade is to be conducted. The last authentic accounts from Vera Cruz are dated October, that town (the only one in the Kingdom) was still under the Kings Government, but the Governor had agreed to surrender it when an adequate force should be sent to take possession, in the United Sates it is asserted that this has already taken place. Iturbide is about 45 years old, a native of Mexico, and held the rank of Colonel in the Spanish army, he has more the character of an enterprising soldier than that of a Politician and has exercised great judgment in the selection of those he has taken as advisers.

Mexico has been known to me since 1811, I have resided there some years, with the special permission of His Catholic Majesty's Government, being employed part of my time by the Lords Commissioners of His Britannic Majesty's Treasury in the important service of procuring nearly ten million of dollars for the Public Excises.

In the conduct of such service opportunity was afforded me of forming an acquaintance with several of the Individuals constituting the present Mexican Government; among them is Don Mariano Almansa, with whom I am intimately acquainted and who held the rank of Counsellor of State in the present Government at Madrid, he is a Creole and possesses considered talent and enterprise. The present opinion seems (and I think not unfounded) that Iturbide's views are of a more ambitious nature than promised in the first instance, and little doubt is entertained but that he will continue at the head of Government, at the Theatre, and in public he has been frequently greeted with the title of "King".

The most decided opposition is evinced to any close connexion with the Government of the U. States, fearing the contiguity of the two Countries by the Province of Texas might tend to increase the ambitious views of the Americans, of which the Mexicans are fully aware. To my knowledge the American government has already endeavored to ingratiate itself with the Independents, and about four years ago it sent an agent to Mexico or head of affairs (Dr. Robinson) who finding no organized Government on the part of the Independents to whom to address himself ultimately fell into the hands of the Royalists, and for a long time was detained prisoner in the Castle of St. Juan de Ulua; I procured many of his papers and documents, which were forwarded to Sir Home Popham then on the Jamaica Station. If I might venture an opinion, I should say that an Agent from this country would be very favorably received, and the advantages likely to accrue in commercial point of view most important. The Mexicans have hitherto been unaccustomed to communicate or hold intercourse with foreigners and at such an important crisis might feel flattered and gratified at being noticed by His Britannic Majesty's Government, and induced to hold out that preference to our commercial relations which other powers will in all probability soon feel anxious to insure.

We have hitherto (tho' clandestinely) enjoyed a large proportion of the trade of that vast Empire, but there is no doubt that under the present state of affairs the advantages to this country might be very considerably increased.

During the last war under a License from the Spanish Government, there was sent from Kingston, Jamaica, to the Port of Vera Cruz alone for a considerable period, an average value of not less than 100 m. dollars weekly, almost entirely of British manufactures. At that period there was a License from America, obtained by the House of Parish whose shipments were to a large amount taking the whole and what was shipped clandestinely, and to other ports, the importations into Mexico could not be less than 20 million of Dollars. These goods although burdened with Bribes, Carriage and Duties to more than double the amount of their original cost met with a ready demand, and were punctually paid for. The population of Mexico is not less than 7 million, and if the trade was once settled on a sure footing, and carried on with reasonable charges an annual consumption of 10 or 12 million of dollars in British manufactured cloths alone, might be reputed, exclusive of Hardware, Glass, Iron, and other more bulky articles. A valuable trade also from our possessions in India to Acapulco, might be looked for, which would entirely supercede that of the Philipian and Manilla Company, and many other advantages obtained by the British Government that cannot now be known or ascertained. I have had a knowledge of the trade of Mexico for many years from a length of residence in Jamaica, Cadiz and Mexico and have had as many opportunities of knowing its nature and extent as most British subjects. I am fully aware that the disturbed state of the Kingdom has prevented the mines being resourceful and impoverished and decreased the Population, which would prevent for a time trade to the usual extent; but it cannot be long before order is restored, and the mighty resources of that country brought into action, when I think it will be seen so far from exaggerating any thing I have stated, it will be found less than the reality.

The Americans are the principal rivals we have to dread, their fine fast sailing vessels, enterprise, and as I before stated, contiguity, give them decided advantage, and no time should be lost in supplying the wants of Mexico, which must be done from some Quarter, and which they are probably at this moment on the alert to accomplish, by endeavouring to establish commercial relations between the two countries.

London, 4th February, 1822,
C. Parker [signature]

Ham Common, George Ha[illegible],[22] Esq, 4 Spring Gardens Terrace

22 [The signature accompanying Parker's is likely to be that of Sir George Harrison, auditor to the Treasury and close advisor to the British Government. This suggests that Parish or Parker sought Treasury advice before submitting his report.]

VIII. Actual state of the different Governments in South America

Buenos Ayres

With respect of the form of Government established by the Independents in the different revolutionized Provinces of South America, it would appear, that <u>Buenos Ayres</u> had at first assumed a controlling influence over all the other <u>Provinces of La Plata</u>.

In March 1816 however a general Congress assembled at Tucuman composed of Deputies from all the Provinces comprehended within the old Vice Royalty of Buenos Ayres (For this Declaration of the Provinces of La Plata 6 [*sic*] July 1816 and subsequent acts and the Constitution framed by the Congress.[23]

This Congress assumed at once the Sovereign Power of the Country, declared its absolute Independence of old Spain, and adopted a Provisional form of Government. Being afterwards adjourned to Buenos Ayres it occupied itself in drawing up a Constitution which was subsequently completed and received the assent of the People.

Buenos Ayres Government

By this Instrument, the Legislative Power is to be exercised by a National Congress composed of two Houses: one of Representatives and one of Senators. The former is composed of delegates elected in the proportion of one for every District containing 25,000 inhabitants. The Deputy must be upwards of twenty-six years of age, must have been seven years a Citizen previous to his nomination, and must possess 4,000 Dollars of Property, or some equivalent which is not well defined in the Article.

The Representatives sit for four years, but half of the Chamber is renewed every two years. The House of Deputies originates all money bills, and has the special right of impeaching Ministers and the high Officers of the State.

23 Vide Walton [Margin note].

The Senate is to consist of the same number of provisional Senators as there are Provinces; of three military Senators; of one Bishop, and three Ecclesiastics; of a representative of each University, and of the Director whose period of Government is ended.

The appointment of the Senators is for twelve years, and they must at their nomination have attained the age of thirty, having been nine years a Citizen. The Legislature is to sit for about six months in the year: they have freedom of speech, and other necessary privileges. They have the power of citing the Ministers before them, to obtain any requisite information. Any of them may originate laws.

When the projects of law have been agreed to by both Houses, they are to be transmitted to the Director for his sanction, who must return them in fifteen days, either with his approbation or objections. If he approve, the Bill becomes a Law; if he state objections, these objections are considered; but if two thirds of the members of both Houses support the original project, their votes constitute a final sanction without a second application to the Director.

The Supreme Director is elected by the two Houses assembled. He is to open the sittings of the Legislature; he appoints all the Officers of the Army, Navy and Envoys, Consuls and others. He chooses and dismisses his Ministers, who are responsible for their conduct while employed under him; all objects of finance, police, public, national, and scientific establishments, as well as all those formed and supported by the funds of the State, are confided to his supreme charge and inspection.

He has the power of pardon, except in cases of State conviction. The Supreme Judicial Power of the State is to reside in a Supreme Court, consisting of seven Judges and two recorders, nominated by the Director; every one of whom must have been a regular Barrister eight years, and have attained the fortieth year of his age. This Court shall, exclusively, take cognizance of all causes relating to Envoys and Consuls from Foreign Nations, all causes in which a Province may be a party, all those concerning public functionaries, all those relating to crimes committed against the Law of Nations. The members exercise their functions during good behavior. The Supreme Court, as well as the other Tribunals, is open to the Public.

Entre Rios & Santa Fe

To this Government all the Provinces of the former Vice Royalty of Buenos Ayres appear to have submitted, excepting those of Entre Rios and Santa Fe, which although consolidated with the rest by a definitive League at the time, have been since, almost without interruption, under the exclusive, and arbitrary command of Artigas, who[24] had separated himself from the general interests of the Buenos Ayreans.

Paraguay

The Province of Paraguay was also under the control of a single Individual, Francia, stiling himself Dictator of Paraguay, and although always on a good understanding with the adjoining Provinces, continued pertinaciously to refuse to enter into the general arrangements made for the other United Provinces.

Government of Chili

The Government of Chili is distinct from that of the United Provinces of La Plata, although the closest intimacy exists between them. The Independence of Chili was proclaimed on the 1° of Jan. 1818.[25] In this Declaration, 'Chili and her adjacent Islands, are stated to form, in fact, and right, a free, independent, and Sovereign State, to be forever separated from the Monarchy of Spain, and to be fully qualified to adopt the form of Government most convenient to their own interests'.

The Supreme Director O'Higgins, in several Proclamations holds out the Prospect of 'a federal form of Government to be established by a General Congress, whenever the circumstances of the War will permit the actual Government to turn their attention to the Subject'.

The Provinces of Cuyo, bordering upon Chili, under the direction of the Buenos Ayrean General San Martin, had taken a prominent part in the Establishment of the Government of Chili, and on the 5th of February 1819 a treaty was signed between the two States, by which they bound themselves, to cooperate for the liberation of Peru, and mutually guaranteed the independence of the State, to be formed out of that Vice Royalty.

State of Relations between Buenos Ayres & Chili and the Mother Country

With respect to the relations of the South American Provinces under the Government of Buenos Ayres and Chili with the Mother Country, they seem to be irrevocably at an end.

24 Although he deserted the Royal Cause at Montevideo and declared for Independence yet [Margin note].
25 Vide Declaration of Independence of Chili, 1 Jan. 1818, Appendix page 15 [Margin note].

The Declaration of Independence both of the Congress at Tucuman in 1816, and subsequently of Chili in 1818, solemnly, and definitively, pronounced their absolute, and Entire independence of Spain, a determination subsequently confirmed by the treatment of the Commissioners sent out in 1820 by the Mother Country to the Rio de la Plata, to endeavour to bring about a reconciliation, and with whom, the Government of the United Provinces positively refused to treat, unless upon the Preliminary basis, of the acknowledgement of their independence, which the Commissioners were not prepared to admit.

The Provinces have hitherto however, in vain appealed to Foreign Powers for any acknowledgement of their political character.

Government of Venezuela

The Government of <u>Venezuela</u> which under the name of the Republic of Columbia[26] extends from the Mouths of the Orinoco to the Pacific and now includes the Provinces of Caraccas, New Granada and Quito with the exception only of Puerto Cabello, Panama and the Capital of Quito which the Spaniards still hold, is very similar to that established at Buenos Ayres. A Congress[27] occasionally meets and Bolivar as chief Magistrate has the principal Direction of Affairs.

Mexican Government

The state of affairs in Mexico is different, and the government is held by a Junta & Regency for Ferdinand, or a Prince of his Family. Events in that Country however have too recently occurred to allow of any certain opinion as to its future Form of Government. It remains take seen whether The Spanish Monarch or his Family will accept the Propositions made to them by the Mexicans.

Actual State of the Independent Provinces

The present state then of the Revolutionized Provinces may be said to be as follows:

<u>Buenos Ayres</u> and the Provinces of La Plata entirely freed from the Mother Country.

26 For a particular account of this Government vide Publication including the Constitution [Margin note].
27 The Federal Constitution of the Congress of Columbia is dated 21 Dec. 1811 [Margin note].

Chili and Peru the same, with the exception of Callao[28] into which place the greater part of the Royal Forces (about 4.000) have been thrown, but with little expectation of being able to maintain themselves.

La Serna wars also with a small force in the interior.

Venezuela and the Provinces of Quito, the Caraccas and New Granada free, with the exception of Porto Cabello & the Province of Panama and the Capital of Quito by the last account still in possession of the Royal Forces.

In Mexico affairs must be considered as still undecided. The Royal Forces in that Country are considerable, supposed to be about 10,000 men, and although tranquil at present, may be still influenced by the Decision of the Mother Country upon the Proposals lately made to her by the Independents. The fortress of Vera Cruz is in the possession of a small garrison of the Royalists.

1821

In the Mother Country, the attention of the Cortes was last year (1821) directed to the State of the South American Provinces.

A Secret Committee was applied to report upon the subject.

This Committee proposed a Plan for the future Government of these possessions which was to be submitted to the Inhabitants for acceptance.

By this It was proposed that the Spanish South American Provinces should be divided into three Governments or Sections de Cortes.

The 1st for the Costa Firme, New Granada and Quito at Santa Fé.

The 2d for New Spain, Cuba, Santo Domingo and Porto Rico at Mexico.

The 3rd for Peru, Chili and Buenos Ayres at Lima.

Each Government to hold its own Cortes which shall send three delegates to General Cortes of Spain; and the whole to be under an Infant to be sent out with the Powers and Attributes of a Vice Roy.

The Spanish Ministry appear to have been averse to the immediate Consideration of the Subject & W. Bardaxi seems to have been inclined to wait till the next year. His opinion however was decidedly against sending out an Infant; He considered that in that case, the Colonies would be for sure lost to Spain. He wished for the mediation of Great Britain:- He particularly deprecated the conduct of General O'Donojú in Mexico whose Convention

---

28 Callao has since been reduced [Margin note, in pencil, probably included by Parish once the report was completed].

with Iturbide would never be ratified; and whom He designated as a Traitor to his Country.

It should be observed, that in the discussions which arose out the Report of the Secret Committee on South America affairs in the Cortes, no less than <u>forty-eight deputies from the South American Provinces</u> appear to have been present as Members of the Cortes. These Deputies presented a petition for the immediate Consideration of the Report, which was rejected.

IX. Appendix of Sundry Public Documents

1. Buenos Ayres Manifesto of Independence, by Pedro Ignacio de Castro Barros and Jose Eugenio de Elias, Buenos Ayres, October 25, 1817[29]

MANIFESTO PRESENTED TO ALL NATIONS BY THE GENERAL AND CONSTITUENT CONGRESS OF THE UNITED PROVINCES OF THE RIVER PLATE, RESPECTING THE TREATMENT AND CRUELTIES THEY HAVE EXPRIENCED FROM THE SPANIARDS, WHICH HAVE GIVEN RISE TO THE DECLARATION OF THEIR INDEPENDENCE.

Honour is a distinction which mortals esteem more than their own existence, and they are bound to defend it above all earthly benefits, however great and sublime they may be. The United Provinces of the River Plate, have been accused, by the Spanish government, before other nations, of rebellion and perfidy; and as such also has been denounced the memorable Act of Emancipation, proclaimed by the National Congress in Tucuman, on the 9th of July, 1816, by imputing to it ideas of anarchy, and a wish to introduce into other countries seditious principles, at the very time the said provinces were soliciting the friendship of these same nations, and the acknowledgment of this memorable act, for the purpose of forming one among them. The first, and among the most sacred of the duties imposed on the National Congress, is to wipe away so foul a stigma, and defend the cause of their country, by displaying the cruelties and motives which led them to the declaration of Independence. This indeed is not to be considered as an act of submission, which may attribute to any other nation of the earth the power of disposing of a fate which has already cost America torrents of blood and all kinds of.

We shall pass over all investigations respecting the right of conquest, papal grants, and other titles, on which the Spaniards have founded their right of dominion. We do not seek to recur to principles which might give rise to problematical discussions, and revive points of argument which have had

---

29 [The manifesto was published in successive instalments in *The Morning Chronicle*, from 5 August 1818. Apart from the title and opening summary, this is William Walton's corrected translation (he corrects the date of the signing of the manifesto, 25 October 1817, not 5 October as published in the *Chronicle*). Walton's translation was published the following year in *Constitution of the United Provinces of South America, Framed, Sanctioned, and Ordered to be Published by the Sovereign and General Constituent Congress, on the 22 April, 1819, Together with the Declaration of Independence, Manifesto, &c*, translated from official copies, with preliminary remarks by William Walton, Esq. London: Hay and Turner, 1819].

defenders on both sides. We appeal to facts which form a painful contrast of our forbearance, with the oppression and cruelty of Spaniards. We will exhibit a frightful abyss which Spain was opening under our feet, and into which these provinces were about to be precipitated, if they had not interposed the safeguard of their own emancipation. We will, in short, exhibit reasons which no rational man can disregard, unless he could find sufficient pleas to persuade a country for ever to renounce all idea of its own felicity, and, in preference, adopt a system of ruin, opprobrium, and forbearance. Let us place before the eyes of the world this picture, one which it will be impossible to behold without being profoundly moved by the same sentiments as those by which we are ourselves actuated.

From the moment when the Spaniards possessed themselves of these countries, they preferred the system of securing their dominion by extermination, destruction, and degradation. The plans of this extensive mischief were forthwith carried into effect, and they have been continued, without any intermission, during the space of three hundred years. They began by assassinating the monarchs of Peru, and they afterwards did the same with the other chieftains and distinguished men who came in their way. The inhabitants of the country, anxious to restrain such ferocious intrusion, under the great disadvantage of their arms, became the victims of fire and sword, and were compelled to leave their settlements a prey to the devouring flames, which were everywhere applied without pity or distinction.

The Spaniards then placed a barrier to the population of the country. They prohibited, under laws the most rigorous, the ingress of foreigners; and in every possible respect limited that of even Spaniards themselves, although in times more recent, the emigration of criminal and immoral men, outcasts, was encouraged -of such men as it was expedient to expel from the Peninsula. Neither our vast though beautiful deserts, formed by the extermination of the natives; the advantages Spain would have derived from the cultivation of regions, as immense as they are fertile; the incitement of mines, the richest and most abundant on the earth; the stimulus of innumerable productions, partly till then unknown, but all estimable for their value and variety, and capable of encouraging and carrying agriculture and commerce to their highest pitch of opulence ; in short, not even the wanton wickedness of retaining these choice countries, plunged in the most abject misery, were any of them motives sufficiently powerful to change the dark and inauspicious principles of the cabinet of Madrid. Hundreds of leagues do we still behold, unsettled and uncultivated, in the space ranging from one city to another. Entire towns have, in some places, disappeared, either buried in the ruins of mines, or their inhabitants destroyed by the compulsive and poisonous labour of working them; nor had the cries of all Peru, nor the energetic remonstrances of the most zealous ministers, been capable of reforming this exterminating system of forced labour, carried on within the bowels of the earth.

The art of working the mines, among us beheld with apathy and neglect, has been unattended with those improvements which have distinguished the enlightened age in which we live, and diminished the attendant casualties; hence opulent mines, worked in the most clumsy and improvident manner, have sunk in and been overwhelmed, either through the undermining of the mineral ridges, or the rush of waters which have totally inundated them. Other rare and estimable productions of the country are still confounded with nature, and neglected by the government, and if, among us, any enlightened observer has attempted to point out their advantages, he has been reprehended by the court and forced to silence, owing to the competition that might arise to a few artisans of the mother country.

The teaching of science was forbidden us, and we were allowed to study only the Latin grammar, ancient philosophy, theology, and civil and canonical jurisprudence. Viceroy, Joaquin del Pino, took the greatest umbrage that the Buenos Ayres Board of Trade presumed to bear the expenses of a nautical school; in compliance with the orders transmitted from court it was closed; and an injunction besides laid upon us, that our youths should not be sent to Paris to become professors of chemistry, with a view to teach this science among their own countrymen.

Commerce has at all times been an exclusive monopoly in the hands of the traders of Spain, and the consignees they sent over to America. The public offices were reserved for Spaniards, and notwithstanding, by the laws, these were equally open to Americans, we seldom attained them, and when we did, it was by satiating the avarice of the Court through the sacrifice of immense treasures. Among one hundred and sixty Viceroys who have governed in America, four natives of the country alone are numbered; and of six hundred and two Captains-General and Governors, with the exception of fourteen, all have been Spaniards. The same, proportionably, happened in the other offices of importance; scarcely, indeed, had the Americans an opportunity of alternating with Spaniards in situations the most subaltern.

Everything, by Spain, was so arranged, that the degradation of the natives should prevail in America. It did not enter into her views that wise men should be formed, fearful that minds and talents would be created capable of promoting the interests of their country, and causing civilization, manners, and those excellent capabilities with which the Columbian children are gifted, to make a rapid progress. She unceasingly diminished our population, apprehensive that, some day or other, it might be in a state to rise up against a dominion, sustained only by a few hands, to whom the keeping of detached and extensive regions was entrusted. She carried on an exclusive trade; because she supposed opulence would make us proud, and inclined to free ourselves from outrage. She denied to us the advancement of industry, in order that we might be divested of the means of rising up out of misery and poverty; and we were excluded from offices of trust, in order that Peninsulars only might hold influence in the country, and form the necessary habits and inclinations, with a view to leave us in such a state of dependence as to be unable to think, or act, unless according to Spanish forms.

Such was the system firmly and steadily upheld by the Viceroys, each one of whom bore the state and arrogance of a Vizir. Their power was sufficient to crush anyone who had the misfortune to displease them. However great their outrages, they were to be borne with resignation, for by their satellites and flatterers, their frown was superstitiously compared to the anger of God. Complaints, addressed to the throne, were either lost in the extended interval of those thousands of leagues it was necessary to cross, or buried in the offices at home by the relatives or patrons of men wielding viceregal power. This system, so far from having been softened, all hopes that even time would produce this effect, were totally lost. We held neither direct nor indirect influence in our own legislation: this was instituted in Spain; nor were we allowed the right of sending over persons empowered to assist at its formation, who might point out what was fit and suitable, as the cities of Spain were authorized to do. Neither had we any influence over the Administration of Government, which might, in some measure, have tempered the rigour of such laws as were in force. We were aware that no other resource was left to us than patience, and that for him who was not resigned to endure all, even capital punishment was not sufficient, since, for cases of this kind, torments, new and of un heard-of cruelty, had been invented, such as made nature shudder.

Neither so great, nor so repeated, were the hard ships which roused the provinces of Holland, when they took up arms to free themselves from the yoke of Spain, nor those of Portugal to effect the same purpose. Less were the hardships which placed the Swiss under the direction of William Tell, and in open opposition to the German Emperor. Less those which determined the United States of North America to resist the imposts forced upon them by a British King; less, in short, the powerful motives which have urged other countries, not separated by nature from the parent-state, to cast off an iron yoke and consult their own felicity. We, nevertheless, divided from Spain by an immense sea, gifted with a different climate, possessing other wants and habits, and treated as herds of cattle, have exhibited to the world the singular example of forbearance amidst degradations, by remaining obedient, when, at the same time, we had the most favourable opportunities of breaking the bond, and putting an end to so unnatural a connection.

We address ourselves to the nations of the earth, and we cannot be so rash as to seek to deceive them in what they have themselves seen and felt. America remained tranquil during the whole period of the war of Succession, and waited the decision of the question then at issue between the Houses of Austria and Bourbon, and with a view to follow the fate of Spain. That would have been a favourable moment to redeem herself from so many hardships;

but she did not do it; rather she ought to arm and defend herself alone, in order to preserve herself united to the parent-state. We, without having direct share or interest in the differences of the latter with other Powers of Europe, have equally felt and partaken in her wars; we have experienced the same ravages, and, without repining, we have endured the same wants and privations, brought upon us by her weakness at sea, and the manner in which we were cut off from all communication with her.

In the year 1806 we were attacked. A British expedition surprised and occupied the capital of Buenos Ayres, through the imbecility and unskillfulness of the Viceroy, who, although he had no Spanish troops, did not know how to avail himself of the numerous resources offered to him in defense of the town. At the end of forty-five days we recovered the capital, and the British, together with their General, were made prisoners, without the Viceroy having had the smallest share in the affair. We implored the Government at home to send us such aid as would protect us from another invasion, with which we were threatened; and the consolation transmitted to us was, a revolting Royal Order, by which we were enjoined to defend ourselves in the best manner we could. In the following year, the eastern bank of the River Plate was occupied by a fresh and stronger expedition, and the fortress of Montevideo was besieged and surrendered. There, more British forces assembled, and an armament was formed for the purpose of again attacking the capital, which, in fact, within a few months experienced an assault; but fortunately the heroic courage of the inhabitants and garrison overcame the efforts of the enemy, and a victory so brilliant compelled him to evacuate Montevideo, and the whole of the eastern bank.

No opportunity more favourable of rendering ourselves independent could have presented itself, if the spirit of rebellion and perfidy had been capable of actuating our conduct, or if we had been susceptible of those seditious and anarchical principles imputed to us. But, why recur to pleas of this kind? We could not be indifferent to the degradation in which we lived. If victory at any time authorizes the conqueror to be the arbiter of his own destiny, we could at any moment have secured our own; we had arms in our hands, were triumphant, without a single Spanish regiment among us capable of resistance; and if victory and force do not suffice to establish a right, we had still other more powerful reasons, no longer to submit to the dominion of Spain. The forces of the Peninsula were not to be dreaded by us; its ports were blockaded, and the seas controlled by British squadrons. Yet not withstanding fortune thus propitiously favoured us, we did not seek to separate from Spain, conceiving that this distinguished proof of loyalty would change the principles of the court, and cause them to understand their real interests.

We miserably deceived ourselves, and were flattered with vain hopes. Spain did not receive a demonstration so generous as a sign of benevolence, but as an obligation rigorously due. America continued to be governed with the same harshness, and our heroic sacrifices served only to add a few pages more to the history of that in justice we had uniformly experienced.

Such was our situation when the Spanish revolution commenced. Accustomed as we were, blindly to obey all the arrangements of the Madrid Government, we tendered our allegiance to Ferdinand de Bourbon, notwithstanding he had assumed the crown by ejecting his own father from the throne, through the means of a commotion excited in Aranjuez. We afterwards saw that he passed on to France, was there detained with his parents and brothers, and dispossessed of that throne he had just usurped. We beheld that the Spanish nation, everywhere overawed by French troops, was in a convulsed state; and that illustrious persons, who either governed the provinces with success, or honourably served in the armies, were assassinated by the people, in a state of open mutiny. That amidst the oscillations to which the administration of affairs was exposed, distinct governments rose up, each one calling itself supreme, and each arrogating to itself the right of commanding over America in sovereignty. A junta of this kind instituted in Seville, was the first that presumed to exact our obedience, and to it the Viceroys compelled us to give it our acknowledgment and submission. In less than two months afterwards, another junta, entitled the Supreme Junta of Galicia, sought from us a similar acquiescence, and sent over to us a Viceroy, with the generous threat, that thirty thousand men would also come over if it should be necessary. The Central Junta was next instituted, yet without our having had any share in its formation; we instantly obeyed, and with zeal and efficacy complied with all its decrees. We sent over succours in money, voluntary donations, and aid of all kinds, in order to prove that our fidelity was in no danger, whatever might be the risk to which it was exposed.

We had been tempted by the agents of King Joseph Napoleon, and flattered by great promises of our situation being ameliorated, if we adhered to his party. We were aware that the Spaniards of the highest class and importance had already declared in his favour; that the nation was without armies, and divested of all vigorous guidance and administration, so necessary in moments of dilemma. We were informed, that the troops belonging to the river Plate, which had been carried over as prisoners to England, after the first expedition of the British here, had been conveyed to Cadiz, and there treated with the greatest inhumanity; that they had been compelled to beg alms in the streets, to avoid dying of hunger; and that naked and without any relief they had been sent to fight against the French. Nevertheless, amidst so many urgent and trying causes of complaint, we remained in the same position till Andalusia was occupied by the French, and the Central Junta dispersed.

In this state of things, an address was published, without date, and signed only by the Archbishop of Laodicea, who had been president of the dissolved Central Junta. By it the formation of a Regency was ordained, and three members who were to compose it were named. A measure, as sudden as it was unexpected, could not fail to surprise and alarm us. For the first time, we were then placed on our guard, fearing that we should be involved in the misfortunes of the mother country. We reflected on her uncertain and vacillating situation, the French being already before the very gates of Cadiz and La Isla de Leon. We were apprehensive of the new Regents, to us totally unknown, since the Spaniards of greatest credit had already passed over to the French, the Central Junta had been dissolved, and its members persecuted and accused of treason in the public prints. We were sensible of the informality of the decree published by the Archbishop of Laodicea, and his total want of powers to establish a Regency. We were ignorant whether the French had taken Cadiz and completed the conquest of Spain, in the meantime that this same decree had been wafted over to as. We were moreover dubious, whether a government rising up out of the dispersed fragments of the Central Junta, would not very soon share the same fate. Intent on the risks to which we were exposed, we resolved to take upon ourselves the care of our own security, until we acquired better information respecting the situation of Spain, and saw that the Government there attained, at least, some degree of consistency. Instead of this, we soon beheld the Regency fall to the ground, and various changes succeeded each other in moments of great public distress and confusion.

Meanwhile we established our own Junta of Government, on the model of those of Spain. Its institution was purely provisional, and in the name of the captive King, Ferdinand. Our Viceroy, Don Baltasar Hidalgo de Cisneros, immediately issued circulars to the interior governors, in order that they might prepare a civil war, and arm one province against the other. The River Plate was soon blockaded by a squadron ; the Governor of Cordova began to organize an army; that of Potosi, and the President of Charcas, caused a division of troops to march to the confines of Salta; and the President of Cusco, presenting himself with a third army on the margins of El Desaguadero, entered into a forty days' armistice, in order to throw us off our guard; but before its termination, commenced hostilities, and attacked our troops, when a bloody battle ensued, in which we lost more than one thousand five hundred men. The human mind shudders at the recollection of the acts of violence then committed by Goyeneche, in Cochabamba. Would to God it were possible to forget this ungrateful and bloody American, who, on the day of his entry into the above place, ordered the honourable Governor and Intendant, Antesana, to be shot; who, witnessing from the balcony of his house this assassination, in a ferocious manner cried out to the soldiery not to shoot him in the head, because he wanted this to place it on a stake ; who, after cutting it off, ordered the lifeless trunk to be dragged along the streets ; and who, by his barbarous decree, authorised his soldiers to become the arbiters of lives and property, allowing them, in possession of so brutal a 'power, uncontrolled to range the streets for several days.

Posterity will be astonished at the ferocity exercised against us by men interested in the preservation of America; and that rashness and folly with which they have sought to punish demonstrations the most evident of fidelity and love, will ever be matter of the greatest surprise. The name of Ferdinand de Bourbon preceded all the decrees of our Government, and was at the head of all its public acts. The Spanish flag waved on our vessels, and served to animate our soldiers. The provinces, seeing themselves in a bereft state, through the overthrow of the national Government, owing to the want of another legitimate and respectable one substituted in its stead, and the conquest of nearly the whole of the mother country, raised up a watch-tower, as it were, within themselves, to attend to their own security and self-preservation, reserving themselves for the captive monarch, in case he recovered his freedom. This measure was in imitation of the public conduct of Spain, and called forth by the declaration made to America, that she was an integral part of the monarchy, and in rights equal with the former; and it had, moreover, been resorted to in Montevideo through the advice of the Spaniards themselves. We offered to continue pecuniary succours, and voluntary donations, in order to prosecute the war, and we a thousand times published the soundness of our intentions and the sincerity of our wishes. Great Britain, at that time, so well-deserving of Spain, interposed her mediation and good offices, in order that we might not be treated in so harsh and cruel a manner. But the Spanish ministers, blinded by their sanguinary caprice, spurned the mediation, and issued rigorous orders to all their generals to push the war, and to inflict heavier punishments; on every side scaffolds were raised, and recourse was had to every invention for spreading consternation and dismay.

From that moment they endeavoured to divide us by all the means in their power, in order that we might exterminate each other. They propagated against us atrocious calumnies, attributing to us the design of destroying our sacred religion, of setting aside all morality, and establishing licentiousness of manners. They carried on a war of religion against us, devising many and various plots to agitate and alarm the consciences of the people, by causing the Spanish bishops to issue edicts of ecclesiastical censure and interdiction among the faithful, to publish excommunications, and, by means of some ignorant confessors, to sow fanatical doctrines in the tribunal of penance. By the aid of such religious discords, they have sown dissension in families, produced quarrels between parents and their children, torn asunder the bonds which united man and wife, scattered implacable enmity and rancour among brothers formerly the most affectionate, and even placed nature herself in a state of hostility and variance.

They have adopted the system of killing men indistinctly in order to diminish our numbers; and on their entry into towns they have seized non-combatants, hurried them in groups to the squares, and there shot them, one by one. The cities of Chuquisaca and Cochabamba have more than once been the theatres of these ferocious acts.

They have mixed our captive prisoners among their own troops, carrying off our officers in irons to secluded dungeons, where during the period of a year it was impossible for them to retain their health; others they have left to die of hunger and misery in the prisons, and many they have compelled to toil in public works. In a boasting manner they have shot the bearers of our flags of truce, and committed the basest horrors with military chiefs and other principal persons who had already surrendered themselves, notwithstanding the humanity we have always displayed towards their prisoners. In proof of this assertion, we can quote the cases of Deputy Matos, from Potosi; Captain General, Pumacagua; General Angulo and his brother; Commandant Munecas, and other leaders, shot in cold blood many days after they had been made prisoners.

In the town of Valle-Grande they enjoyed the brutal pleasure of cutting off the ears of the inhabitants, and sent off a basket filled with these presents to their headquarters; they afterwards burnt the town, set fire to thirty other populous ones belonging to Peru; and took delight in shutting up persons in their own houses before the flames were applied to them, in order that they might there be burnt to death.

They have not only been cruel and implacable in murdering, but they have also divested themselves of all morality and public decency, by whipping old religious persons in the open squares, and also women, bound to a cannon, causing them previously to be stripped and exposed to shame and derision.

For all these kinds of punishment they established an inquisitorial system, seized the persons of several peace able citizens and conveyed them beyond seas, there to be judged for supposed crimes; and many they have sent to execution, without any form of trial whatever.

They have persecuted our vessels, plundered our coasts, butchered their defenceless inhabitants, without even sparing superannuated priests, and, by orders of General Pezuela, they burnt the church belonging to the town of Puna, and put to the sword old men, women, and children, the only inhabitants therein found. They have excited atrocious conspiracies among the Spaniards domiciliated in our cities, and forced us into the painful alternative of imposing capital punishment on the fathers of numerous families.

They have compelled our brethren and children to take up arms against us, and, forming armies out of the inhabitants of the country under the command of their own officers, they have forced them into battle with our troops. They have stirred up domestic plots and conspiracies, by corrupting with money, and by means of all kinds of machinations, the peaceful inhabitants of the country, in order to involve us in dreadful anarchy and then to attack us in a weak and divided state.

In a most shameful and infamous manner they have failed to fulfil every capitulation we have, on repeated occasions, concluded with them, even at a time when we have had them under our own swords; they caused four thousand men again to take up arms after they had surrendered, together with General Tristan, at the action of Salta, and to whom General Belgrano generously granted terms of capitulation on the field of battle, and more generously complied with them, trusting to their word and honour.

They have invented a new species of horrid warfare, by poisoning the waters and aliments, as they did when conquered in La Paz by General Pinelo; and in return for the kind manner in which the latter treated them, after surrendering at discretion, they resorted to the barbarous stratagem of blowing up the soldiers' quarters which they had previously undermined.

They have had the baseness to tamper with our generals and governors, by availing themselves of and abusing the sacred privilege of flags of truce, exciting them to act traitorously towards us, and for this purpose making written overtures to them. They have declared that the laws of war, observed among civilized nations, ought not to be practised towards us; and their General, Pezuela, after the battle of Ayouma, in order to avoid any compromise or understanding, had the arrogance to answer General Belgrano, that with Insurgents it was impossible to enter into treaties.

Such has been the conduct of Spaniards towards us, since the restoration of Ferdinand De Bourbon, to the throne of his ancestors. We then believed that the termination of so many sufferings and disasters had arrived; we had supposed that a king, schooled by the lessons of adversity, would not be indifferent to the desolation of his people, and we sent over a commissioner to him [Bernardino Rivadavia], in order to acquaint him with our situation. We could not for a moment conceive that he would fail to meet our wishes as a benign prince, nor could we doubt that our requests would interest him in a manner corresponding to that gratitude and goodness which the courtiers of Spain had extolled to the skies. But anew and unknown species of ingratitude was reserved for America, surpassing all the examples found in the histories of the greatest tyrants.

In the first moments of his restoration to Madrid, he declared us to be in a state of mutiny, but since then he has refused to hear our complaints, to admit our requests; and, as the last favour we could expect from him, he has offered to us unconditional pardon. He confirmed the viceroys, governors, and generals, whom at his return he found carrying on their works of butchery. He declared it to be a crime of high treason for us to presume to frame a constitution for ourselves, in order that the administration of our own affairs might not depend on a tyrannic, arbitrary, and distant government, under which we had groaned during three centuries — a measure which could alone be offensive to a prince, the enemy of justice and beneficence, and consequently unworthy of governing.

By the aid of his ministers, he then applied himself to the forming of large armaments, with a view to employ them against us. He has since caused numerous armies to be conveyed over to these countries, in order to consummate the work of devastation, fire, and robbery. He has caused the first felicitations of the potentates of Europe, on his return to Spain, to be used as pleas in order to engage them to refuse us all aid and succour, and thus behold us tear each other to pieces with an eye of indifference. He has made special regulations for cruising against vessels belonging to America, containing barbarous clauses, and ordering that the crews shall be hung. He has forbidden, with regard to us, the observance of the laws of his naval regulations, framed according to the rights of nations, and denied to us all that we grant to his subjects when captured by our cruisers. He has sent over his generals with certain decrees of pardon, which they cause to be published for the purpose of deceiving weak and ignorant minds, and under a hope to facilitate their entry into the towns; but at the same time he has given to them other private instructions; and authorized by these, as soon as possession is gained, they hang, burn, plunder, confiscate, and connive at private assassinations, plotting all kinds of injury against those thus feignedly pardoned. In the name of Ferdinand De Bourbon, it is, that the heads of patriotic officers, who have been taken prisoners, are placed on the highways; that one of our commanders of a light party was killed with sticks and stones; and that Colonel Camargo, after also being murdered with blows by the hand of the villain, Centeno, had his head cut off, which was sent as a present to General Pezuela, with this revolting notification, 'that this was a miracle of the Virgin del Carmen'.

Such is the extent and force of the evils and sufferings which have impelled us to adopt the only alternative left to us. We have long and deliberately meditated on our fate, and casting our eyes everywhere around us, we have beheld nothing but the vestiges of those elements by which our situation was necessarily distinguished, opprobrium, ruin, and patience. What had America to expect from a king who ascends the throne, animated by sentiments so cruel and inhuman? From a king who, before he commences his ravages, hastens to prevent any foreign prince from interposing in order to restrain his fury? From a king who, with scaffolds and chains, rewards the immense sacrifices made by his own subjects of Spain to release him from the captivity in which he laid? Those very subjects who, at the expense of their own blood and under every species of hardship, had, without any intermission, fought to redeem him from prison, and till they had again placed the diadem on his head? If men, to whom he is so much indebted, only for forming to themselves a constitution, have received death and imprisonment as a return for their services, what could we suppose was in reserve for us? To expect from him and his butchering ministers benign treatment, were to seek among the tigers of the forest the magnanimity of the eagle.

Had we hesitated in our resolve, we should have be held repeated among us the sanguinary scenes of Caracas, Carthagena, Quito, and Santa Fe; we should have implicated the ashes of eighty thousand persons who have been victims of the enemy's fury, whose illustrious memories would have risen up in judgment against us, and demanded vengeance ; and we should have called down upon ourselves the execration of so many future generations condemned to serve a master at all times ready to ill-treat them, and who, owing to his impotency at sea, has been completely disabled from protecting them from foreign invasions.

In consequence whereof, and impelled both by the conduct of Spaniards and their king, we have constituted ourselves independent, and prepared for our own natural defence and against the ravages of tyranny, by pledging our honour, and offering up our lives and property. We have sworn to the King and Supreme Judge of the universe, that we will not abandon the cause of justice ; that we will not suffer that country which he has given us to be buried in ruins and immersed in blood spilled by the hands of our executioners ; that we will never forget the obligations we are under of saving our homes from the dangers by which they are threatened, and the sacred right vested in our country to demand from us every sacrifice, in order that it may not be polluted, crimsoned with blood, and trampled underfoot by usurpers and tyrants. We have engraved this declaration on our hearts, in order that in its behalf we may never cease to combat; and while we manifest to the nations of the earth the reasons which have so powerfully induced us to adopt the present measure, we have the honour to proclaim it as our intention to live in peace with all, even with Spain herself, from the moment she is desirous of accepting it. — Given in the Hall of Congress, Buenos Ayres, this 25th day of October, eighteen hundred and seventeen.

Dr. Pedro Ignacio de Castro y Barros, President.
Dr. Jose Eugenio de Elias, Secretary.

2. Exposition of the Proceedings of the Supreme Government of the United Provinces of South America, during the present administration, by Juan Martin de Pueyrredon, Buenos Ayres, July 21, 1817[30]

The evils which hard, in succession, since the year 1810, occasioned our calamities, and retarded the progress of our sacred cause, appeared to have all conspired to assail us at the same moment, threatening to reduce our political existence to its last agonies, towards the close of 1815. The few remaining forces which we had saved from the unhappy field of Sipesipe seemed to be on the point of dissolution. The army which had been organized in the province of Cuyo, for the purpose of marching upon Chili, beheld itself insecure even in its entrenchments. The enemy, proud of his victories, had already laid his plans to entrammel the inhabitants of those districts, who were distracted by opposite councils, and who dared not indulge a hope that, through our means, they might be shielded from the impending dangers. The national treasury was not only inadequate to the satisfaction of the demands upon it, but even to provide for the most urgent wants. The public spirit of the different provinces had lost sight of the common danger, and occupied itself exclusively in the visionary project of seeking liberty in the dissolution of every tie. Discord had taken possession of all hearts, expelling every generous and honourable sentiment. The citizens of the same land displayed their valour only in mutual destruction or distrust; assailing their best friends and benefactors. Subordination amongst the military was disregarded by the lowest subalterns. The public authorities were only respected as they gave countenance to crime, to error, to licentiousness. It grieves me, fellow-citizens, to speak of it, but I must be faithful to truth when I undertake to trace the revolting picture which our country then exhibited to the contemplation of the world; the acknowledgement of our errors can bring upon us no disgrace, when made with the virtuous resolution of correcting them; nor am I the first friend of his country who has deplored our past melancholy situation. Pardon me, therefore, if I proceed. Calumny with her baleful train, had seated herself in the midst of us, scattering her poisons through the minds of our most respectable fellow citizens. The capital of the State, which, in the midst of the most trying difficulties, had preserved a certain dignity of character, now appeared to be the focus of all the passions which distracted every part of the country. Fractions of every party were here encountered in a state of the utmost exasperation, while the imminence of the public dangers served but as the pretext for the indulgence of mutual revenge; accusing one

30 [*The Morning Chronicle*, 19 December 1817, British Library Newspapers. Accessed 25 April 2020].

another with the origin of the general distresses, and breathing, mutually, the most injurious suspicions.

The magnanimous people of Buenos Ayres, to whom the praise cannot be denied of having impoverished themselves in affording aid to brethren engaged in the same glorious cause, were on the point of experiencing a re-action, whose consequences would have proved radically destructive to the character and existence of La Plata. Anarchy, in a word, had lighted up a universal conflagration. Nor was this all; when now it might have been supposed that the measure of our afflictions had been full, the troops of Portugal made their appearance on the northern borders of this river, availing themselves of our discords; for these unhappily, unknown to ourselves, had but too well seconded the interests of the neighbouring Court. New dangers here presented themselves, new occasions to sow discords, and a new impulse was given to the torrent of personal enmities, rendering even loyalty suspicious. It is no easy task, fellow-citizens, to draw a just picture of our misadventures, or to enumerate the perils over which your firmness has happily triumphed. You all remember that the evils which thus assailed us, began to diminish at the very moment when we had yielded to despair. The Supreme Congress, into whose hands the people had confided their safety, had just been installed at Tucuman. Those who were called upon to be the legislators of their country, and to fix its destiny, by the wisdom of their councils, were compelled more than once to exert their courage, and to encounter with intrepidity the dangers which threatened to profane this last asylum that remained to our country in its misfortunes. The prudence, the integrity, the fortitude of this august body, presented to the Provinces the delightful spectacle of an authority which captivated their submission, not less by the just title of its elevated origin, than by the animated zeal, and vigorous energy which it displayed in the first steps of its illustrious march. The boldest passions were compelled to renounce their extravagant designs; and if in some districts they had the temerity to attempt new excesses, the celerity with which they were suppressed, scarcely allowed time to their authors to sue for mercy. The seditious, notwithstanding, still harboured the design of putting vigilance to sleep, in order that they might snatch the opportunity of insulting whatever was most respectable. It was at this crisis that the Supreme Representation, deigned to invest me with the honourable, but awful distinction of Supreme Director of the State. This was not the first time I had been clothed with authority; and that I had already experienced the bitter mortification attendant upon it, was too well known, not to regard my acceptance as a sacrifice. At that time a Member of the Supreme Body, I knew well the mass of difficulties that would weigh upon me; but even these, in the midst of anxiety and fears, urged my submission to the Supreme will.

I had no right to expect that my elevation would meet the approbation of everyone; and the calamity of the times caused me to fear that my election might give rise to new disturbances. The result did not disappoint my anticipations. I saw myself compelled to subdue the hearts of my personal enemies; but I now considered my person as exclusively devoted to the public cause. Invested with the Chief Magistracy, I set off from the bosom of the Supreme Congress, for the province of Salta, and had the good fortune to compose the loud dissentions which had set at variance the citizens and the soldiers; and, having prepared the elements which afterwards procured for the Saltanians their well-earned fame. I proceeded to the army, examined its situations, inspected the fortifications, and, giving such orders as the occasion might require, I returned to Tucuman, where I had the proud satisfaction of hastening, by my influence, the memorable act and solemn declaration of our independence. I pursued my journey to the capital of Cordova, where, according to previous arrangement, I was expected by general San Martin, in order to settle the places for rescuing Chili from the power of the Spaniards. From Cordova, with what painful inquietude did I stretch my view towards the agitated population of Buenos Ayres. I appeal to you, fellow-citizens, as the witnesses of the well-founded causes of my fears; and permit me, passing by the perils of my transit, to fix your attention on the first days of my arrival in this capital. What violence of passions! How many jarring interests! My resolution was taken. I hastened to fulfil the obligations of my oath. I announced to the people that the past should be forgotten, that those who deserved well of their country should be rewarded.

Fellow-citizens, I have not failed in my promises, nor shall I ever have reason to repent me of my conduct. To this course, and to your virtues, it is due, that the constituted authorities have been supported in despite of the boldest innovators; to this am I to attribute the reconciliation of those who before regarded themselves as having reason to be my enemies; to this, to say all in a word, it is due, that obedience to the lawful authorities, and the love of order, constitute at present the prevailing temper of the provinces over whose destinies I have the honour to preside as Chief Magistrate. It were a presumptuous folly to assert, that this has been established on foundations that are proof against every attempt; the present age offers but too many examples of how fallible, in these particulars, are all political institutions; but how disgraceful ought we to consider the conduct of those who meditate a repetition of those mournful scenes in our country; it is proper to hope that, in future, restless spirits will be more easily repressed than in the earlier part of the present administration. Then it was, that the spirit of anarchy claimed our first attention; yet we were by no means free from other assailants, whom it was necessary to oppose with our utmost efforts. The interior provinces were threatened by the near approach of the enemy, with a more numerous and effective force than had ever been brought into the field; to concentrate our own was impossible, from the want of means to transport them hundreds of leagues, and from their already occupying posts from which they could not be spared. Moreover I experienced the most painful embarrassment of mind, when compelled to choose between two extremes equally perilous -to abandon the districts of the interior, and the army which covered them, to the utmost hazard; or to desist from the attempt to reconquer Chili, exposing the province of Cuyo to subjugation. I at length adopted the course inspired by courage, baffling the plans of the enemy's Generals, La Serna and Marco. The Patriot Army, against which that of Lima was intended to operate, was rapidly reinforced, the discipline and subordination which had been lost during the periods of our reverses were in a short time restored. Its present strength, respectability, and efficiency is known to you, in common with the rest of our fellow-citizens; and more would you have seen, if the enemy who now flies before us, beaten and humbled, had not encountered a rampart of loyalty and valour in the province of Salta.

The army of Cuyo, far from giving way to that of Peru, maintained its ground, until regiments were marched from Buenos Ayres to its reinforcement; new regiments were created with a rapidity almost incredible, through the noble devotedness and generous liberality of that province, in order to accelerate the final preparations for setting on foot the stupendous design which had been formed of scaling the Andes: whose successful issue will afford to other nations some means of estimating the respectability of our power, as it has struck terror into the minds of our enemies, has kindled gratitude in the hearts of our brethren of Chili, and erected the most splendid monument to the power and glory of our country.

The army of this capital was organized at the same time with those of the Andes and of the interior; the regular force has been nearly doubled; the militia has made great progress in military discipline; our slave population, has been formed into battalions, and taught the military art as far as it is consistent with their condition. The capital is under no apprehension that an army of 10,000 men can shake its liberties, and should the Peninsularians send against us thrice that number, ample provision has been made to receive them.

Our navy has been fostered in all its branches; the scarcity of means under which we laboured until now, has not prevented us from undertaking very considerable operations, with respect to national vessels; all of them have been repaired, and others have been purchased and armed, for the defence of our coasts and rivers; provision has been made, should necessity require it, for arming many more, so that the enemy will not find himself secure from our reprisal even upon the ocean.

Our military force, at every point which it occupies, seems to be animated with the same spirit; its tactics are uniform and have undergone a rapid improvement from the science and experience which it has borrowed from warlike nations. Our arsenals have been replenished with arms, and a sufficient store of cannon and munitions of war have been provided to maintain the contest for many years; and this, after having supplied articles of every description to those districts which have not as yet come into the union, but whose connexion with us has been only intercepted by reason of our past misfortunes.

Our legions daily receive considerable augmentations from new levies; all our preparations have been made, as though we were about to enter upon the contest anew. Until now, the vastness of our resources were unknown to us, and our enemies may contemplate with deep mortification and despair, the present flourishing state of these provinces after so many devastations.

The office of Major-General has been re-established, for the purpose of giving a uniform direction to our armies, in order to foster the militia in all its details, and to regulate the system of military economy. The General Officers and those of a lower grade, occupied in those duties, will lighten the labours of the Government, at the same time rendering more practical the progress and improvement of which the military force is susceptible, thus forming by degrees a body of expert soldiery, who will at once be an honour to their country, and serve as its firmest pillar in times of danger.

Whilst thus occupied in providing for our safety within, and preparing for assaults from without, other objects of solid interest have not been neglected, and which hitherto were thought to oppose insurmountable obstacles.

Our system of finances had hitherto been on a footing [entirely inadequate to the unfailing supply][31] of our wants, and still more to the liquidation of the immense debt which had been contracted in former years. An unremitted application to this object has enabled me to create the means of satisfying the creditors of the state, who had already abandoned their debts as lost, as well as to devise a fixed mode by which the taxes may be made to fall equally and indirectly on the whole mass of our population; it is not the least merit of this operation, that it has been effected in despite of the censures with which it was attacked, and which are but little creditable to the intelligence and good intentions of their authors. The result has been, that there now circulates in the hands of the capitalists a sum equivalent in its value to one million of dollars, which was deficient before the adoption of the measures by which it was produced. To the same measures are we indebted for the receipt of two hundred and sixty-eight thousand dollars, in the treasury of the custom-house, in the short time which has elapsed since my decree of the 29th of March. At no other period have the public exigencies been so punctually supplied, nor have more important works been undertaken.

The people, moreover, have been relieved from many burdens, which, being partial, or confined to particular classes, had occasioned vexation and disgust. Other vexations, scarcely less grievous, will by degrees be also suppressed, avoiding, as far as possible, a recurrence to loans, which have

---

31 [The phrase in brackets is not included in the newspaper and has been taken from Brackenridge's translation, in Brackenridge, 1820: 314].

drawn after them the most fatal consequences to States. Should we, however, be compelled to resort to such expedients, the lenders will not see themselves in danger of losing their advances. To shew these practical results is to make the best reply to censure; if it be the intention to do justice to the zeal and intelligence of public officers, the inconveniences and difficulties must be weighed with the good that has been effected. It is an idle vanity to seek perfection in the labours of men.

One of the mischiefs attendant on the administration of the National Treasury, was the existence of many superfluous officers; with respect to this, the proper reformations have been made, especially in relation to the armories and public works. The attention of the Government is continually alive in this branch of its duties, and it is not without hopes of being able to see abundance restored, even in the midst of the unceasing attention required by war, and of the many undertakings that have been set on foot for the advancement of the general prosperity.

Such has been the extension of our southern frontier over plains and deserts, well adapted to the formation of wealthy settlements; a project, whose accomplishment was not in the reach of former Governments, in spite of repeated attempts to subdue obstacles which the present Administration has had the good fortune to surmount. The unfortunate inhabitants of our plains have not only been gratuitously supplied with suitable lands, on which to fix their habitations, but have been furnished with the means of cultivating them to advantage.

Such has been the re-establishment of the college heretofore named San Carlos, but hereafter to be called the Union of the South, as a point designated for the dissemination of learning to the youth of every part of the State, on the most extensive scale; for the attainment of which object, the Government is at the present moment engaged in putting in practice every possible diligence. It will not be long before these nurseries will flourish, in which the liberal and exact sciences will be cultivated; in which the hearts of those young men will be formed, who are destined at some future day to add new splendour to our country.

Such has been the establishment of a military depot on our frontier, with its capacious magazine -a necessary measure to guard us from future dangers; a work which does more honour to the prudent foresight of our country, as it was undertaken in the moment of its prosperous fortunes; a measure which must give more occasion for reflection to our enemies, than they can impose upon us by their boastings.

This exposition is not made with a view to enhance the value of these services which our country has a right to demand as a debt, but to offer an irrefragable proof to the people, that prudence and circumspection are the virtues which are required to secure the fruits of their heroic efforts. For the rest, reflecting minds calculating the labours of the Government by the immense disparity between the present state of our affairs, and what they were 15 months ago, will do justice to the zeal which has effected changes so important. They will no less give credit for many other acts, of a nature to manifest themselves less fully to the public. I have already mentioned the difficulties which embarrassed me, in respect to our exterior relations: and if I had opposed less firmness in resisting the violence of a party, a breach with a neighbouring nation would be the inevitable consequence. The course pursued by me in this particular, leaves unimpaired our right to the invaded territory, convinced that pacific measures, so long as the honour of the country requires no other, will be productive of more salutary effects, than a resort to violence, without necessity.

A period there has been, you will remember, fellow-citizens, in which the provinces were threatened with the sight of the nascent order and tranquillity subverted under pretexts of the most injurious suspicions against the constituted authorities. It was that period which occasioned more trouble to my mind, than any other during my administration. I will cheerfully renounce my claims to the public gratitude for the sleepless nights spent in watching over its safety, if it will appreciate the sacrifice I have made, the pain it has given to my heart, to have been compelled to adopt the rude and violent measures which at that crisis saved the State from ruin. But the necessity and justice of my proceedings, and the happy consequences which have attended them, leave me no room to repent.

Under the same circumstances, my conduct shall be the same. I will extinguish all the natural feelings of my heart, sooner than consent to the repetition of scenes, which weaken our power, and sink our national glory to the lowest degradation.

Fellow-citizens, we owe our unhappy reverses and calamities to the depraving system of our ancient metropolis, which, in condemning us to the obscurity and opprobrium of the most degraded destiny, has sown with thorns the path that conducts us to liberty. Tell that metropolis that even she may glory in your works! Already have you cleared all the rocks, escaped every danger, and conducted these provinces to the flourishing condition in which we now behold them. Let the enemies of your name contemplate with despair the energies of your virtues, and let the nations acknowledge that you already appertain to their illustrious rank. Let us felicitate ourselves on the blessings we have already obtained, and let us shew to the world that we have learned to profit by the experience of our past misfortunes.

JUAN MARTIN DE PUEYRREDON
Buenos-Ayres, July 21 [1817]

3. Report on the State of the Republic of La Plata, by J. Graham, 1818[32]

SOUTH AMERICA [1818]

The following is a Report from Mr. Graham, one of the Commissioners sent by the United States' Government to inquire into the state of the Republic of La Plata. It is addressed to Mr. Q. Adams, the Secretary of State (from the New York Papers):

The country formerly known as the viceroyalty of Buenos Ayres, extending from the north-western sources of the river La Plata to the southern cape of America, and from the confines of Brazil and the ocean to the ridge of the Andes, may be considered that which is called 'the United Provinces of South America'.

Under the royal government, it was divided into the intendencies or provinces of Buenos Ayres, Paraguay, Cordova, Salta, Potosi, Plata, Cochabamba, La Paz, and Puno. Subsequently to the revolution, in the year 1814, another division was made, and from the provinces of Cordova, Salta, and Buenos Ayres, were taken those of Cuyo or Mendoza, Tucuman, Corrientes, Entre Rios, and the Banda Oriental. The others, it is believed, retained their former boundaries, and, with the exception of Paraguay, are generally called 'Upper Peru'.

This widely extended country embraces almost every variety of climate and soil, and is capable of almost every variety of production. A large part of it, however, particularly on the west side of the river La Plata, and southerly towards Cape Horn, is deficient in wood, even for fuel, and in water; that which is found is generally brackish.

Although three centuries have passed by, since the Spaniards made their first settlement in this country, and some considerable towns and cities have grown in it, yet its general improvement and population have by no means kept pace with them; for the lower provinces have been almost entirely abandoned to the immense herds of cattle which graze on their plains, and require only the partial care of a comparatively few herdsmen; and the inhabitants of Upper Peru have been engaged more generally in the business of mining than was favourable to improvement or population. Certain small districts have peculiar advantages, are said to be well cultivated, and very productive: but

---

32 [*The Morning Chronicle*, 24 December 1818, British Library Newspapers. Accessed 4 June 2020].

agriculture has in general been very much neglected. It is, in a great degree, confined to the vicinity of the towns and cities, and may be said to limit its supplies to their demands. This state of things, combined with the regulations of the former government, the influence of climate, and the force of example, has stamped the character of indolence upon that class of society usually considered as the labouring class. The same causes have not operated, at least with the same force, upon the other inhabitants of the country: hence they are more industrious, and more active; their manners are social, friendly, and polite. In native talents they are said to be inferior to no people; and they have given proofs that they are capable of great and persevering efforts; that they are ardently attached to their country, and warmly enlisted in the cause of its independence.

It is not necessary for me to enter into a detail of the causes which led to the revolution in 1810. The most immediate, perhaps, are to be found in the incidents connected with the two invasions of the country by the British, in the years 1805 and 1806, and in the subsequent events in Spain, as they had a direct tendency to show to these people their own strength, and the incapacity of Spain to give them protection or enforce obedience. The ground-work was, however, laid in the jealous and oppressive system adopted at a more early period by the kings of Spain, whose policy it seemed to be to keep within as narrow limits as circumstances would permit the intelligence, wealth, and population of that part of America subject to their dominion, as the surest means of preserving an empire which they considered the great source of their wealth and power.

[In 1810, manuscript note] The revolution having been auspiciously commenced in the city of Buenos Ayres, was warmly and zealously supported by the great mass of the people descended from the Spaniards; but the native Spaniards, as well those domesticated in the country as those in the service of the king, were almost all opposed to it, particularly at the time and under the circumstances it took place. Dissensions were the immediate result, and their long-standing jealousy and distrust of each other have, by subsequent events, been heightened into deadly hostility, which time alone can wear away. These dissensions have been considered as one of the causes that produced those which subsequently took place among the patriots themselves, and which have been most serious obstacles to the progress of the revolution. Other obstacles, however, have been presented by the royal government at Lima, which has hitherto not only been able to sustain itself there, but has found means, by enlisting the native Peruvians in its service, to send at different times considerable armies into the upper provinces of La Plata, where the war has been carried on from the commencement of the revolution to the present day with various success; the great extent and peculiar character of the country, and the want of resources, having prevented either party from making a blow decisive of the contest. When we came away, the advantage in that quarter was on the side of the Spaniards, as they were in possession of the provinces of Upper Peru, which had, to a certain degree at least, joined in the revolution, and some of which are represented in the Congress. Everywhere else they have been obliged to yield up the government and abandon the country, or submit to the ruling power. The peculiar situation of Montevideo, on the east side of the river La Plata, open to the sea, and strongly fortified, enabled the Spanish naval and military forces, at an early period in the revolution, to make a stand there; they were ultimately obliged to surrender it not, however, until long-protracted, and perhaps ill-directed, efforts on the part of the assailants, had given rise to many jarring incidents between those that came from the opposite shores of the river; probably the effect, in part at least, of ancient jealousies, kept alive by the individual interests of particular leaders; these have been followed by events calculated to produce a still greater alienation; and, although several attempts have been made to bring about a union, they have hitherto been unsuccessful. The provinces of the 'Banda Oriental' and the 'Entre Rios' on the eastern side of the river, under the direction of General Artigas, are now at war with those on the western side, under the government of the Congress at Buenos Ayres.

This war has originated from a combination of causes in which both parties have, perhaps, something to complain of, and something to blame themselves for.

General Artigas and his followers profess a belief that it is the intention of the government of Buenos Ayres to put them down, and oblige them to submit to such arrangements as will deprive them of the privileges of self-government, to which they claim to have a right. They say, however, that they are willing to unite with the people on the western side of the river; but not in such a way as will subject them to what they call the tyranny of the city of Buenos Ayres. On the other hand, it is stated that this is merely a pretext; that the real object of General Artigas, and of some of his principal officers, is to prevent a union on any terms, and to preserve the power they have acquired, by giving an erroneous excitement to the people who follow them: that it is wished and intended to place these provinces on a footing with the others: that the respectable portion of their inhabitants are aware of this fact, and anxious for a union; but are prevented from openly expressing their sentiments from a fear of General Artigas, whose power is uncontrolled by law or justice; and hence the propriety and necessity of aiding them to resist it. Armies have accordingly been marched within the present year into these provinces; but they were not joined by a number of the inhabitants, and were defeated with great loss.

This war is evidently a source of great injury and regret; and, at the same time, of extraordinary irritation to both parties; for, independently of other causes of recrimination, each accuses the other of having brought about that state of things which threatens to place a most important and valuable portion of their country in the hands of a foreign power, who has invaded it with a regular and well-appointed army, and is gradually taking possession of commanding points, from which it may be difficult for their united force hereafter to dislodge them. That they will unite is, I think, to be calculated on, unless some event disastrous to the cause of the revolution itself takes place; for their mutual interest requires a union. But more of moderation and discretion may be necessary to bring it about than is at this time to be expected from the irritated feelings of some of the principal personages on both sides.

The city of Santa Fe, and a small district of country around it, also refuse to acknowledge the authority of the government of Buenos Ayres.

In Paraguay the events of the revolution have differed from those in any other province, as the inhabitants of that country have uniformly resisted the efforts of the other provinces to unite with them. After having aided the Spanish authorities placed over them, to repel a military force which had been sent to overthrow them, they themselves expelled from their country these authorities, and established a government of their own, totally unconnected with that of the other provinces, with whom they manifest an unwillingness to keep up even a commercial intercourse. This has given rise to a suspicion in the minds of some that there is a secret predilection among them for the ancient order of things. But, from what is said of their cold and calculating character, from the safe position of their country, and its capacity to supply its own wants, it is probable that their object is to husband their resources, and profit by the exertions of others, without giving their own in aid of them; and possibly, in case of ultimate failure, to place their conduct in a less objectionable point of view before the government of Spain. Whatever may have been their motives, they have hitherto contrived to escape in a great measure the evils of war. Their resources, in men and money, are said to be considerable, and no country is more independent of foreign supplies.

Their conduct furnishes a striking contrast to that of the people of Buenos Ayres, who entered into the revolution with unbounded zeal and energy, and have ever been ready to meet the difficulties of so great an undertaking. This circumstance connected with their local situation, greater resources, and more general information, and perhaps the fact of their having been the first to get power into their hands, have had the effect to give them a controlling influence over the revolutionary government, which has not failed to excite, in some degree, the jealousy of the other provinces, and amongst themselves a feeling of superiority little calculated to allay that jealousy. Great evils were at one time apprehended from this state of things; but the Congress which met at Tucuman, in March, 1816, composed of deputies from the several provinces then united, assumed the sovereign power of the country, boldly declared its absolute independence, and adopted a provisional form of government, which is understood to have the effect of allaying dissensions, and of introducing a more regular administration of public affairs.

It will be seen from the documents in your possession, that this provisional constitution recognizes many of the principles of free government: but with such drawbacks as are little calculated to enforce them in practice. Great allowances are doubtless to be made for the circumstances of the times, and the danger and difficulty of tearing up ancient institutions, or of adapting new principles to them. But, after due allowance for all these considerations, it did not appear to me that so much had been done for the cause of civil liberty as might have been expected, or that those in power were its strongest advocates. It is generally admitted, however, that some changes for the better have been made. Much care seems to be taken to educate the rising generation, and as those who are now coming on the theatre of action have grown up since the commencement of the revolution, and have had the advantage of the light thrown in by it, it is fair to suppose that they will be better prepared to support and administer a free government than those whose habits were formed under the colonial government of Spain.

The commerce and manufactures of the country have grown beyond its agriculture. Various causes, however, have contributed to lessen some branches of manufacture since the revolution, but commerce is understood to have been increased by it. A much greater variety and quantity of foreign goods are imported, and a greater demand is opened for the productions of the country. The city of Buenos Ayres is the seat of this commerce. From it foreign and some domestic goods are spread through the interior, as far as Chili and Upper Peru; and, in return, the various productions are drawn to it. This trade is carried on principally by land, as is that between the different provinces, though some small portion of it finds its way up and down the large rivers forming the La Plata, which is itself not so much a river as a great bay. The abundance of cattle, horses, and mules, and of some other animals peculiar to the country, which are used in the mountainous regions of Peru, furnish facilities for transportation not to be found in any other country so little improved; hence the price of transportation is very low, and the internal trade greater than it otherwise would be, though it had been materially lessened in some important branches by the war with Peru, and the system adopted in Paraguay.

The export and import trade is principally in the hands of the British, though the United States and other nations participate in it to a certain degree. It is depended on as the great source of revenue to the state; hence they have been tempted to make the duties very high, and to lay them upon both imports and exports, with the exception of lumber and military stores. This circumstance, connected with the fact that payment is demanded at the custom-house before the goods are delivered, has led to a regular system of smuggling, which is said to be carried to great excess, and doubtless occasions the official returns to fall short of the actual amount of the trade. This may be the reason why they were not given to us. The articles imported are almost every variety of European and East India goods, principally from England; rum, sugar, coffee, tobacco, cotton, and timber from Brazil ; lumber of almost every description, cod-fish, furniture, gin, and some smaller articles, from the United States, together with military stores; which, however, find their way into the country directly from Europe, and are thus furnished at a cheaper rate than we can sell them. The principal articles of export are taken from the various animals of the country, tame and wild, from the ox to the chinchilla; copper from Chili, and some of the precious metals, drawn principally from Peru; but as gold is worth seventeen dollars the doubloon, and passed by tale at that rate, very little of it is exported; hence the currency of the country is gold; for they have no paper money. The 'Libranzas', or bills of credit, issued by the government, are, however, an article of traffic among the merchants, as they are received in payment of one half of the duties. No distinction is made in favour of the trade of any nation, save only that the British merchants have some peculiar facilities granted them in relation to their letters, which are an object of taxation, at least so far as applies to those sent out of the country.

In the official statements given to us, and to which I beg leave generally to refer for information as to the foreign relations, the productions, military and naval force, revenue, and population, the latter is stated at 1,300,000, exclusive of Indians. This is understood as comprehending the population of all the provinces; but, as some of them are not under the government at Buenos Ayres, I have thought it proper to annex the several estimates I have collected of the population of each province, as they may serve to give some general information on that point. The most immediate difficulty felt by the government, whilst we were in the country, seemed to arise from the want of money: for, although the debt was small, their credit was low. It had not been found practicable to adopt a system of finance adequate to the exigencies of the times, though it would seem, from the statement given to us, that the revenue of the last year exceeded the expenses. The important events of the present year in Chili, of which you are informed, will doubtless have the effect to raise the credit of the country, and to lessen the pressure upon it, at least for a time, and will probably leave the government more at leisure to attend to its internal affairs.

When we came away, it was understood that a committee of the congress was engaged in drafting a new constitution, the power of forming and adopting it being exclusively vested in the congress. Whether it will assume a federal or a national character, is somewhat doubtful, as there are evidently two parties in the country, whose views in this respect are very different, and it is believed that they are both represented in the congress. The one party is in favour of a consolidated or national government; the other wishes for a federal government, somewhat upon the principles of that of the

United States. The probability seems to be, that, although there might be a majority of the people in the provinces generally in favour of the federal system, it would not be adopted upon the ground that it was not so well calculated as a national government to provide for the common defence, the great object now in view. The same general reason may be urged, perhaps, for giving to the latter, should it be adopted, less of a republican character than probably would have been given to it in more quiet and peaceful times. There is danger too, as the power of forming and adopting the constitution is placed in the hands of a few, that the rights and privileges of the people may not be so well understood or attended to as they would have been had the people themselves had a more immediate agency in the affair. It is not to be doubted, however, that it will at least have a republican form, and be bottomed upon the principles of independence, which is contended for by all descriptions of politicians in the country who have taken part in the revolution, and will, it is believed, be supported by them, in any event, to the last extremity.

Their means of defence, of which they are fully aware, are, in proportion to their numbers, greater perhaps than those of almost any other people, and the duration and the events of the war have strengthened the general determination never to submit to Spain. This determination rests upon the recollection of former sufferings and deprivations; upon a conscientiousness of their ability to defend and to govern themselves; and upon a conviction that, in case of submission on any terms, they would, sooner or later, be made to feel the vengeance of the mother country. These considerations doubtless have the most weight upon those who have taken a leading part. They, of course, use all their influence to enforce them, and thus to keep up the spirit of the revolution. In this they probably have had the less difficulty, as although the sufferings of the people have been great, particularly in military service, and in raising the contributions necessary for that service, yet the incubus of Spanish power being thrown off, and with it that train of followers who filled up almost every avenue to wealth and consequence, the higher classes have been awakened to a sense of advantages they did not before enjoy. They have seen their commerce freed from legal restraints, their articles of export become more valuable, their supplies furnished at a lower rate, and all the offices of government, or other employments, laid open to them as fair objects of competition. The lower classes have found their labour more in demand, and better paid for; and their importance in society greater than it formerly was.

They are yet, however, from their indolence, general want of education, and the great mixture of 'castes' among them, in a degraded state, but little felt in the affairs of the government. The stimulus now given will operate to produce a change in them for the better, and, it is to be presumed, will gradually have its effect, as their docility, intelligence, and activity, when called into service, give evidence that they are not deficient in natural or physical powers.

Labour, as it becomes more general, will become less irksome to individuals, and the gradual acquisition of property which must necessarily result from it in such a country, under a good government, will doubtless produce the happy effects there which it has uniformly produced elsewhere, and more especially in countries where the population is small when compared to the extent of territory.

I am very sensible that I may have been led into errors of fact, or inference. In that case I can plead honesty of intention, and the difficulty of collecting at a single point, and within a limited time, correct information; or of analyzing that which was collected, respecting a people in a state of revolution, who are spread over an immense country, and whose habits, institutions, and language, are so different from our own.

I have only to add, that we were politely received by the Supreme Director, who made every profession for our government, and every offer of accommodation to us, as its agents, which we had a right to expect, and that the people manifested on all occasions the most friendly dispositions.

Estimate of the Population of the Provinces of Buenos Ayres, Cordova, Tucuman, Mendoza or Cuyo, and Salta, under the Names of the different Towns or Districts which send Representatives to the Congress.

By an imperfect census, taken, it is believed, in 1815, Buenos Ayres contained 98,105, excluding troops and transient persons, and Indians.

		By more recent estimates	
	Excluding Indians	Excluding Indians	Excluding Indians
Buenos Ayres	105,000	120,000	250,000
Cordova	75,000	75,000	100,000
Tucuman	45,000	45,000	20,000*
Santiago del Estero	45,000	60,000	
Valle de Catamarca	36,000	40,000	
Rioja	20,000	20,000	
San Juan	34,000	34,000	
Mendoza	38,000	38,000	
San Luis	16,000	16,000	
Jujuy	25,000	25,000	
Salta	50,000	50,000	
	489,000	523,000	

	By more recent estimates		
	Excluding Indians	Excluding Indians	Excluding Indians
Provinces of Upper Peru			
Cochabamba	100,000	120,000	200,000
Potosi	112,000	112,000	250,000
Plata, or Charcas	112,000	112,000	175,000
La Paz			300,000
Puno (Under the name of)			30,000+
Santa Cruz de la Sierra			150,000+
Oruro			50,000+
Paraguay			300,000
Banda Oriental and Entre Rios	50,000		

*Probably the town only.
+Under the various names of Santa Cruz de la Sierra Majos, and Chequitos.
Note: It is not understood that any part of the province of Corrientes, or that of the city or district of Santa Fe, is included in this estimate; and some districts of some of the other provinces may be omitted.

Together with the Reports from our Commissioners, were transmitted to Congress the several Documents therein referred to, comprising the following papers:

APPENDIX

A. Funes's outline.

B. The Manifesto of Independence by the Congress of Buenos Ayres.

C. Declaration of Independence of Chili.

D. Translation of various documents furnished by the Government of Buenos Ayres.

E. Provisional Salute.

F. Original Reports of the Secretary at War of Buenos Ayres.

H. Correspondence between Alvarez and Agent of Artigas.

4. Report on South America, by C. A. Rodney, 1818[33]

MR. RODNEY'S REPORT TO THE SECRETARY OF STATE

Sir, I have now the honour to submit to your consideration, my report on the subject of the late mission to South America, embracing the information derived from the various sources within my power, so far as I had an opportunity of improving the advantages possessed.

With the history of the conquest of the Spanish possessions in America, you, must be familiar. They were principally, if not exclusively, achieved by private adventurers. When completed, a most oppressive system of government, or rather despotism, was established by the Parent Country.

These extensive regions were originally swayed by two viceroys. The dominions of Spain, in North America, were under the government of the Viceroy of Mexico; and all her possessions in South America were subject to the control of the Viceroy of Peru.

The remoteness of some parts of the country from the residence of the viceroy at Lima occasioned, in 1718, the establishment of another viceroy-alty at Santa Fe de Bogota, in the kingdom of New Grenada. In 1731, New Grenada was divided, and a number of the provinces composing that kingdom were separated from it. These were put under the jurisdiction of a captain-general and president, whose seat of government was at Caraccas.

In 1566, Chili was erected into a separate captain-generalship; in 1773, a new viceroyalty was established at Buenos Ayres, comprehending all the Spanish possessions to the east of the Western Cordilleras, and to the south of the river Maranon.

This immense empire seems, according to the laws of the Indies, to have been considered a distinct kingdom of itself, though united to Spain, and annexed to the crown of Castile. In this light it is viewed by Baron Humboldt, in his Essay on New Spain.

With some slight shades of difference in the regulations established in these governments, the prominent features of their political institutions exhibit a striking resemblance, as the general system was the same.

Their commerce was confined to the parent country and to Spanish vessels exclusively. They were prohibited, under the penalty of death, to trade with

33 [*The Morning Chronicle*, 26 December 1818, British Library Newspapers. Accessed 4 June 2020].

foreigners. The natives of Old Spain composed the body of their merchants. Though this part of the system had, previously to the revolution, been relaxed, in some degree, particularly by the statute of free commerce, as it is styled; the relief was partial, and the restrictions continued severe and oppressive.

All access to the Spanish settlements was closed to foreigners; and even the inhabitants of the different provinces were prohibited from intercourse with one another, unless under the strictest regulations.

The various manufactures that might interfere with those of Spain were not permitted. They were prevented, under severe penalties, from raising flax, hemp, or saffron. In climates most congenial to them, the culture of the grape and the olive was prohibited. On account of the distance of Peru and Chili, and the difficulty of transporting oil and wine to these remote regions, they were permitted to plant vines and olives, but were prohibited the culture of tobacco. At Buenos Ayres, by special indulgence of the viceroys, they were allowed to cultivate grapes and olives merely for the use of the table.

They were compelled to procure from the mother country articles of the first necessity; and were thus rendered dependent on her for the conveniences of life, as well as luxuries. The Crown possessed the monopoly of tobacco, salt, and gunpowder.

To these oppressive regulations and restrictions was added an odious system of taxation. From the Indians was exacted a tribute in the shape of a poll-tax, or a certain servitude in the mines, called the mita. A tenth part of the produce of cultivated lands was taken, under the denomination of tithes. The alcavala, a tax varying from two and a half to five per cent, on every sale and resale of all things moveable and immoveable, was rigidly exacted, though, in some cases, a commutation was allowed. Royal and municipal duties were laid on imports, and on the tonnage, entrance, and clearance of vessels, under the different appellations of almoxarifasgo, sea-alcavala, corso, consulado, armada, and armadilla. To these may be added the royal fifths of the precious metals, the most important tax in the mining districts. Besides all these, there were stamp taxes, tavern licences, and sums paid for the sale of offices, of titles of nobility, papal bulls, the composition and confirmation of lands, with a number of others of inferior grade.

Under the Spanish monarchs, who had early obtained from the Pope the ecclesiastical dominion, and thus had united in their royal persons all civil and religious authority, a most oppressive hierarchy was established, with its numerous train of offices and orders, succeeded by the Inquisition.

The posts of honour and profit, from the highest to the lowest, were filled, almost exclusively, by natives of Old Spain. The principal code of laws, thus maintaining the supremacy of Spain over those distant regions, almost locked up from the rest of the world, emanated from the Council of the Indies, established by the King, in which he was supposed to be always present. The Royal Rescripts, the recopilations of the Indies, and the partidas, furnished the general rules of decision; and when these were silent or doubtful, recourse was had to the opinions of professional men.

This system was generally executed by the viceroys, captains-general, and by the tribunals of justice, with a spirit corresponding with the rigorous policy that produced it. To this form of government, the country had for centuries submitted with implicit obedience, and probably would have continued to submit much longer but for events in this country, and the changes in Europe. The sagacious minds of many able writers, penetrating into the future, had predicted, at some distant date, a revolution in South America, before that in North America had commenced. From the period of the successful termination of our own struggle for independence, that of the inhabitants of the South has been with more confidence foretold; and there is reason to believe it has been hastened by this fortunate event. The conduct of Spain, during the war of our revolution, was calculated to make a lasting impression on her colonies. This result was then foreseen by intelligent politicians; many were surprised that she could be so blind to her own interests, after she had on one occasion manifested the strongest suspicion of Paraguay; for to her scrupulous jealousy of this power the expulsion of the Jesuits from that country, in 1750, is to be attributed.

The wars that arose from the French Revolution have produced in Europe changes of the greatest magnitude, which have had an immense influence on the affairs of South America. When Spain joined France against the combined Princes, she exposed her distant possessions to British hostilities. The great naval power of England gave her ready access to the American colonies. Engaged in an arduous contest, she was prompted by her feelings and interests to retaliate on Spain the conduct she experienced from her during the war of our independence. Encouraged, perhaps, by the counsels of her enemies, the first symptoms of insurrection in the continental possessions of Spain were exhibited in the year 1797, in Venezuela. These were succeeded by the attempts of Miranda in the same quarter, which were accompanied or were followed, since the vacillating state of the Spanish monarchy, by revolutionary movements in Mexico, Grenada, Peru, Chili, and Buenos Ayres; and from which scarcely any part of the Spanish dominions in America has been entirely exempt.

The occurrences that led the way to the subsequent important events in the provinces of La Plata, were the invasion of the British, under Popham and Beresford, in the year 1806, and their expulsion, a few months afterwards, by the collected forces of the country, under Liniers and Pueyrredon. These incidents fortunately gave to the people a just idea of their own strength; and they afterwards repelled, with a firmness and bravery that did them great honour, the formidable attack of the British under General Whitelocke.

The wretched state to which Spain was reduced, by the policy, the power, and the arts of Napoleon; the resignation of Charles IV in favour of Ferdinand VII, and the renunciation of both in favour of Napoleon, were productive of the most important results. They threw the kingdom into the greatest confusion. The alternate successes and disasters of the French armies produced a new era in Spain. The people, generally, revolted at the idea of being governed by the brother of Napoleon, to whom he had transferred the crown. Juntas were established, who acted in the name of Ferdinand, then confined in France. These were substituted for the ancient Cortes, and the regular counsel of the nation, to which, in times of imminent danger, they ought to have recurred agreeably to their usages. Conflicting authorities produced a distracted state of affairs. In the scenes that ensued, the proper attention was not paid to the American provinces. Their conduct towards them was versatile and inconsistent: they were lost sight of or neglected, until it was too late. Conceiving they were abandoned by the parent state, they thought it justifiable to act for themselves. It was not very long before the inhabitants of Buenos Ayres, embracing the example of their brethren in Spain, established a junta, which assumed the reins of government, and finally in the year 1810, sent off the Viceroy Cisneros, and his principal adherents. For a summary of events subsequent to this period, until the time of my departure, I beg leave to refer to the outline subjoined (Appendix A), from the pen of Dr. Funes, drawn up, in part, at my request. Without vouching for the perfect accuracy of the work, I think, from the information received, it will probably be found to contain, in general, a correct and impartial sketch of the prominent transactions and occurrences.

In perusing this interesting document, I have to lament, that its pages are marked with some cases of severity and cruelty, which seem almost inseparable from great revolutions. It must, however, be consoling to observe, that they appear to have passed through the state which might possibly have rendered examples necessary, and to have arrived, perhaps, at that stage, when the passions becoming less turbulent, and the people more enlightened, a milder system may be expected to prevail.

Their dissensions have produced most of their calamities. In such seasons they were naturally to be expected. But their disputes have been principally healed by the prudent and energetic measures of the Congress, which commenced its sittings in Tucuman in the year 1815, and adjourned in the year following from thence to Buenos Ayres, where it remained in session, occupied with the task of forming a permanent constitution. This respectable body, besides acting as a convention, or a constituent assembly, exercises temporarily legislative powers. Their sittings are public, with a gallery of audience for citizens and strangers. The debates are frequently interesting, and are conducted with ability and decorum; they are published every month for the information of the people.

The dispute with Artigas, the chief of the Orientals, has not been adjusted. This, with a certain jealousy of the superior influence of the city of Buenos Ayres on the general affairs of the provinces; the conduct of the government of Buenos Ayres towards the Portuguese, and the high tariff of duties, which I understand have been since reduced, appeared to constitute the principal causes of dissatisfaction at the time of my departure.

The declaration by Congress of that independence which they had for many years previously maintained in fact, was a measure of the highest importance, and has been productive of an unanimity and a decision before unknown. This summit of their wishes was only to be reached by slow and gradual progress. The public mind had to be illumined on the subject by their pulpits, their presses, and their public orations. The people were to be prepared for the event. When the season arrived, they cut the knot which could not be untied. The declaration of independence was adopted in the directorship of Mr. Pueyrredon, on the 9th day of July, 1816. It was succeeded by an able exposition of the causes that extorted it, to justify, to their fellow-citizens and to the world, the measure they had deliberately voted to support with their fortunes and their lives.

Believing the latter paper might be thought worthy of perusal, a translation has been annexed (Appendix B).

The salutary influence of this bold and decisive step, was at once felt throughout the country. It gave new life and strength to the patriotic cause, and stability to the government. The victories of Chacabuco and Maipo, achieved by the arms of Chili and Buenos Ayres, have produced and confirmed a similar declaration of independence by the people of Chili, which is also annexed (Appendix C), and cemented the cordial union existing between the confederate states. The consequence has been, that, within these extensive territories, there is scarcely the vestige of a royal army to be found, except on the borders of Peru.

Having thus, in connexion with the succinct account given by Dr. Funes, traced the principal events, since the revolution in Buenos Ayres, I shall proceed to state the result of the information received, according to the best opinion I could form of the extent, population, government and resources of the United Provinces, with their productions, imports and exports, trade and commerce.

The late Viceroyalty of Buenos Ayres, of which that city was the metropolis, was by many considered the largest, as well as the most valuable of all the Spanish dominions in South America, extending in a direct line, from its north to its south boundary, a distance of more than two thousand miles; and from its eastern to its western not less than eleven hundred.

It was composed, at the commencement of the revolution, of the nine provinces, or intendencies following: Buenos Ayres, Paraguay, Cordova, Salta, Potosi, La Plata, Cochabamba, La Paz, and Puno.

Watered by the great river La Plata and its numerous tributary streams, which afford an easy communication with countries of an immense extent, and furnishing an easy access to the treasures of South America, it has always been regarded by Spain as one of her most precious acquisitions. Enjoying every variety of climate to be found between different and distant latitudes, and blessed with a large portion of fertile soil, it is capable of producing all that is to be found in the temperate or torrid zones. Immense herds of cattle and horses graze on its extensive plains, and constitute at this time their principal source of wealth. The mines of Potosi are also included within its boundaries. There are no woods for a very considerable distance from Buenos Ayres. No forest trees are to be seen on the widely extended Pampas, except at intervals a solitary umboo. After passing the Saladillo in a northerly direction, the woods begin, and proceeding in the upper provinces, the hills appear, and mountains rise in succession, interspersed with rich valleys. On the east side of the rivers La Plata and Parana, the country is said to be very fine. The Entre Rios is represented as capable of being made a garden spot; and the Banda Oriental presents hills and dales, rich bottoms, fine streams of water, and at a distance from the great river, on the banks of the smaller streams, some excellent wood land. Between Maldonado and Montevideo, the east ridge of the Cordilleras terminates on the river La Plata.

Since the revolution, five more provinces have been erected, making in all fourteen within the limits of the ancient viceroyalty; viz. Tucuman, taken from Salta; Mendoza or Cuyo, taken from Cordova; Corrientes, Entre Rios, comprising the country between the Uruguay and the Parana, and the Banda Oriental, or eastern shore of the river La Plata. The two last were taken from the province of Buenos Ayres, which was thus reduced to the territory on the south side of that river. The subordinate divisions of the country, with the principal towns, will be found in the Appendix to this Report, with an account of the produce or manufactures of the different districts (Appendix D).

Of the fourteen provinces into which the ancient Vice-royalty is now divided, five were, at my departure, principally occupied by the royal forces (which, in consequence of the victory of Maipo, were expected soon to retreat to Lower Peru), or partially under their influence, viz. Potosi, La Plata, Cochabamba, La Paz, and Puno; and the nine following independent de facto of Spain, were in the possession of the patriots, viz. Buenos Ayres, Paraguay, Mendoza, Cordova, Tucuman, Salta, Corrientes, Entre Rios, and Banda Oriental. But Paraguay and the city of Santa Fe act independently of Buenos Ayres, though Paraguay is not on unfriendly terms with them, and it is hoped by some will before long join the union. Entre Rios and the Banda Oriental, under General

Artigas, in the character of chief of the Orientals, are in a state of hostility with Buenos Ayres.

Montevideo, the capital of the eastern shore, was occupied by a Portuguese army, and a squadron of ships of war from Brazil blockaded the ports of Colonia and Maldonado, and prohibited the entrance of neutral vessels, unless they paid them the same duties on their cargoes, that were charged on the importation of the goods when landed in the country.

The territory of the United Provinces is computed to contain 150,000 square leagues, though it probably exceeds that quantity. The lands occupied in the country, remote from the cities, are generally converted by their owners into estancias, or large grazing farms for cattle, and chacras for growing grain. The small farms or quintas, in the neighbourhood of cities, are in fine order. Those around Buenos Ayres, which furnish their market with an ample supply of fruit and vegetables, are, by irrigation, in the highest state of culture.

The population, exclusive of the Indians, is now calculated at 1,300,000; but, adding the civilized Indians only, who are of great importance, it would in all probability exceed two millions.

The whole population consists of natives of Old Spain, and their descendants, born in the country, or, as they style themselves, South Americans; of Indians civilised, or unreclaimed, with different 'castes', or mixed blood; of Africans, and their descendants, or Negroes and Mulattoes.

I could not ascertain, with satisfaction, the population of the different provinces: the province of Buenos Ayres contains about 120,000, whilst the population of Entre Rios, and Banda Oriental is computed at fifty thousand.

The city of Buenos Ayres contains a population of 60,000. The inhabitants of this place appear to be amiable, and an interesting people. They are considered brave and humane; possessing intelligence, capable of great exertions and perseverance, and manifesting a cheerful devotion to the cause of freedom and independence.

There is also a certain mediocrity and equality of fortune prevailing among them, extremely favourable to a union of the popular sentiment, in support of the common weal. Many industrious mechanics and enterprising merchants are, however, increasing their estates, and adding to the stock of capital in the country.

The people of the province of Buenos Ayres, residing out of the city, are, generally speaking, poor, and rather indolent, though a hardy race and when excited to action, they become zealous defenders of the liberties of their country. They are capable of great improvement, and, under the influence of a good example when a change takes place in their habits and manner of living, they bid fair to become useful and industrious citizens.

The inhabitants of Cordova are said to be more superstitious, and more industrious, but less patriotic. This is principally attributed to the loss of the trade with Peru, occasioned by the revolutionary war.

Tucuman, I was informed, possessed an excellent population.

The people of Mendoza, or Cuyo, are moral, industrious, and patriotic. They have sacrificed largely at the shrine of independence, supporting with zeal and confidence the cause of their country; whilst the citizens of Santa Fe are represented as immoral and insubordinate, and manifesting, on most occasions, an extreme jealousy of their neighbours.

The population of Entre Rios and Banda Oriental is perhaps not inferior in valour to that of Buenos Ayres. Nor is it deficient in military skill, particularly in carrying on a partisan warfare, for which its troops are admirably adapted. Their other good qualities have been probably somewhat impaired by the system pursued in that quarter, where they have been compelled to give up everything like civil avocations, and to continue without any regular kind of government, under the absolute control of a chief, who, whatever may be his political principles or professions, in practice concentrates all power, legislative, judicial, and executive, in himself.

The general Congress of the United Provinces, assembled at Buenos Ayres, on the 3d of December, of 1817, established, by a provisional statute, a temporary form of government, which will be found in Appendix marked E.

The Congress is comprised of deputies from the different provinces. It actually consists of twenty-six members. But, as a representative is allowed for every 15,000 citizens, it would be more numerous, if all the provinces had sent delegates in that ratio of population.

With some exceptions, and particularly of that palladium of our rights, which is unknown to the civil law, the trial by jury, the provisional constitution will be found, on an attentive perusal, to contain a distinct recognition of many of the vital principles of free government. A church establishment also, that of the Catholic faith, is contrary to our ideas of religious freedom; though a measure adopted from necessity, perhaps, by them.

It declares, that all power, legislative, judicial, and executive, resides in the nation. The Congress are to be chosen by electors, who are to be voted for by the people in the primary assemblies. The cabildos, or municipalities, are to be elected immediately by the citizens. It recognizes the independence of the judiciary, and declares the tenure of office, with respect to the superior judges, to be during good behaviour. It provides for the election of a chief magistrate by Congress, removable when they choose to appoint a successor, and responsible for the execution of the duties of his office, which are defined and limited. In the oath of office, he is sworn to preserve the integrity and independence of the country.

The three great departments of state, of the treasury, and of war, are distinctly marked out, and their respective powers and duties assigned.

On some subjects it enters more into detail than is usual with us, particularly in those of their army, navy, and militia. But this, perhaps, in their situation, was necessary.

It provides that no citizen shall accept a title of nobility, without forfeiting the character of citizenship.

It provides, also, against general warrants, and the arrest of individuals, unless on probable proof of guilt.

It contains a salutary provision, that a judge, having original jurisdiction, before taking cognizance of the cause, shall use all possible means of reconciling the parties. This constitution is but temporary. The Congress are engaged in the task of forming a permanent one. In the meantime, no alteration can be made in the present, unless with the consent of two thirds of the members. In this manner some alterations have been adopted.

The subject of a permanent constitution was before a committee of sixteen members of Congress. There was a difference of opinion prevailing among them on the point of a confederated or a consolidated government. If they should adopt the former, they will frame the constitution, in all probability, nearly after the model of that of the United States. Should they decide on the latter, it is highly probable they will incorporate the leading features of our system into their form of government.

They seem to concur in the proposition to have a chief magistrate elected for a term of years, and a representative legislature, to consist of two branches. A senate, to constitute the most permanent body, and a house of representatives, whose term of service shall be of shorter duration.

Perhaps it would be better for them to delay the completion of this all important task, after the example of the United States, until a period of peace. Their present provisional statute is an improvement on those which preceded it; and we may expect their proposed constitution will be still more perfect, as they advance in the knowledge of those principles on which republican governments are constituted.

But, however free in theory this provisional statute may be, it is undoubtedly true that, unless administered agreeably to its letter and spirit, it will not afford security to the citizen. Whether any infractions have occurred since the date of its existence, I cannot pretend to determine, not being in full possession of the facts.

When we recollect that they have the benefit of our example, it may reasonably be expected that they will, in general, adhere to the constitution. They have also the fatal result of the French Revolution, warning them of the dangers of its excesses, of which they appear to be sensible.

The productions and the manufactures of the different provinces will be found in Appendix D; but I was unable to procure any satisfactory estimates of the probable value or amount in each province. There is, however, a considerable internal trade carried on in the interchange of various articles between the several provinces; cattle, horses, and mules, furnish a considerable source of barter: with the latter, Peru is usually supplied; the Paraguay tea is a great article of trade throughout the country. The brandy, wine, raisins, and figs, of Mendoza and San Juan, are becoming important; the hides of oxen, the skins of the vicuna and guanaco, with a number of fine furs, afford valuable articles of exchange. These, with the foreign goods transported in every direction from Buenos Ayres, very readily, by oxen and mules, which also furnish the means of carrying their native productions to their sea-ports, form a branch of trade of great magnitude, considering the population of the country.

Their exports are calculated, with some degree of accuracy, at ten millions of dollars. These consist principally of ox-hides, jerk beef, and tallow, the present great staples of the country. A variety of furs and peltries, some grain, copper, mostly brought from Chili, with gold and silver, in bullion and coin, chiefly from the mines of Potosi.

The imports are computed to be about equal to their exports. British manufactures form the principal mass, and they are to be had in great abundance. They consist of woollen and cotton goods of every description; some of them wrought to imitate the manufactures of the country; ironmongery, cutlery, hardware, saddlery, hats, porter, ale, and cheese, are among the remaining articles.

From the United States they receive lumber of all kinds, and furniture of every description; coaches and carriages of all sorts, codfish, mackerel, shad, and herring, leather, boots, and shoes, powder, and munitions of war, and naval stores, ships and vessels, particularly those calculated for their navy, or for privateers.

From Brazils, they receive sugar, coffee, cotton, and rum.

From the north of Europe, they receive steel and iron; and from France, a number of articles of its manufacture.

Their foreign commerce is principally carried on by British capitalists, though there are some Americans, a few French and other foreign merchants, also settled at Buenos Ayres; they are all placed, I believe, on the same footing of equality.

The revenue of the state may be estimated at about three millions of dollars annually; but their system of finance is very imperfect; and, although their debt is small, their credit is low. They have hitherto avoided the issuing of paper money, and they have no established bank; but they have sometimes anticipated their revenue, by giving due bills receivable in payment for duties or goods imported, or articles exported; the impost furnishes the principal part of the revenue. A copy of their tariff, as at first established, was some time since transmitted, I believe, to the department of state; in this, the duties were generally specific and high. I understand they have been lately reduced, as their exorbitancy had occasioned much smuggling.

Voluntary contributions from those friendly to the revolution, and forced loans from the Old Spaniards, have constituted another portion of their funds. To show the public capital adequate to all exigencies, their different civil, military, and naval establishments have been taken into view, and are comprised in the estimate furnished—a thing unusual with us; but they have omitted their public lands, which, if a prudent use be made of them, must, at no distant day, become a very productive source of revenue to the State.

The mines of Potosi, which, in all probability, will very soon fall into their hands again, may furnish them with a considerable supply of the precious metals. It is stated, on respectable authority, that so late as the year 1790, the amount of gold and silver coined at Potosi in that year was calculated to have been 299,846 dollars in gold, and 2,983,176 dollars in silver. The state of their army, and the condition of their navy, will be seen by a reference to the original return presented (Appendix F).

Their army is composed of regular troops, civicos, and militia. In one or other of these classes, they are educated to the military art; and, as far as I had an opportunity, and was capable of judging, they appeared to be well acquainted with the elements of their profession. Their forces, according to the paper furnished, are estimated at nearly 30,000 men. They are composed of 1,296 artillery, 13,693 infantry, and 14,718 cavalry; of which 12,143 are troops of the line, 7,041 are civicos, and 10,573 militia. These form the different armies of the centre of Peru, of the Andes, of Cordova, and the auxiliary forces in the Entre Rios. This statement, however, only includes the militia of the province of Buenos Ayres itself. Their supply of arms and munitions of war is ample, as will be seen by the statement annexed on that subject.

Their navy is small, and some of their vessels are laid up in ordinary. A list of them, as well as of their privateers, will be found in Appendix F.★ Their private armed vessels are subjected to very strict regulations, agreeably to their prize code, which is among the original papers presented and herewith delivered. It may be proper in this place to introduce the subject of the irregular conduct of the privateers under the patriot flag, against which the Commissioners were directed to remonstrate. Having taken an opportunity of explaining to Mr. Tagle, the Secretary of State, the proceedings of our government relative to Amelia Island and Galveston, agreeably to their instructions, the Commissioners embraced a suitable occasion to urge the just cause of complaint, which the malpractices of private armed vessels, wearing the patriot colours, had furnished our government; on both topics they had long and interesting conversations. With the conduct of the government respecting Amelia Island and Galveston, Mr. Tagle expressed himself perfectly satisfied; and he disclaimed for his government any privity or participation in the lodgments made at those places, by persons acting in the name of the patriots of South America.

In reference to the acts of cruisers under the patriot flags, he said he was sensible that great irregularities had occurred, though his government had done everything in their power to prevent them, and were willing, if any instance of aggression were pointed out, to direct an inquiry into the case, and if the facts were established, to punish those concerned, and redress the injured individuals. He professed his readiness to adopt any measures that would more effectually prevent a recurrence of such acts, in which he expressed his belief that the privateers of Buenos Ayres had rarely participated, though the character of the government had suffered from the conduct of others. He stated that they had on one occasion sent out some of their public vessels to examine all cruisers wearing the Buenos Ayrean flag, to see that they were lawfully commissioned, and to ascertain whether they had violated their instructions.

Amongst the causes of dissatisfaction to which I have alluded, the preponderance of the capital has been mentioned. Its great weight in the scale of national affairs is to be ascribed to its greater exertions in the national cause. These are owing to its comparative wealth, and to its active, intelligent, and enterprising population. The armies that have been raised in this city and the neighbouring country, with the supplies in money, and munitions of war drawn from these sources, have been truly extraordinary.

It would be a difficult task to make an exact calculation, or to form even a probable estimate, but all seemed to concede the superior merit claimed on account of their exertions, when compared with their wealth and population; and it is not unlikely that Buenos Ayres has, in consequence, assumed a higher tone, and acquired a controlling influence, which she has sometimes abused.

Another source of discontent is the unfortunate dispute between the Banda Oriental and Buenos Ayres, which had an influence on the proceedings of the latter towards the Portuguese.

The original cause of division may be traced to a jealousy long subsisting between the rival cities of Montevideo and Buenos Ayres. This has become habitual, and has extended to the country. Private interests and personal views have also increased their dissensions. General Artigas (who bears the character of chief of the Orientals, as has been already stated, and has also assumed that of Protector of the Entre Rios and Santa Fe) was originally in the royal service, a captain in a provincial corps. In this he continued for some time after the revolution had commenced at Buenos Ayres. But, in the year 1811, taking offence, as it is said, at some conduct of the Spanish commandant of Colonia, he abandoned the royal cause, and entered into the service of the patriots. So early as the year 1813, when acting against Montevideo, he became dissatisfied with Sarratea, the commander-in-chief from Buenos Ayres. On his removal from the head of the army, he quarrelled with General Rondeau, who, it was supposed, would have been acceptable to him, and finally withdrew, before the siege of Montevideo was finished under General Alvear. For this conduct, Posadas, when he succeeded to the government, treated him as a deserter from their service. By a proclamation, he offered a reward for his apprehension, and set a price upon his head—an act which General Artigas never forgot or forgave.

During the subsequent directorship of Alvear, he induced the cabildo of Buenos Ayres to issue a similar proclamation against General Artigas. When Alvear was dismissed, the people of Buenos Ayres endeavoured to atone for their conduct, by burning, with every mark of ignominy, the degrading proclamation. They also addressed a conciliatory letter to the General, and received from him a corresponding answer. These were preliminary to a fruitless attempt at reconciliation, made by the director, ad interim, Colonel Alvares, who succeeded Alvear. The correspondence on this occasion is annexed (Appendix H). Other endeavours to reconcile him have failed, notwithstanding the changes in the office of director at Buenos Ayres. On one occasion the proposition was made, that the Banda Oriental should remain independent of Buenos Ayres, and merely send deputies to the General Congress, to concert measures against the common enemy. On another, when the Portuguese army was approaching the frontiers of the Banda Oriental, an effort was made by Pueyrredon to reconcile him, and to unite him in the common defence. Ample supplies of arms and munitions of war were offered, and some furnished; but this attempt also failed.

In order that a fuller view of this subject may be had, I have subjoined a translated copy of an animated letter from General Artigas to Mr. Pueyrredon (Appendix I.) It is but justice to add, that General Artigas is thought, by persons entitled to credit, to be a firm friend to the independence of the country. To express a decided opinion on this delicate question would scarcely be expected of me, as my position did not command a view of the whole ground. I had not the satisfaction to be derived from a personal interview with General Artigas, who is, unquestionably, a man of rare and singular talents. But if I were to hazard a conjecture, I think it not improbable that in this, as in most family disputes, there have been faults on both sides. It is to be lamented that they are in open hostility. The war has been prosecuted with great animosity; and, in two late engagements, the troops of Buenos Ayres have been defeated with great loss. By some it was said, that the inhabitants of the eastern shore were anxious that a reconciliation should take place, whilst the people in the country preferred their present state.

I must not omit to take a glance at the situation of Paraguay. This province presents a singular spectacle. It stands aloof from the rest. The people, with the aid of the few remaining royal troops, repulsed an army sent to compel them to join the common standard. Very soon afterwards they expelled the royalists, and set up for themselves. Since this period, they appear to have adopted a partial non-intercourse system. But Buenos Ayres, on one occasion, succeeded in obtaining an understanding with them. Some suspect that they are secretly inimical to the existing order of things, and wish to keep themselves within their shell, that, in case of a change, they may profit by future events; others calculate with some confidence on their ultimate union with Buenos Ayres, with which at present they indulge a limited and reluctant intercourse. Paraguay is under the immediate control of a person named Francia, who styles himself Director of Paraguay.

From the domestic concerns of the provinces, we naturally turn to their foreign relations. On this subject the Commissioners were informed, that they had nothing more than a friendly understanding with any foreign nation. With the Portuguese government, they concluded an arrangement in 1812, under the mediation, it is said, of the British, with respect to the Banda Oriental. They have since had a correspondence with them on the subject of their entrance into that province, and the forcible occupation by the Portuguese army of the city of Monte Video, of which a copy is annexed (Appendix J). This will present the state of affairs between Buenos Ayres and the Brazils, which has been the theme of much discussion. The superior naval force of the Portuguese, stationed in the river La Plata, could have effectually blockaded all the ports of Buenos Ayres. By this means they would have prevented supplies of arms and munitions of war, and entirely destroyed the great source of revenue to the state, the duties on imports and tonnage, at a season when money was much wanted.

For about this period Buenos Ayres had a powerful army to contend with on the side of Peru, and had taken the burden of the renewed contest of Chili with Spain. Under such circumstances they were in some measure obliged to adopt a cautious and moderate policy. Their conduct in this respect seems to have been coerced. Their unhappy state with the Orientals had also an influence on their measures, they alleged that the restless conduct of Artigas had furnished the Portuguese a pretext for the invasion; but it is probable that they will ultimately break with the government of Brazils.

The British government has, through their official agents, entered into commercial stipulations with General Artigas, as the chief of the Orientals, on the subject of their trade with the eastern shore. A copy of this instrument will be found in Appendix K.

The government of Buenos Ayres have a confidential person in Europe, soliciting from England and other Powers, it is said, assistance of every kind, and a recognition of their independence. England has a consul, who, with her naval commander on that station, appeared to conduct the confidential affairs of the British cabinet with the government of Buenos Ayres.

What effects the victory of Maipo will produce abroad, it would be hazardous in me to conjecture. Whether, like the capture of Burgoyne, it will procure for the United Provinces foreign alliances, I cannot pretend to say.

From a source which is entitled to credit, I was informed that the raising and embarkation of Osorio's army in Peru was not accomplished without serious difficulties. Alternate force and persuasion were used to collect them, and nothing but the name, character, and promises of their General, could have induced them to go on board of the vessels prepared for the purpose, at the port of Callao. Some of them were actually in a state of mutiny, notwithstanding they were told they would be received with open arms by their brethren in Chili.

The forces finally embarked, agreeably to an account furnished by a gentleman of undoubted veracity on the spot, consisting of the following troops:

One company of artillery	70
One ditto sappers and miners	81
regiment of Burgos	900
ditto of San Carlos infantry	907
ditto of Arequipa	1,000
Arequipa dragoons	160
Lamas	144

	3,262

This army was composed of all the regular soldiers they could spare from Lima, who were united, at Talcaguna, to the Royal forces left in Chili. By the battle of Maipo it has ceased to exist. The probable effects in Peru, and other parts of South America, may be conjectured, but cannot be affirmed. The same Gentleman who has been mentioned, and who is conversant in Peruvian affairs, apprehended that important changes would result. I cannot conclude this paper without drawing your attention to a rapid survey of the reforms and improvements in the province of Buenos Ayres, produced by the Revolution, and its influence on knowledge, society, and manners.

The effects of the Revolution are visible in the changes produced in the state of society. The difference in the freedom of acting and thinking, which preceded the revolution, must necessarily be great. The freedom of commerce must have given a spring to exertions of native enterprise and intelligence, while the active scenes of war and politics, for the last ten years, have awakened the genius of the country, which had so long slumbered. The generation now on the stage may almost be said to have been reared under a new order of things. The common stock of ideas among the people has been greatly augmented; the natural consequence of the important political events which daily transpire, and in which every man, like the citizen of Athens, feels an interest. The newspapers are everywhere circulated, together with the manifestos of the government, which is obliged to court the approbation of public opinion on all measures of moment. It is not very unusual for the same countryman, who, a few years ago, never troubled himself about anything beyond the narrow circle of his domestic concerns, to purchase a newspaper on coming to town as a matter of course, and, if unable to read, to request the first one he meets to do him that favour. The country curates are, moreover, enjoined to read the newspapers and manifestos regularly to their flocks. The spirit of improvement may be seen in everything. Even some of those who are under the influence of strong prejudices against the revolution, frequently remark the changes for the better which have taken place. Their habits, manners, dress, and mode of living, have been improved by intercourse with strangers, and the free introduction of foreign customs, particularly English, American, and French. Great prejudices prevail against whatever is Spanish. It is even offensive to them to be called by this name—they prefer to be identified with the aborigines of the country. The appellation which they have assumed, and in which they take a pride, is that of South Americans.

A powerful stimulus must necessarily have been given to their industry, by two important circumstances—the diminution in prices of foreign merchandize, and the great increase in value of the products of the country, with the consequent rise of property. Though the grounds in the neighbourhood of cities are highly improved, as I have already stated, agriculture, comparatively speaking, is in a low condition. In general the lands are badly tilled. The plough is rarely used, and the substitute is a very indifferent one. But notwithstanding the disadvantages of the present method of culture, I was informed by reputable persons, that the average crop of wheat is not less than fifty bushels per acre in good seasons.

On the subject of religion, especially, the change in the public mind has been very great. The Catholic faith is established as that of the state, but there are many advocates, both in conversation and in writing, of universal toleration. Some members of congress are said to be strongly in favour of it; but the ignorant and superstitious part of the people, together with the regular clergy, would not be satisfied with such a measure—while the liberality prevailing among the better informed classes is such as to secure a virtual toleration for the present. Besides, from the circumstance of there being no sects in the country, such a provision may wait the progress of liberality in public opinion. In fact, the human mind has been set free on all matters of a general abstract nature, although the liberty of the press is circumscribed in some degree with respect to strictures on public measures and men, and the established religion; but there is neither inquisition nor previous licence.

They acknowledge the Pope as a spiritual head merely, and do not think him entitled to any authority to interfere with their temporal concerns. His Bull in favour of the King of Spain against the colonies, which may be almost regarded as an excommunication, produced little or no sensation.

The number of monks and nuns was very great in Buenos Ayres, when compared with other portions of the Spanish dominions. They have diminished since the revolution. There was at one time a positive law passed, forbidding any one to become a monk or a nun; but they were obliged to repeal it, and it was afterwards passed with some modifications. The restrictions substituted, aided by public opinion, have nearly produced the desired effect. Few of the youth of the country apply themselves to the study of theology, since other occupations, much more tempting to their ambition, have been opened to their choice. Formerly the priesthood was the chief aim of young men of the best families, who were desirous of distinction; as, in fact, it constituted almost the only profession to which those who had received a liberal education could devote themselves; which will readily account for the circumstance of so many of the secular clergy directing their attention, at present, almost exclusively to politics. The regular clergy, who are not permitted by the nature of their profession, to take part in the business of the world, or to hold secular offices, are many of them Europeans; but those of them who are natives, take the same lively interest in passing events, with the other classes of the community.

They have gone cautiously to work in reforms in the different branches of their municipal laws, and the administration of them. The number of offices has been considerably diminished, and responsibility rendered more direct and severe. The judiciary system has undergone many improvements, and nearly all the leading features of the law, which did not harmonize with the principles of free government, have been expunged, though some of the former evils still remain. The barbarous impositions on the aborigines have been abolished -the odious alcavala, and other obnoxious taxes, modified, so as to be no longer vexatious-slavery, and the slave trade, forbidden in future- and all titles of nobility prohibited, under the pain of loss of citizenship. The law of primogeniture is also expunged from their system. In the provisional statute, as has already been stated, nearly all the principles of free representative government are recognized, accompanied, it is true, with certain drawbacks, for which they plead the necessity of the times, but which they profess their intention to do away, on the final settlement of the government -a consummation anxiously desired by all classes of inhabitants. The example of France has warned them not to attempt too much at first; they have followed the plan of the United States in the introduction of gradual reforms, instead of resorting to violent and sudden innovations and revolutions.

Next to the establishment of their Independence by arms, the education of their youth appears to be the subject of the most anxious interest. They complain that every possible impediment was thrown in the way of education previous to the revolution; that, so far from fostering public institutions for this purpose, several schools were actually prohibited in the capital, and the young men were not without restraint permitted to go abroad for their education. There was a college at Cordova, at which those destined for the bar, or the priesthood, completed their studies, upon the ancient monkish principles. Another, called San Carlos (now the Union of the South), had been opened at Buenos Ayres, but was afterwards converted into barracks for soldiers. It is an immense building, more extensive, perhaps, than any which has been dedicated to learning in this country; and it has lately been fitted up at a very great expense. The school was to have opened in May or June last, on a more modern and liberal plan of discipline and instruction. The library of the state is kept in an adjoining building; it occupies a suite of six rooms, and contains nearly 20,000 volumes, the greater part rare and valuable. It is formed out of the library of the Jesuits, the books collected in the different monasteries, donations from individuals, and an annual appropriation by the government, and contains works on all subjects and in all the languages of the polished nations of Europe. A very valuable addition has been lately made of several thousand volumes, brought to Buenos Ayres by M. Bonpland, the companion of the celebrated Humboldt.

Besides the university of Cordova, at which there are about 150 students, there are public schools in all the principal towns, supported by their respective corporations. In Buenos Ayres, besides an academy in which are taught the higher branches, and the college before mentioned, there are eight public schools, for whose support the corporation contributes about seven thousand dollars annually; and, according to the returns of last year, the number of scholars amounted to 864. There are five other schools exclusively for the benefit of the poor, and under the charge of the different monasteries. These are supplied with books and stationery at the public expense. There are also parish schools in the country, for the support of which a portion of the tithes has been lately set apart. It is rare to meet with a boy ten or twelve years of age, in the city of Buenos Ayres, who cannot read and write. Besides the scholars thus instructed, many have private tutors. In addition to all this, I must not omit to mention the military academies supported by government at Buenos Ayres and Tucuman, at which there are a considerable number of cadets.

There are no prohibited books of any kind; all are permitted to circulate freely, or to be openly sold in the book-stores; among them is the New Testament in Spanish. This alone is a prodigious step towards the emancipation of their minds from prejudices. There are several book-stores, whose profits have rapidly increased; a proof that the number of readers has augmented in the same proportion. There had been a large importation of English books, a language becoming daily more familiar to them. Eight years ago, the mechanic art of printing was scarcely known in Buenos Ayres; at present there are three printing offices, one of them very extensive, containing four presses. The price of printing is, notwithstanding, at least three times higher than in the United States; but, as there is no trade or intercourse with Spain, all school books used in the country, some of them original, are published at Buenos Ayres; the business is, therefore, profitable and rapidly extending. There are many political essays, which, instead of being inserted in the newspapers, are published in loose sheets; there are also original pamphlets, as well as republications of foreign works. The constitutions of the United States, and of the different states, together with a very good history of our country, and many of our most important state papers, are widely circulated. The work of Dean Funes, the venerable historian of the country, comprised in three large octavo volumes, considering the infancy of the typographic art in this part of the world, may be regarded as an undertaking of some magnitude. There are three weekly journals or newspapers published in the city, which have an extensive circulation through the United Provinces. They all advocate the principles of liberty and republican forms of government, as none other would suit the public taste. The year before last, it is true, one of the papers ventured to advocate the restoration of the Incas of Peru, with a limited monarchy, but it was badly received. No proposition for the restoration of hereditary power of any kind, as far as I could learn, will be seriously listened to for a moment by the people. Even the ordinary language has changed. They speak of 'the state', 'the people', 'the public', 'country', and use other terms, as in the United States, implying the interest that each man takes in what appertains to the community. The first principle constantly inculcated is, 'that all power rightfully emanates from the people'. This, and similar dogmas form a part of the education of the children, taught at the same time with their catechism. It is natural that the passion for free government should be continually increasing.

A fact may be mentioned to show the solid advancement they have made, which is, that the number of votes taken at their elections increases every year. In becoming habituated to this peaceful and orderly mode of exercising their right of choosing those who are to be invested with authority, the tumultuous and irregular removal, by a kind of general oratory or acclamation, of those who have been chosen, will gradually cease.

Rather than disturb the order of society, they will endure with patience, until the time arrives for effecting a regular and constitutional change. Since the election of the present Director, none of these tumults, before so frequent, have occurred. These tumults have seldom been attended with bloodshed; yet they produce great confusion and disorder, and give rise to habits of insubordination, at the same time that they are ruinous to the character of a nation.

The viceroyalty of Buenos Ayres differed from the rest in one important particular. It contained no nobility, or, if any, very few. This may be regarded as a favourable circumstance in their society. Another favourable feature, very necessary to the successful administration of their affairs, is the conduct of many individuals who have filled the highest office of state, in descending from that dignified situation to inferior posts, and discharging their duties with alacrity. Thus we behold General A. Balcarce, who was formerly Director, acting as second in command to Colonel San Martin. Colonel Alvarez, also a Director at one period, now serving in the staff under the chief of that department, General Azcuenaga, and General Rondeau, once elected to the chair of state, is at present employed in a minor office. There are others who have occupied the same elevated post, who have retired to the station of private citizens.

The general capacities of the United Provinces for national defence are also important in many respects. The nature and extent of the country afford the inhabitants numerous advantages over an invading army. The ease with which their herds of cattle may be driven to distant places, beyond the reach of an enemy, and the rapid movements which the troops of the country can make, from the ample supply of horses and mules, are circumstances of great consequence in a military view. Even the towns, not fortified, from the manner in which they are built, and from the construction of their houses, furnish powerful means of defence, as the British army, under General Whitelocke, experienced in their attack on Buenos Ayres.

I am sensible that, in the course of these statements and remarks, some inaccuracies and errors must have occurred, but they have been unintentional. I have only to add, that the reception of the commissioners at Buenos Ayres, by the chief magistrate, was friendly and flattering.

From every class they met with a cordial welcome. The people, in general, appeared to be very much attached to the American character, and to the Government and citizens of the United States.

Should anything further occur, it shall be made the subject of a future paper.

I have the honour to be, with great respect,
Your most obedient Servant,
C. A. Rodney

5. Proclamation of the Independence of Chili, by Bernardo de O'Higgins, Miguel Zanartu, Hipolito de Villegas y Jose Ignacio Zenteno, January 1, 1818[34]

Proclamation of the Independence of Chili

Force has been the supreme reason which for more than 300 years has compelled the people of the New World to venerate as a dogma the usurpation of their rights, and to seek in that usurpation itself the origin of their greatest duties. It was certain that the termination of this constrained submission must one day arrive, although it was impossible to anticipate the exact period. The resistance of the weak against the strong gives a character of sacrilege to their pretensions, and often throws discredit on the justice in which they are founded. It was reserved for the 19th century to see America reclaiming its rights without the guilt of having forfeited them, and to show that the period of its suffering could last no longer than that of its weakness. The revolution of Sept. 18, 1810, was the first effort that Chili made to fulfil her high destinies, to which time and nature impelled her; her inhabitants proved at that time the energy and firmness of their determination, encountering the vicissitudes of a war, in which the Spanish Government had evinced that its policy with respect to America would survive the overthrow of all abuses. This undisguised violence naturally inspired in them the resolution of separating forever from the Spanish monarchy, and proclaiming their independence in the face of the world. But the existing circumstances of the war not permitting the convocation of a national congress to sanction the public wish, we determined to open a register, in which all the citizens of the state should freely and openly vote for themselves upon the urgent necessity of independence, declared by the Government, whether it should be delayed or not; and the result having been that the whole of the citizens have irrevocably decided for the declaration of independence, we have thought fit to exercise that extraordinary power with which the nation has authorized us in this particular case, to declare solemnly, in their name, in the presence of the Most High, and to make known to the great confederacy of the human race, that the continental territory of Chili, and her adjacent islands, form in fact and right a free, independent, and sovereign state, to remain for ever separated from the monarchy of Spain, with full power to adopt what mode of Government may be most conducive to her interests. And in order that this declaration may have all the force and solidity which ought to characterize the first act of a free people, we confirm it with the honour, life, fortunes,

34 [*The Times*, 6 June 1818, p. 3, The Times Digital Archive. Accessed 4 June 2020].

and all the social relations of the inhabitants of this new state: we pledge our word, the dignity of our office, and the glory of the arms of the country, and we command that the original act in the archive of the municipality of Santiago, be deposited, together with the books of the Great Register, and that it may be circulated among all the people, armies, and corporations, in order that the emancipation of Chili may be sworn to and be for ever sealed.

Given in the Directorial Palace of Conception, the 1st day of January, 1818, confirmed by our own hand, I signed by the nation, and countersigned by the ministers and secretaries of the state, in the departments of Government, &c.

BERNARDO O'HIGGINS

MIGUEL ZANARTU

HIPOLITO DE VILLEGAS

JOSE IGNACIO ZENTENO

After this proclamation, there follows an address of the representatives of the Buenos-Ayres Government to the Supreme Director of the newly-erected state of Chili, expressive of the joy of the former at the recovered freedom of the latter, their ardent wishes for their prosperity, and their desire to assist them in preserving the rights which they had gained. He was answered in terms of ardent gratitude, and with wishes of indissoluble union between the two States.

6. Special treaty between the states of Buenos-Ayres and Chili, Antonio Jose de Yrisarri and Gregorio Tagle, February 5, 1819[35]

SOUTH AMERICA

SPECIAL TREATY BETWEEN THE STATES OF BUENOS-AYRES AND CHILLI

His excellency the Supreme Director of the United Provinces of the Rio de la Plata, and his excellency the Supreme Director of the State of Chili, in possession of the powers conferred on them by the provincial constitutions of the respective states, desiring to put a period to the tyrannical domination of the Spanish government in Peru, and to bestow on its inhabitants that liberty and independence of which they are so unjustly deprived, and with a view to giving that assistance which the inhabitants of Lima have solicited of both the contracting states, have resolved to conclude the present treaty.

For this purpose the contracting parties have named as their plenipotentiaries, to wit:

On the part of his excellency the Supreme Director of the United Provinces of the Rio de la Plata, Don Gregorio Fagle [*sic*], Minister of State in the Departments of the Government and Foreign Affairs.

And on the part of the Supreme Director of the State of Chili, Col. Don Antonio José de Yrisarri, Officer of the Legion of Merit and Minister of State:

Art. 1. Both contracting parties, agreeing with the desire manifested by the inhabitants of Peru, and especially by those of Lima the capital, that they should aid them with an armed force, in order that they may drive thence the Spanish government, and establish that which shall be more analogous to their physical and moral constitution, the said two contracting parties oblige themselves to undertake an expedition which for that purpose is already prepared in Chili.

Art. 2. The combined army of the United Provinces and of Chili, directed against the actual authorities at Lima, and in aid of these inhabitants, shall cease to exist in that country the moment it has established a government by

35 [*The Times*, 29 May 1819, p. 2, The Times Digital Archive. Accessed 4 June 2020].

the free will of the inhabitants, unless being required by that government, and being suitable to the circumstances of both the contracting parties, the three estates of Chili, the United Provinces and Lima, should agree that the army remain for a period in the same territory. In that case, the generals empowered, or the other ministers of Chili and the United Provinces, must treat upon this point with the government which shall be established in Lima; the execution of such treaties being always subject to the respective ratification of the supreme authorities of Chili and the United Provinces.

Art. 3. In order to avoid all cause of disagreement between the two contracting states and the new one which is to be formed in Peru, respecting the payment of the expenses of the liberating expedition, and desirous of removing henceforth all pretext which may be formed by the enemies of America, in order to attribute to that expedition interested motives which are utterly foreign to it, both contracting parties agree not to treat of levying these expenses, before they can be arranged with the independent government of Lima; the combined army observing, both till then and subsequently, such conduct as is conformable to its object, which is to protect and not to act in hostility to these in habitants, respecting all which both governments shall give express orders to their respective generals.

Art. 4. The statements of the expenses of the liberating expedition and of the Chilian squadron which conducts it, from the time of its passing into the Pacific sea for that purpose, shall be presented by the ministers or agents of the governments of Chili and of the United Provinces, to the independent government of Lima, arranging with it amicably and conveniently the quantities, periods and manners of the payments.

Art. 5. The two contracting parties mutually guarantee the independence of the state which shall be formed in Peru, when its capital is liberated.

Art. 6. The present treaty shall be ratified by his Excellency the Supreme Director of the United Provinces of Rio de la Plata, and by his Excellency the Supreme Director of the State of Chili, within the space of 60 days.

Dated and signed in the city of Buenos Ayres, on the 5th of Feb. 1819.

ANTONIO JOSE DE YRISARRI
GREGORIO TAGLE

7. Manifesto of Chili to other Nations, by Bernardo O'Higgins and Miguel Zanartu, February 12, 1818[36]

MANIFESTO ADDRESSED BY THE SUPREME DIRECTOR OF CHILI TO OTHER NATIONS,

EXHIBITING THE MOTIVES IN JUSTIFICATION OF THE REVOLUTION OF THAT COUNTRY, AND THE DECLARATION OF ITS INDEPENDENCE, DATED CHILI, FEBRUARY 12, 1818.

When the justice of the Cause of America is no longer an object exclusively consigned to the pens of Philosophers, who so eloquently anticipated its defence, that their writings were condemned by the Inquisition; when all civilized Nations are now engaged in examining this Cause, judging rather by the probable issue of the struggle, than by the rectitude of the principles of our right to emancipation, in which they are all unanimously agreed; for these principles are no other than those proclaimed by Spain herself, in the maintenance of her own sovereignty, and in the vindication of her resistance against the oppression of the French; in fine, when succeeding generations have no need to have recourse to the Press to learn the history of our events, better preserved in the pages of liberty, from age to age, by tradition; it might seem unnecessary to explain the reasons which have induced the Inhabitants of Chile to declare their Independence, if custom, and respect for the dignity of other Nations, at whose side we are about to range ourselves, did not make it requisite, and if it were not justly expected as due to our own honor.

For the happiness of Mankind, that gloomy era is now no more, when the Learned of Europe lamented the shameful state of the Colonies, at the same time that it was considered a crime in us to complain. At that epoch, even all the recollections of the Conquest were forbidden, save only to praise the bloody arm of the Usurpers, by whom it was effected. Those days of chivalry, when the absurd practice of personal conflict prevailed, and which gave birth to the pretended right of the strong, exist no more; but this right, obscure in itself, was as inconsistent as are violence and consent, for without the latter no man can permanently exercise dominion over his fellow-creatures. The abuse undermined the very foundation of the right erected upon it; because,

---

36 [The manifesto was published in successive instalments in the *Morning Chronicle*, from 15 June 1818. We have kept the title given in the newspaper, but this version is taken from the *British and Foreign State Papers*, 1835, pp. 821–834. Notes 120 to 139 are the document's own].

either the Subjects were free to recover their liberty by force, or the means by which they were deprived of it were illegal.

Such is the fact with respect to America. Spain invaded our Coasts under the sacrilegious pretence of Religion, profaned by false Apostles,-men who came to preach the Gospel, but searched only the mines of the mountains, as the surgeon, who comes to bleed, looks after the blood-vessel; but she never afterwards attempted to legalize her hideous title, at least by that expedient which Statesmen devise to give validity to the famous diploma of Conquest, the consent and ratification of the People. Instead of this, America, without the least participation in the Cortes which has been convened, and subservient to the capricious will of the Monarch, was bound by the superstitious observance of an Oath, administered without authority by a Municipal Officer, who had improperly procured his Office by purchase; was precluded from discussing the motives of her passive obedience; and was condemned, in short, to slavery, without the privilege of remonstrance: she would have lost, with the liberty of speech, even the recollection of her wrongs, if it had been as easy to forget as to be silent. But these evils were repeated by a fixed system in the policy of the Tyrants, and, our complaints being drowned in the noise of our chains, the insolence of the Oppressor increased with our patience.

The miserable residue of the Aborigines, who have survived so many millions of victims, and who move and rove about in different Bodies, like the piles of sand in a desert, still preserve in their mournful history the memory of their persecutions, and shew very clearly their repugnance to the yoke of their Invaders, by the perpetual War which they carry on against our Frontiers, to the interruption of our tranquillity. What argument, then, can Spain produce in her favor, hated as she is by the Natives, and resisted by the sons of the Conquerors, so soon as they were able to make known their wishes, without the impending fear of the dungeon? We claim that right which a Slave may claim against a cruel Master; the right of a man who, arrived at the age of maturity, is able to provide for himself by his own exertions and industry; the right of a person whose minority has expired, but who is generous enough not to call his Guardian to an account; the right of a Steward, who, having become richer than his Employer, instead of expecting protection, can offer support. But all these examples fall very far short of our case: we hold this land as our Country by birth-right; we here first saw the light, and received the civilization of the age.

All the efforts of tyranny cannot prevail against this right of Nature. By virtue of this right, we now compose an Association of Men, equally as free as those originally conquered. Yet Spain, not less cruel to us than to them, adhering to her system of death and desolation, has afflicted us, by her Laws, with all the horrors committed during the Conquest. Let us pass over in silence that Code of the Indies, which is calculated only for the education of Slaves, under the ecclesiastical feudalism of the Curates, and the inhuman control of the *Encomiendas*. That abject portion of the species, for whom the barbarous Decrees of an Isabella, the Ferdinands, Philips, and Charleses, were promulgated, exists no longer in our community. A more enlightened People have succeeded those abominations, who are, of course, the more sensible of the infamy of the 3 centuries preceding. The Sister Provinces, which have before us constituted themselves into Independent States, have already exhibited to the World a picture of vexations so horrid as to excite the astonishment of Nations at our sufferings and our patience, and have saved us the trouble of repeating them in this Manifesto; for the system of oppression, cruelty, and devastation, and the degradation of servitude, increased by the contrivances of the most inhuman despotism, have been universal.

The object of Government being no other than to procure to men the security and prosperity of society, how could it have been supposed that the people of America would have submitted to misery and humiliation? Who would have believed that Americans, possessing the most precious Country in the Universe, would have submitted to live upon it only to moisten its fields with their tears, and to obey sacrilegious Edicts prohibiting the productions of Nature? for olive-trees and vines were ordered to be pulled up by the roots in Chile[37] that we might receive oil and wine from the Peninsula. Were we to receive from Cadiz the Regulations of our passive Trade? Were we, in this exclusive intercourse, to live fettered by restrictions similar to those exercised by the Government of Juan Fernandez, over its miserable convicts? Were we to see our Coasts abandoned to the enterprise of every Invader, whilst Spain was draining from us 50,000,000 of dollars in Duties, under the pretence of their defence, with Vessels which never appeared but to commit hostilities against ourselves? Were we to be excluded from an intercourse with other Nations, and to be condemned to buy for 10, what they could have sold to us for 1; and to see all Foreigners driven from Chile, together with the literature of their languages?[38] Was it to be expected that, under a monopoly of every kind, even of ideas, the freedom of the Press, and of speech, prohibited, and our University forbidden from discussing the pretended prerogatives of the Monarch of the Indies, lest the titles of his void and shameful dominion should be known; that, when our Archives were filled with Regulations of etiquette and ceremonies, about the Appeals called the 1,500, bought with the substance and the despair of the Petitioner[39], and about *pecuniary privileges*,

---

37 By a Royal Command, by advice of the Council of the Indies (Cedula of 15th October, 1767).

38 An Order of the 1st of September, 1750.

39 A famous Appeal in Spanish Jurisprudence, known by the name of 1,500, from the Supreme Court in Spain, where, to revise the case, it was necessary to give bail for that amount of reals. The slowness of its proceedings passed for a proverb, and, by the People, the name of 1,500 was understood to be the number of years for the Trial. (Translator).

which, from the distance of 3,000 leagues, were distributed to the highest bidders, we should be indifferent to our fate, and receive with cheerfulness these gifts of our Masters?

Was it practicable for them, amidst the intelligence of the age, to preserve their pretensions, after we had become ashamed of so many years of suffering, after our rude infancy was past, and when we had become more remarkable for our unfortunate habitual obedience, than the Conquest of America for its importance to the 3 Quarters of the Globe then known? Has not the moment yet arrived for cancelling the debt contracted by the pledge of the jewels of Isabella for the Expedition of Columbus? Are we still to be debtors, after the millions exported to Madrid? No: the Revolution of Spain, and the obstinacy of our Oppressors, have placed in our hands the power of casting off the burden. To suffer this favourable occasion to be lost is to become responsible to Posterity. To learn our rights from the instructions given by Spain herself, and yet not to secure them in a solid *independence*, would be a crime deserving the execration of our sons, and the opprobrium of the present generation. We have declared it, and the sighs forced from us by the hostilities of our unreasonable Enemies, shall be softened by the satisfaction of securing to the offspring of the Conquerors, that *liberty* of which the Spaniards stripped their Ancestors.

We wish to be, we can be, then we ought to be, free.

Here is a conclusion, drawn most precisely from antecedents, as evident *in fact as in right*. We shall not question Spain any more about the rights she can plead against us. Let us consider those she has alleged in support of her own Sovereignty, after the imprisonment of Ferdinand; let us examine her conduct; let us compare her proceedings with ours; and, mindful of her circumstances and station, we must inevitably decide in favor of the justice of our own Cause.

The news of the Coronation of Ferdinand reached us together with the tidings of his imprisonment, and the mysterious accounts of the scenes of the Escorial, Aranjuez, and Bayonne. At that very time, the Junta of Seville invited us to send Deputies to the *Central Government*, although, as America formed no part of such centre, it was quite unworthy of that name; for the first time, America was then declared *to be an integral part of, and equal in rights to the rest of the Monarchy, and to be no more a Colony, or Factory, than the Territory of other Nations*; she was informed of the establishment of the Provincial Juntas, their object, form, and attributes; she heard asserted the noble privileges of man, the sacred principles of the social compact, the rights of the People, and received the invitation to the exercise of Sovereignty, which had been held before by the King as their Agent, but who was then disabled from continuing his functions in consequence of his captivity; finally, she was assured of the happy prospect of having a Constitution, to restrain the arbitrary conduct of the Government, and to guarantee to the Citizen the protection of the Law, by his Representatives in a National Congress.[40]

This ray of light was too strong not to penetrate the most obscure mind, not to raise the most apathetic spirits. The idea of the Sovereignty excited that instinct of *independence* which is natural to man. Although united to the fate of the Peninsula, it formed in the heart a contest between the habitual wish for the prosperity of the Mother Country, and the necessity of providing for ourselves, in the event of that Country falling before the victorious Armies of France. The cautious and suspicious activity of our Chiefs, inclined opinions to this side, and induced us to believe, that the generous declarations of the Liberals on the other side of the Atlantic, were mere artifices to maintain America yoked to the chances of fortune. Every criticism on the events of Spain was, at the same time, deemed treason; and to repeat the animating Proclamations of her Government, was considered as the sound of perfidy. Our Assemblies were closely watched, and every man of intelligence had a centinel placed over him. This was the plan formed in the closets of the inferior Tyrants. At Venezuela, the Citizens Ortega, Rodriguez, and Sanz, were exiled from their families, by the Governor Emparan; and Roxas, Ovalle, and Vera, in Chile, by Governor Carrasco. The former Governor ordered his Assessor to be admitted to his functions by force; and Carrasco, surrounded by bayonets, gave possession to a like Officer of the first seat in the Cabildo. At that moment, fears began to rise superior to hope, and personal freedom to engage the sentiments of the People. Entertaining doubts of the fidelity of our Chief, the Inhabitants observed that his conduct was at variance with the promises of the Spanish Government. And we learnt from Spain, that the greater part of her Ministers, Councillors, Generals, Nobles, and Bishops, had adhered to the French Party.[41] We noticed the removal from Office of the Peninsular Authorities; the inactivity of their Successors; and the expedient adopted by the People for their safety, in the erection of Provincial Juntas. The news of one having been established at Buenos Ayres, put Chile in motion. Carrasco hoped to pacify it, by the hypocritical recall of the Exiles; which was detected and treated as a fraud; and the Governor was deposed. The Spaniards residing at Santiago were the most strenuous for his removal; and the command was conferred on Brigadier Count de la Conquista, as Senior Officer, according to ancient regulations. The Oidores trembled at the sight of this alteration, which seemed to them a presage of the downfall of their authority: their consciences accused them of having subscribed too readily, by their *advice*, to the treacheries of Carrasco. They believed that the occasion for *promoting discord*, agreeably to the *Secret Order* of the 15th April, 1810, had arrived; and, in fact, they excited it between the

---

40 Orders of the 19th and 20th March, and 30th September, 1808; of the 1st and 22nd January, and Manifesto of the 28th October, 1809.
41 Orders of the 28th July, 1808; and 14th February, 23rd March, and 24th May, 1809.

Americans and Spaniards. A meeting was proposed, of the most respectable Persons of both Parties; and the result was, the convocation of the People for the 18th of September. On this ever memorable day was established the Supreme Junta, to rule over the Country, *in the name of Ferdinand the VIIth*, with submission to the Regency erected in Spain over the ruins of the Central Junta. The sympathy then felt for the misfortunes of a suffering King, habitual respect, and the spirit of imitation, were more powerful than the sense of our rights. Yet, moved by the course of events, the intelligence of the age, and a just regard to our interests, there were heard, even then, some voices for independence.

Our new Government was approved of by the Regency. But this approbation was but a snare for the candor and generosity of the Chilenos, and to sacrifice them to the contemplated bloody invasion which was ordered to be made by the Viceroy of Peru. We ought to have anticipated this, after having seen our brethren in Buenos Ayres proscribed, Caracas blockaded, and the tyrant Melendez directed to practice the most cruel severities.[42] Thus, in the midst of our most frank intercourse with Lima, in the season when our produce was exported to Callao, when 120,000 dollars had just been acknowledged to have been received in Spain, from our Consulado[43], and 200,000 dollars from our Treasury, together with a voluntary contribution to assist Spain in her afflictions, that, as if waiting for this assistance, to proceed to our extermination, Pareja landed at San Vicente with the Army of devastation, *in the name of Ferdinand the VIIth.*

Then was brought to our recollection what the Regency had told us[44], that, to this name would be forever united the epoch of the regeneration and happiness of the Monarchy in both Hemispheres; that our destinies would no longer depend on the Viceroys and Governors; that they were in our own hands; and we asked ourselves, what that equality of rights was, with which they had flattered us, if, on making use of it, they judged us 'guilty of *high treasonable innovation!*' We looked to the causes that produced the Regency in Spain, and we reasoned thus: 'The People of the Peninsula have founded their Revolution on no other title than the *exigency of circumstances.* Why should not the People of America be the proper judges, as well as the People of Spain, to decide whether they are, or are not, under the same pressing necessity? From the moment that the Regency and the Cortes proclaimed, as the only basis of their authority, the Sovereignty of the People, they lost all pretension to command any People who might wish to exercise their own. If the Sovereignty emanates from the Spanish People, and if that People have no power over America, which, like Spain, is an integral part, if not the principal part of the Nation, why can we not ourselves represent the King, and act in

42 Orders of the 2nd August and 4th September, 1810.
43 Letter from the Spanish Government of 15th August, 1810.
44 Manifesto of the 14th February, 1810.

his name, as is done by the same Persons who declare us to be Rebels? Have they received from the captive Monarch some Special Commission, which has not reached us, besides the Order from Bayonne, to admit the new dynasty of Napoleon, which they resist with so much heroism? That which is in them a virtue and a right, cannot be with us a crime. If Spain refuse to submit to the French, although they intend to govern her in the name of Ferdinand, and by virtue of his resignation, with more reason shall we repulse those who bring War to us in the same name, because we have preserved him at the head of our Government, and have lavished an undeserved gratitude to Persons who were Traitors to their own principles'.

We were thus undeceived as to the true meaning of those theories, as brilliant as they were seducing; and we discovered on the reverse of the talisman, that, under pretence of restoring Ferdinand to the Throne, usurped from his Father, they concealed the fraudulent design of stamping upon us and our Posterity a more fatal Slavery than we had yet endured, and that this was their urgent motive for ordering all our Schools to be closed, that we might be employed only in remitting to Spain men, money, and other supplies, with blind obedience.[45] We cast our eyes on the Map; we considered the natural and political position of Spain, and we were amazed that we had not, for so many years, dropt the curtain in this Comedy, where the Performers, from the small theatre of a peninsular angle of Europe, have kept in silent admiration a whole World, without tiring and disguising it by the uniformity of a plot, conducted through the wiles of mere intrigue, and the detection of which would be like the discharge of a thousand lightnings on the Spectators.

We reflected, and said to ourselves, 'Shall 22,000 square leagues, and 1,000,000 of Inhabitants, animated with the spirit and discretion of the Araucanos, continue subject to a part of the Old Hemisphere, which begs its resources from us, which perishes without them, lives by them, and endeavors to destroy us with them? Since when has the order of the social relations been so overturned, that the lame must assist his crutches, that the infant's mouth must change the milk into blood, and vomit it in the face of its nurse? that the needy must rise up, and seek to command his benefactor? Whence did that Legislation spring, by which neither mature age, nor sound judgment, nor wealth, nor adequate means of government, nor superiority of force, nor any of the many elements favorable to individual liberty, can procure freedom to a whole Nation? Who has dictated that Code, which directs that the treacherous and the ungrateful be applauded by the offended, and have their conduct sanctioned? And who has deprived us of our intellect, that we cannot discover the cruelties of Spain, even in the impudent gifts of her favors?

45 Order of the 30th April, 1810.

Called to the Cortes, with '*an equal representation*', we see 1 Member for every 30,000 Peninsulars, and that 1,000,000 of us is barely a sufficient number to elect 1! There the suffrage is popular; here it is consigned to the Vote of a President, under the sanction of Corporations. There the form of Election does not vary; here each Mail brings us new forms, in order that we shall never be represented in any other manner than by *Substitutes*, introduced with as much legality as were the Deputies of the Congress of Bayonne: some of them are unknown to the People they are to represent; others are expressly objected to by their Constituents; not 1 of them has proper Credentials, and every one of them would be elected by Peninsular influence.[46] There they trade freely with all Nations; whilst here they shut our Ports even to Vessels from England, to whose alliance Spain owes all her power; and they are not ashamed to declare as null and void, a Decree of the 17th March, 1809, which, it was supposed, was favorable to a Free Trade.[47] There, all Foreign Periodical Papers, and Literary Productions, and the liberal opinions of Statesmen and Philosophers, which were formerly stifled by despotic terror, but now render homage to Nature and to the elements of Civilization, are freely circulated; but here they have proscribed even National Productions, the Liberty of the Press, and all Writings relating to the Spanish Revolution, except the Ministerial Papers of the Regency, and have recommended to the Inquisition the most scrupulous and responsible vigilance[48]; pretending that, to enlighten the People, it was only necessary to send 20 Missionaries, to complete the number of them in Chile, *in order that the Holy Religion should not suffer for want of Ministers*. Such is, in 1810, the language of the Regency, which orders our Treasury to pay the passage of those Fanatics, to the great horror of our Priests, and of the piety and intelligence of the Country.[49]

Such is the grand system of equality and distinction which they offer to us. Such is the compliment that they have substituted for the deceits with which they formerly robbed the artless Indians of their treasures, and with which they seek to deprive us of our feelings and our instinct; accompanying their overtures with bayonets, that they may exterminate us, in case we should rely on the faith of their promises. What decency and circumspection in these pretended *Sovereigns!*'

Whilst occupied with these circumstances, and by the light of the fire of the War which they had kindled, we felt ashamed of our improvidence and generosity, and an universal cry of Independence was the effect of the remorse elicited by justice and the sight of our evils. The least of the motives we were contemplating would have justified the declaration of our Independence.

46 Orders of the 6th October, 1809, and 29th March, 1810.
47 Orders of the 27th June, and 10th July, 1809.
48 Cedula of the 1st January, 1809, and Orders of 31st April, 1810.
49 Of the 13th and 19th July, 1810.

Satisfied, however, with the hope of a triumph which, by undeceiving our Aggressors, should reduce them with the arms of persuasion, we delayed this august act, to which we were impelled by nature, time, and our successes. We fought and vanquished. Our arms, covered with glory, in the Battles of Yerbas-Buenos, San Carlos, el Roble, Concepcion, Talcahuano, Cucha, Membrilla, and Quechereguas, brought us to that crisis when the Forces of the new General Gainza, having been driven within the small Precincts of Talca and annihilated, we might have dictated the Law to the Man who brought to us the Spanish Constitution; that crafty Document, which, under the appearance of Liberty, contained only the conditions of Slavery, for America, which had not concurred in its formation, nor under which could she have been fairly represented by 31 Substitute Deputies, legislating amidst the 133 Spanish Representatives. We could wish to consign to eternal oblivion that fatal epoch, in which all the intrigues of perfidious Spain were contending against the magnanimity and open ness of the Chilian character. Who could have believed that, at a crisis so favorable to our interests, and so fatal to the self-styled *National Army*, the Capitulation of the 3rd May, 1814, would have been concluded!

It is necessary to save ourselves the shame of analysing it. Suffice it to say, that, it having been ratified by our Government, guaranteed by the mediation of Commodore Hillyar, with Powers from the Viceroy of Peru, accepted by the Chief of the Army of Lima, our Troops with drawn, the Prisoners restored to the Enemy, and the People obliged to acknowledge the Peace solemnly proclaimed, it became necessary to assist the Invaders, whom it was then impossible to remove, and to accept its nullity as an apology for their remaining employed in Treasons at Talca, which place was to have been evacuated in 30 hours. They had scarcely left that City, and crossed the Maule, when Gainza made every exertion to repair his losses; he recruited, assembled, and disciplined, another Army, which he stationed in the Province of Concepcion; he spent, in recruiting, all the money which was destined, through him, to repair the losses sustained by the Inhabitants; he laid hands on all our funds; he appointed Judges; and, in a word, he acted as Lord and Master of the very Territory which he had agreed to evacuate in 2 months, until the arrival of Ossorio, who renewed hostilities, and threatened to put everything to fire and sword, unless we surrendered at discretion[50], and opened our bosoms to the Proclamation and Pardon of his Vizier.[51] It was too late to trust in the caresses of the Lion, who concealed bis claws under the folds of the Standard of War: we knew the consequences of the pardons already granted in Mexico, Venezuela, Quito, Huanuco, and Upper Peru. The summons excited our alarm; more especially because, with the news of the Restoration of Ferdinand to the

50 Summons of the 20th August, 1814, from Chillan.
51 Proclamation and Pardon of the Viceroy of Lima, 14th March.

Throne, we had received his Decree, annulling the Regency, the Cortes, their Orders and Constitution, and maintaining the established Authorities in both Hemispheres.

We did not wish to call upon the Satellites of Tyranny to shew their right to spread devastation in the Country; but only the right that supported their present aggression, and converted their *Royal* Army once more into a *National* Army. If they had weakness enough to become the sport of a versatile Government, was that a reason why the People should deliver themselves up to the sword, and the implacable designs of their assassins? They cannot any longer quote the Constitution as an authority; as it did not give them any right or claim to obedience, any more than the Constitution, however beneficial and admirable, which was made by Joseph Napoleon, has given him over the Peninsula. Ferdinand has re-assumed his Sceptre, and torn to pieces that celebrated Act. And now, by what new Act, have the Americans re-established the authority of the son of Maria Louisa, which, although null in its origin, he had himself abdicated and lost, by repeated and subsequent acts of infamy and cruelty?

Let us recall to our recollection the scenes of the Escorial, Aranjuez, and Bayonne. In 1807, Ferdinand is declared a Traitor to his Father, and unworthy of succeeding to the Crown. In 1808, the scene changes at Aranjuez, and Charles IV, treated with violence by the same Faction which was stifled at the Escorial, cedes the Crown to the Son, who is proclaimed amidst the disturbances of the Court. The old Pupil of Godoy escapes to France, to seek the protection of the Emperor; who, in the Conferences of Bayonne, causes the Diadem to be restored, in order to accept it himself, and place it upon the head of his Brother Joseph.

These royal comic Transactions have been represented to us by the Central Junta and Regency, under the veil of exalted exclamations, in order to move all our sensibility in behalf of the misfortunes of that Youth, with whose party they have been engaged. And hence it is, that they have despatched Executive Orders to America, to apprehend the parent King, and his suite, in case they appear on these Coasts, and to send them back to Spain under arrest.[52] The tender enthusiasm, excited by our compassion and our hopes, having subsided, who can discover less violence in the Renunciation of Bayonne, than in that of Aranjuez? Was the presence of Bonaparte more imposing to Ferdinand, than the presence of a mob at the gates of his palace, to Charles IV? The Bourbons have abandoned the Nation, against the will of the People, and they have, by this act, lost even those obscure rights upon which their Dynasty was founded. A Nation left without a Chief, in consequence of their domestic quarrels, could not belong to those Emigrants. Ferdinand, from

52 Cedula of the 12th August, 1808, and Orders of 1st March, 1809, and 26th June, 1810.

Valençay, could not keep in his hand the extremity of the cord, or, more properly speaking, of the chain, which fastened America.

When Spain declared War against Denmark, she said in her Manifesto -'If this Power is oppressed, and is subject to the will of Napoleon, Spain declares War against her as against a Province of France'.[53] Why do they not hold the same language with respect to Ferdinand, who was a Prisoner, or rather, voluntarily gave himself up to the disposal of the Emperor? Will the world ever forget the base, horrid, and sacrilegious denunciation, by which he betrayed the Baron de Kolli, who was engaged in rescuing him from the Castle of Valençay, with the assistance and credentials of George III.[54] Treating as false the Report of Mr. Bertheny, the Commander of the Fort, in which he states, that Ferdinand, in his communication, had dared to assert, 'that England continued to shed blood in his name, being deceived by the false idea that he was forcibly detained there'; supposing even that Ferdinand's Letter to Napoleon, requesting him to adopt him for his Son, be also a fabrication, (but of neither of which accusations has he cleared himself), is not the infamy of such a denunciation sufficient to deprive the denunciator of the character of a Prince? How can they attempt to blind us with an Oath, taken without our consent, to bind our consciences at an epoch full of perplexities and tumultuous afflictions, at the sight of promises which have never been fulfilled, and under circumstances that have long ceased to exist? But with the Commissioners engaged in the destruction of America, the threat never changes: their object is to annihilate her; and it is the same thing with them to commit hostilities in the name of the Constitution, or in the name of the Despot who tramples under foot the same Constitution which they came to announce to us.

Such has been the conduct of Ossorio in Chile; it is necessary to repeat it, he enters with the sword in one hand, and the Code in the other. We shewed him, (although he knew it himself beforehand), that it has been annulled by Ferdinand, with the same facility, that he fights for the Law, or for the Enemy of the Law. Can Justice, a virtue in variable, and constantly the same in all times and climates, be supported upon contradictory bases and discordant interests? No: it was not Justice that gave to the Tyrant the Victory of the 2nd of October, 1814: it was not Justice that suggested to him to set fire to the Hospital, where our wounded Soldiers were: it was not Justice that fired the gun on the Victims who fled for refuge to the Churches of Rancagua: Justice did not authorize the violences by which these sanctuaries of Religion and innocence were polluted. Justice did not put into their sacrilegious bands the vases of priesthood, to be used in their bacchanalias. Justice did not cover with blood the roads from Talcahuano to the Capital, that these traces of

---

53 Manifesto of the 4th October, 1809.
54 Vide the Documents in the work *El Español*, No. 2, 30th May, 1810.

death might serve to shew the way to the headquarters of the Sicarios, where our most respectable Citizens, wandering in the mountains, were obliged to present themselves, to be transported to the rock of Juan Fernandez. Justice did not sharpen the knife which murdered the 9 Persons in the Prisons, under the pretence of a supposed conspiracy, without any other trial than the ferocity of the perpetrators of the catastrophe of Quito. It is not Justice that has cast into the Casemates[55] so many deserving Individuals, who have been snatched from their families, without any form of Trial, and are now lamenting over their orphanage, and the refusal of an Exchange of Prisoners; the Vizier of Peru, sacrificing the lives of his own mercenaries, rather than ameliorate the fate of our fellow Citizens.

It was not Justice that erected the 4 scaffolds, for the recreation of the coward modern Baptus[56], and which he ordered to be immediately taken away from the public square, at the news of the Triumph of the 12th of February, 1817, the anniversary of which day we celebrate (Chacabuco). Justice granted to Chile that day of glory and splendor, well satisfied that, by 21 years sufferings, we had atoned for our unnatural submission, and for our blindness in not perceiving that, by such submission, we betrayed the sacred rights of our Country, called in question the necessity of *independence*, and the sincere wishes of the People, who proclaimed it with so much the more eagerness, because they had learnt, at the school of tyranny, that Independence is the only desirable end of this bloody struggle of 7 years; that the imbecility and impotence of our Aggressors and of the Despot they serve, had become evident; that the idol and its renown had fallen to the ground; and that we ought no longer to be guilty of the weakness of invoking him, when Spain herself, after being chilled by his ingratitude, on his re-ascending the Throne, tears herself in the convulsion of a paralysis that carries her to her final destruction.

Such is the state of that unfortunate Nation, which is rendered less miserable by the fierceness of the monster, than by his obstinacy in keeping it engaged in this destructive struggle, in which, after having lost all the acquisitions of the First Conquest, it will remain excluded forever from the only relations by which it might have repaired the losses of 25 years. Spain existed by America; it now receives nothing from it, and is obliged to exhaust all its means in combating it. It can no longer deceive us, owing to the state of poverty which devours it. Should a miraculous effort enable it to send over some gladiators, they would not, without reluctance, abandon their native soil, to descend to the grave at such a distance from their home; and they would soon be convinced, that they were engaged in an undertaking in which any ephemeral

---

55 Horrible dungeons in the Callao of Lima.
56 Marco, successor of Ossorio, is not less remarkable for his cruelties than for his effeminacy, resembling that of Baptus, so much despised in ancient Greece. The above mentioned tyrannical acts are recorded judicially in our Archives.

triumph they might obtain, would resemble only that of the bird, which cuts the air that closes upon it again after it has passed. The condition of Morillo, with the best Army that Spain has sent out, and of all the other Divisions, is a proof of this. Whilst they occupy one Place, the Insurrection rages in another; and thus all the dispersed masses of the Invaders are ultimately consumed in the midst of the conflagration. The combustion is universal, the space immense, and the fire of the Revolution inextinguishable.

We will not belong to an insignificant Nation, from which we want nothing, but which, being in want of us, seeks only to destroy us. We will not belong to a Nation which is unfaithful to its promises, violates its engagements, and is contradictory in its principles; which dares to assert pretensions to its decrepit usurpation, in behalf too of a dynasty which has divested itself even of all appearance of right; and which would make us a reproach, to the rest of our brethren, who have nobly emancipated themselves, to the improvement of the age, which venerates Liberty as the Goddess of Civilization, to our children, who, from the prospect of the future, await the happy moment when they are to enter without trouble into the enjoyment of the days of order, honor, and peace, which their Fathers will have bought for them with their blood, to all the human race, who can now rest, in abundant places of refuge in these regions, blessed by their Creator, but who were formerly shut out by proud ambition from the hospitality of men who were unwilling to become Slaves, to Nature, which placed in our minds a sense of shame and spirit which is incompatible with Slavery,-and, finally, to Heaven itself, which has unfolded to us the list of the Nations, and has pointed out the place we are to occupy in the rank of those which are independent.

[1818–19]
Chile has at length obeyed the call. The solemn Act of the 1st of January, 1818, is the expression of the general voice, and the result of every individual determination. She has not deferred her Revolution until the convocation of a Congress, which it would be difficult to assemble during the effervescence of War; she has herself dictated the measure which, under all the circumstances, would have been sanctioned by her Representatives, who are faithful to their trust and the confidence of their Constituents. When the latter shall depute them, the Representatives will ascend the altar of the Law, invested with all the plenitude of Sovereignty required to proclaim it. That epoch approaches as the expiring remnant of our Enemies flies away terrified. In the meantime, to defend the great Charter of our Rights, every Citizen runs spontaneously to arms. A veteran Army of 12,000 brave men, and the general embodying of the Militia, without exception, are the pledge and eternal foundation of our INDEPENDENCE.

Free Nations of the Universe! who behold the basis of your Sovereignty secured, by the new monument of justice upon which Chile has raised its own, decide, in this fatal struggle, between humanity and the vain spirit of domination; teach Spain, that the welfare of the People is the origin and object of all Government, and ask her, then, which is to yield? By uniting your voices to ours, you will stop the blood which overflows vigorous America, and draws the last breath of expiring Spain. If you are touched by our destinies, convince her of her impotence, and of the mutual advantages of our Independence: let her be softened by her own misfortunes, and by those which we have suffered during 3 centuries; inspire her with a natural feeling towards her fate and ours; and when, dispassionately weighing the consequences that threaten her, she shall lay down her arms, and sacrifice to justice and liberality the illusions which precipitate her to her ruin, you may assure her, upon our honor, that generous Chile will open her heart to the friend ship of her brethren, and participate with them, under the glorious empire of the Laws, in all the benefits of their mutual INDEPENDENCE.

Directorial Palace of Chile, 12th February, 1818.

BERNARDO O ' HIGGINS

MIGUEL ZANARTU, *Secretary of State*

8. Independence of Chili, Santiago de Chili, Feb. 16, 1818[57]

INDEPENDENCE OF CHILI

Extraordinary Gazette of Buenos-Ayres, March 5

The people of Chili have raised themselves to the rank of independent nations, by their magnanimous resolution of announcing, in the face of the whole world, their decided will to belong only to themselves, and to maintain this declaration with all their power. They cannot go back without covering themselves with disgrace, and without becoming the laughing-stock of the nations who have a resolution that does the Chilians so much honour. The provinces of the Rio de la Plata, through the medium of their deputy, Don Thomas Guido, have been the first to recognize the new rank of this kingdom, as appears by the documents subjoined, and his Excellency the Supreme Governor has ordered that, for three successive nights, there shall be an illumination in the capital, beginning tomorrow, when there shall be a salute from the fortress at sun-rise, at midday, and in the evening, with such other demonstrations of joy as are usual on days of public festival, and which his Excellency leaves to the option of the patriotic citizens. Communicating this disposition to all the towns of the union, that they may act as becomes them on so glorious an occasion.

Official Letter of the Deputy of the Provinces.

Most Excellent Sir,

On the 12th of the month, at half-past 10 in the morning, the independence of Chili on the Spanish monarchy was proclaimed and solemnized with oaths by the Supreme Chief, the Magistrates, and all the public bodies, ecclesiastical, civil, and military, and by an immense multitude collected in the great square of the capital, after the declaration of their sentiments, by the reading of the proclamation of their independence, the motives which justified it, and the unanimous will of the whole people, for their political emancipation.

The flag of the United Provinces, in the hands of the Governor of Santiago, and the national flag of Chili, which is in my hands, shall authenticate this act, which is unquestionably the most magnificent and imposing of all those which the history of the New World presents since its ominous conquest. My heart is transported with joy to communicate to your Excellency this grand

57 [*The Times*, 6 June 1818, p. 3, The Times Digital Archive. Accessed 4 June 2020].

event, on which the zeal of your administration has had so much influence; and I feel honour in informing your Excellency, that on the day of the public congratulations to the Government of this nation, I recognized, in virtue of the power with which I was entrusted, in the name of your Excellency, the sovereignty of Chili and its absolute independence in terms of the address given in number 2d, as a proof a proof of the liberality of the system pursued by the United Provinces, and of the pleasure with which they hail the freedom of their brethren.

Whoever has observed the spirit of this nation, in the act of abjuring the dominion of the Kings of Spain, the enthusiasm and joy of every citizen, at the new elevation of their country, and the demonstrations of love and gratitude to the state of the Rio Plata, must agree, that neither law nor time can oppose the impulses of nature and justice, that the elevation of a firm character has superseded the degradation of a colony, and that Chili will be no more the patrimony of the tyrannical and arbitrary dynasty of Spain, but the asylum of liberty and the country for all the men on the globe.

Let your Excellency glory in an event so fortunate for the cause of the Americans, and while I transmit you an account of the various remarkable incidents of this happy period, deign to receive the congratulation which I offer to my country for the liberty of this delightful region. God preserve your Excellency for many years, &c.

Santiago de Chili, Feb. 16. 1818.

His Excellency Thomas Guido, to his Excellency the Supreme Director of the United Provinces of South America.

9. Report concerning Chili, by T. Bland, 1819[58]

American Intelligence
[From the National Register]

BLAND'S REPORT CONCERNING CHILI

The readers of the *National Register* have already been furnished with the reports of Mr. Rodney and Mr. Graham, relative to the current situation of Buenos-Ayres and the United and Independent provinces of La Plata. Mr. Bland has also made an official statement respecting the same provinces, together with a report concerning Chili and his mission thither, which the President communicated to Congress on the 15th instant.

We have not been enabled, this week, to introduce into our pages either of these latter documents in whole or in part: but a friend, who has read with attention the report concerning Chili, has favored us with an accurate abstract of its contents, which we have now the pleasure of laying before our numerous patrons.

Mr. Bland, it will be recollected, was, in pursuance of instructions from the President, left by his colleagues, Mr. Rodney and Mr. Graham, at Buenos-Ayres; whence, on the 15th of April, 1818, he departed for Chili, and on the 20th of the same month arrived at Mendoza, on the eastern side of the Andes, having traveled, by the way of the post-road, a distance of about 900 miles. He left Mendoza on the 24th of April, and, crossing the Andes, reached Santiago de Chili on the 5th of May; the whole route being, perhaps, about 1,200 miles. At this latter place Mr. Bland presented himself to Don Antonio Jose Irisarri, Secretary of State, through whom he obtained an interview with Don Bernardo O'Higgins, the Supreme Director of Chili. He was received with much cordiality by the Director, with whom he had, at different times, very interesting conversations, touching the present and future probable condition of Chili, and the friendly sentiments which the United States entertained towards that Country.

In the several interviews which Mr. Bland had with the Supreme Director, he represented to him the good disposition which the Government of the United States cherished towards the independent authorities of Chili, and the cause in which they are engaged; the sympathy which the free citizens of North America felt for the sufferings of those who were contending for liberty and emancipation from the yoke of Old Spain in the southern part of

58 [*The Times*, 20 January 1819, p. 2, The Times Digital Archive. Accessed 4 June 2020].

the American continent; and portrayed to him the benefits to be derived from the establishment of the representative system, by the immediate formation of a Congress.

To these observations O'Higgins answered, that he was not insensible to the friendship of the United States; that it was his intention to institute a free government, as soon as Chili waş entirely freed of her enemies, and sufficiently tranquillized for the purpose; but that the present moment was inauspicious for the commencement of so great a work; that in times of public peril the presence of a Congress had been found extremely pernicious; that Mexico had been lost by a congress; that the congress of Venezuela once lost that Country; and that Buenos-Ayres had been endangered by a congress: lately, indeed, he admitted, the latter had learnt to act more in concert, and with greater propriety.

The Supreme Director having intimated that it was expected the United States would recognize the independence of Chili, and that the Chilians would grant special favours in commerce to the nation, (and it would be gratifying if the United States should be the nation) first making such recognition, Mr. Bland replied, that the single object of his mission was to make inquiry as to the true posture of affairs in Chili; that the United States would be thankful for any favours of the kind, but that they did not ask for them; that all they desired was to be put on a footing with other nations, and were willing to rely, as to any advantages in commerce and navigation, on the skill and industry of their merchants and seamen; that he had repaired to Santiago in order to procure, upon the spot, accurate knowledge of the country, of its institutions, and of its capacities in peace and in war; that the Government of the United States only wished to see its way clearly, and would make no improper use of this information; and that any particulars communicated to him from authority might be considered as confidential, or otherwise, just as the Supreme Director might deem proper.

The Supreme Director, O'Higgins, admitted the propriety of authentic information, in order that the Government of the United States might act intelligently with regard to South American affairs, and told Mr. Bland that he would cause an official statement to be made out respecting the condition and resources of Chili, and placed in his hands for that purpose; which promise the Supreme Director Complied with. This statement makes a part of Mr. Bland's report concerning Chili.

During the intercourse between Mr. Bland and O'Higgins, the former explained to the latter the motives which actuate the President in the seizure of Amelia Island, and in driving the banditti from Galveston; and told him, that the freebooters who had been forced from those places were not the only armed vessels whose officers and crews had interrupted the lawful commerce of the United States, for that some of the privateers cruising under regular Patriot commissions had committed depredations upon their trade; that the United States would, at all hazards, defend the fair traffic of her citizens; and that they would do so even against the Chilians, however painful it might be to crush in the germ a growing intimacy between the two people, and which promised to be in the sequel fruitful of benefits to them both.

O'Higgins did not even know where Amelia Island and Galveston were situated, until Mr. Bland explained the positions to him. He decidedly approved of the conduct of the President in driving of the pirates from thence, inasmuch as it tended to preserve the character of the Patriot cause from imputations of an injurious nature: he had heard of outrages committed by private armed vessels sailing under some of the independent flags of South America; but that whatever might have been the behaviour of the vessels acting under commissions from other states, no charge of the kind could justly be brought against the Chilians; that in fact, with the exception of some fishing-boats, it was not until very lately that the Government of Chili had any vessels of war under its control; and that he had taken great care, by giving proper instructions, and by placing suitable superintending officers on board, to prevent any departure from the rules of naval warfare prescribed by the law of nations.

In one of the conversations which took place, Mr. Bland told the Supreme Director, that when he was at Rio Janeiro (where, it will be recollected, the commissioners touched, on their way to Buenos Ayres), he had learnt through Mr. Sumter, the Minister of the United States, from the Spanish Minister resident there, that Great Britain had been induced to take an active part in favour of Old Spain, and had influenced the Allied Sovereigns of Europe to interpose for the adjustment of differences between her and her colonies: and that the plan of adjustment was to be something like that which had been formerly rejected by the Cortes, and might be found in a work that had been published in England, entitled 'An Outline of the Revolution in Spanish America'.

At first O'Higgins did not believe in the truth of the information which Mr. Bland had received; he said that the British would hardly do so, as they wanted the commerce of Spanish America: but shortly after, meeting with him again, the Supreme Director said he was then convinced of it; for he had seen Capt. Shirriff, of the British frigate *Andromache*, in Santiago, who had told him that he had in his possession papers on the subject, with which he was going to Lima, in Peru. O'Higgins further remarked, that all attempts to reconcile the South Americans, short of the acknowledgment of their independence, would be fruitless; and that a return to allegiance under the government of Old Spain was wholly out of the question.

On the 9th July Mr. Bland, having received the statistical information which the Supreme Director had promised him, took leave of him and of the Secretary of State Irisarri. O'Higgins expressed his intention of writing a letter to the President; but whether he did so or not, Mr. Bland had not distinctly related.

On the 10th of July Mr. Bland left Santiago de Chili; the 11th he arrived at Valparaiso; and on the 15th July he sailed thence in the brig America, Captain Daniel Rea, and arrived, by the way of Cape Horn, at Philadelphia, on the 29th October, 1818.

The narrative of Mr. Bland's communications with the Supreme Director forms but a small portion of his Report concerning Chili. He furnishes in addition a very copious description of that region of our hemisphere, in which he now and then lets his fancy get the better of his judgment. But, from the mass of pages which he has written, circumstances of a highly interesting complexion may be selected.

From Mr. Bland's account, it would seem that Chili is a country (excluding the Magellanic tract, or New Chili) of about 1,000 miles in extent on the sea coast; that it has many excellent ports convenient for foreign trade; that it is a country fruitful in grain, wine, and oil, and productive in gold, silver, copper, and tin; that it is destined to be the granary of that part of the world; that its population is about 1,200,000 souls; that 100,000 of these are under the domination of the Patriots, the remainder being under the jurisdiction of the Royalists; that there are about 50,000 Indian slaves in all Chili; and but very few slaves of the African race. All the mechanical arts and agriculture are in a rude state, and the roads and pathways in a neglected condition. The principal articles of export are the metals already mentioned, together with wheat, flower, hemp, cordage, hides, tallow, jerked beef, vecunia, guanaca, chinchilla skins, figs, raisins, &c. Of 4,000,000 of dollars' worth of imports, in the course of last year, two millions in value were from England, one from the United States, and one from Buenos-Ayres. The articles furnished from the United States are chiefly tobacco, windsor chairs, saddlery, and furniture. Of European commodities, Mr. Bland thinks the manufactures of France and Germany are preferred. The stocks of cattle are numerous and fine; the horses are active, spirited, serviceable, and cheap; but the mules are the common beasts of burden. The soil and climate of Chili are different in different places: from the Straits of Chacao to the river Biobia, it is woody, fertile, and salubrious, and is inhabited by the Araucanians, or natives: from the Biobio to the river Maule, the country is the same, but the population is Spanish: from the Maule to the Aconcagua, still fertile, but no forests: from the valley of Aconcagua the mine country presents itself, which is less fruitful on the surface: after the mine country, the dreary desert of Atacama, upwards of 300 miles in extent, affords a protection to the Chilians from any invasion by land from Peru. From the Straits of Chacao to the river Maule, it rains at any season; at Santiago de Chili there is no rain for seven months in the year; and beyond Capiapo rains are hardly known. Mr. Bland divides the country into two regions -the one variable and humid, and the other invariable and dry. Fuel, in some parts, is scarce; but it is said there is plenty of pit-coal on the banks of the Biobio, near Conception. The Archipelago of Ancud, or Chiloe, contains 47 islands; it is a considerable fishery, and will be a nursery for seamen. There are only three carriage-roads in all Chili. The fertile part of the soil is situated in vallies, surrounded for the most part by hills and mountains; and the inhabitants of these vallies communicate with each other principally by mule paths. Mr. Bland describes the people generally as being 'mild, amiable, brave, and uninformed'. Santiago is the capital, and contains about 40,000 souls. The Royalists have possession of Penco, and a considerable district around Conception, which is their strong hold; they retain, also, Valdivia and Chiloe. The patriot army, at a medium, (for Mr. Irisarri and Mr. Bland differ on this point) is about 6,000 strong, 2,000 of which negroes from Buenos-Ayres; there are no Chilian officers in it, above the rank of Captain, with the exception of O'Higgins, who is a Brigadier under San Martin, and Colonel Raymon Freyere. The navy consists of but three or four indifferent vessels, but would be increased by the addition of two new ships of war, to be called *San Martin* and *Chacabuco*, built at New York, and for which purpose Messrs. Aguirre and Gomez were, a considerable time since, sent to the United States from Buenos-Ayres with money. A superior naval force is indispensable to enable the Chilians to invade Peru, for the desert of Atacama prevents them from marching thither by land. The Chilians have no seamen of their own.

The revenue of the Government in Chili is derived from duties on imports and exports; from an excise which is laid upon almost everything that is sold, from a direct tax, the mines, papal bulls, printed indulgences for the living and the dead, a crusade tax, tithes, forfeited estates of the Jesuits, voluntary contributions, and from confiscated estates of the enemies of the Patriot cause. The officers of the customs and the judges of the commercial courts receive no regular salaries, and a duty is imposed on merchandise to compensate them; in addition, traders quicken their exertions by presents or bribes. There are 10,000 monks and nuns in the country. The church holds one-third of the landed property of the state. The church lands are farmed out to tenants, who let them again to under-tenants, and these last work them with slaves: thus three sets of idlers are supported upon the product of the industry of the labouring class. In addition to their landed estates, the religious institutions have what are called their censos, or money lent out at an interest to five per cent per annum, to the amount of ten millions of dollars. Besides their share of the tithes, which the state still permits them to draw, the clergy have the annats, or first fruits, which yield to each curate between two and three hundred dollars per annum.

The government of Chili, it seems, is needy, and has made some progress towards laying hands on the enormous property of the priests. Indeed, neither monks or nuns, according to Mr. Bland, are treated with much ceremony; some of the former have been turned out of their dwelling places, which have been occupied for military purposes, and some of them have been tried for treasonable practices.

The most immediately interesting part of the Report is that which gives the history of the Chilian revolution, and the change of parties among the Patriots. There have, it appears, been two powerful factions in that country of the revolutionists themselves. At the head of one were the Carreras; the Larrains formed the other, with O'Higgins at their head. At the beginning of the contest for independence, the Carrera faction prevailed. It would seem, however, this party did not manage affairs in a judicious manner; for at the battle of Rancagua, against the Royalists, fought on the 2d of October, 1814, the Patriots were entirely defeated, and fled over the Andes. They were rallied at Mendoza by San Martin, who identified himself with the Larrain faction, and having obtained a reinforcement of 2,000 negroes from Buenos-Ayres, crossed the mountains, and, on the 12th February, 1816, fought the battle of Chacabuco, defeated the Royalists, and took their commander, Marco, prisoner. This may be called the second epoch of the revolution in Chili. The Carrera party was, of course, put down, and the Larrains, with O'Higgins as chief, confirmed themselves in power by the victory of Mapu, obtained on the 5th April, 1818, with the particulars of which the reader is no doubt well acquainted. It is greatly to the dishonour of the Larrains that they seized this moment of success to put to death two of the most distinguished of the Carreras. They were sacrificed under judicial forms, and on the pretext of treason. Their execution was a foul and bloody murder, to gratify the vengeance of the reigning faction.

The closest intimacy subsists between the Governments of Chili and Buenos-Ayres. O'Higgins told Mr. Bland, that there was nothing which Buenos Ayres could ask of Chili that would not be granted: and that Buenos-Ayres would act in like manner towards Chili. All the inhabitants of Buenos Ayres are naturalized citizens of Chili. The Supreme Director, by way of characterizing the intimacy, said they were as two bodies actuated by one soul. Mr. Bland thinks, however, that this connexion is to the disadvantage of the Chilians, and conceives that it will not be lasting.

Under the faction of the Carreras, at the commencement of the revolution, the press, for the first time, was introduced into Chili. Before that period all books and papers, prior to their entrance into the country, were inspected and approved by the Holy Inquisition in Spain or at Lima. The name of the first paper was the *Aurora*. It was printed weekly, at a printing-office sent from New York, and managed by three citizens of the United States, edited by Camilla Henriquez, now of Buenos-Ayres. The opposite party also published a paper, which they called the *Aurora*. It was edited by Irisarri. At this time there are four weekly papers issued at Santiago; and none are published anywhere else in Chili; their names are the *Ministerial Gazette*, which is the acknowledged paper of the Government, *El Argos*, *El Duende*, and *El Sol*.

They are all printed at the same press, and edited by clerks and officers of the Government. Two other printing-presses had been carried there for sale, but they were not saleable articles. Newspapers and pamphlets are conveyed free of postage, and books are imported free of duty.

The reader may recollect that, after the battle of Maypu, the Viceroy of Peru was desirous of effecting an exchange of prisoners, and sent on board the United States' sloop of war *Ontario,* Captain Biddle, from Lima, an officer to Valparaiso and Santiago for the purpose. It turned out, however, on investigation, that the Royalists had a few or no Chilian prisoners, that those which they formerly had having been confined is one of the islands of the Archipelago of Chiloe, were released by the Patriots after the battle of Chacabuco. The Patriots, on the contrary, had about 8,000 Royalist prisoners, and were willing they should be exchanged for any prisoners which the Royalists held belonging to Buenos Ayres; but, owing to some contempt manifested in relation to the Patriot authorities, no cartel was agreed upon.

Incidentally speaking of Peru, Mr. Bland says, that one-third of the population of that country are whites of unmixed blood, and two- thirds mulattoes and negroes; the latter, in general, as well informed as the whites.

10. Decrees from the Protector, by Joseph de San Martin, August 3, 1821[59]

SOUTH AMERICA

The Ministerial Gazette Extraordinary of Chili, published at Santiago on the 29th of August, contains a copy of an official dispatch from General San Martin to the Supreme Director of the Republic of Chili. The dispatch, after stating the succeed which had attended the Liberating Army in its progress to Lima, explains the situation of that country, and the reasons which induced General San Martin to continue to hold the command of the army. It also contains a copy of the Decree issued on that occasion by General San Martin, which is as follows:

DECREE OF DON JOSEPH DE SAN MARTIN, CAPTAIN GENERAL AND CHIEF OF THE LIBERATING ARMY OF PERU, GRAND OFFICER OF THE LEGION OF MERIT OF CHILI, PROTECTOR OF PERU, &. &.

On undertaking to complete the important object of establishing the liberty of this country I was induced by no feeling other than a desire of forwarding the sacred cause of America, and of promoting the happiness of the people of Peru. A great portion of those wishes have been realised; but the work will remain incomplete unless I labour to fix on a sure basis the security and future prosperity of the inhabitants of this region of the world.

Since my arrival at Pisco I announced in a Proclamation that from the necessary consequences of the events which had occurred, I had found myself invested with the Supreme Authority, and that I was responsible to my country for the exercise of it. Those circumstances have not varied, for as yet there is in Peru some open enemies to combat with, and therefore the necessity continues of my retaining in my hands the political and military authority.

I hope that on my taking this step, the justice will be done to me of not attributing false motives to my actions; and that all will believe I am actuated by no views of ambition, but solely by my desire of forwarding the public service. It is already well known that I seek only for tranquillity and retirement after a life sufficiently agitated; but I feel that I am still bound by every moral sanction, which requires me to offer at present to my country the

---

59 [We have been unable to locate the original source used by Parish].

sacrifice of my dearest wishes. The experience of ten years of revolution in Venezuela, Cundinamarca, Chili, and the United Provinces of La Plata, have given to me a clear knowledge of the evlls [*sic*] occasioned by a hasty and unseasonable convocation of the Congress, while there remain any enemies in this country; first, therefore, let us secure our independence, and then let us think of establishing liberty on a solid foundation. The religious scrupulosity with which I have fulfilled my word during the course of my life, gives me a right to be credited: and I now most solemnly pledge it to the people of Peru, that at the moment when the country is liberated from its enemies, I will resign my command, in order to make room for that Government which will think proper to elect. The frankness with which I speak, ought to give a new guaranty of the sincerity of my intentions. I could have regulated that the electors chosen by the citizens of the liberated departments should appoint a person to hold the reins of Government, until the re-union of the representatives of the Peruvian nation; but as I have been invited by the simultaneous and repeated expression of a great many persons of high character and decided influence in this capital, to preside over the administration of the State, I felt assured that the people are desirous of my continuing so to do; and on the other hand, having obtained the free assent of the people who are protected by the Liberating Army, have considered it as the most decorous and suitable line of conduct to follow that which must lead to the tranquillization of all the citizens who are zealous for the possession of freedom.

When I shall have the satisfaction of renouncing the command and of giving an account of my operations to the representatives of the people, I am certain that I shall not then receive from any person the name of having been led on by the venality, despotism, and corruption which have been the distinguishing characteristics of the agents of the Spanish Government in America. To administer unbiassed justice to all, by giving a recompense to the virtuous and patriotic, and by chastising vice and sedition wherever I may find them, shall be the rule by which my conduct will be regulated, while I continue placed at the head of the Nation.

I will then entrust to the interests of the country the installation of a vigorous government, which may preserve it from those evils which are produced by war, licentiousness and anarchy:

For which purpose I DECREE and DECLARE as follows:

1. That from this day there are united in my person the supreme political and military command of the five departments of Peru, under the title of PROTECTOR.

2. That the Ministry of States and of foreign relations is to D. John Garcia del Rio.

3. That of War and of the Marine to Lieut. Colonel D. Bernard Monteagudo, War Auditor of the Army and Navy.

4. That of the Home Department to Doctor D. Hippolito de Unanue.

5. That all the orders and official communications shall be affirmed by the appropriate Secretary and countersigned by me, and that all communications addressed to me shall be sent through the respective Secretaries.

6. That the necessary regulations shall be as soon as possible formed, for the establishment of a better system of administration, and for the better service of the public.

7. That this Decree shall continue to have force and effect until the assembly of the Representatives of the Peruvian nation, and that it shall cease to have effect when they shall have determined on the form and manner of Government.

Given at Lima, August 3, 1821, in the second year of the freedom of Peru.

JOSE DE SAN MARTIN

11. Recognition of the Independence of Chili by Portugal, by Juan Manuel de Figueiredo, Buenos Ayres, August 11, 1821[60]

SOUTH AMERICA

RECOGNITION OF THE INDEPENDENCE OF CHILI

[From the Government Gazette of Chili]

SANTIAGO, SEPT. 29.

LETTER FROM THE DEPUTY OF HIS MOST FAITHFUL MAJESTY WITH THE GOVERNMENT OF BUENOS-AYRES TO THE ENVOY FROM CHILI WITH THE SAME GOVERNMENT.

His Most Faithful Majesty, my Sovereign, at the time of his return to Europe, thought fit to recognize the fact of the independence of the provinces of the Rio de la Plata, which are in obedience to their respective Governments, and to enter into those intimate relations of friendship which he had long wished to maintain with the people of the territories adjoining to his kingdom of the Brazils; and it was only a fatal concurrence of circumstances, equally experienced in the interior of both countries, or indeed rather the vacillating policy of the states of Europe, which could have prevented his Majesty from manifesting before the present epoch the whole extent of his liberal views.

His Most Faithful Majesty, well persuaded of the legitimacy of a Government, the existence of which is proved by the fact of the obedience of the people, only waited for a conjuncture in which the union of all wills might be demonstrated, in order to treat with the respective Governments on the firm basis of sound policy, on the immutable relation of reciprocal interests, the ties of commerce, alliance, and friendship, calculated to secure the perpetual enjoyment of that peace which is always the most desirable object of the people of all nations.

In pursuance of these principles, his Majesty has been pleased to appoint me his agent to the Government of your State, authorizing me, as he has authorized me by credentials, to aid and promote all the interests of commerce and the Crown.

In the instructions given me by the Minister Secretary of State for Foreign Affairs, I am authorized to treat with the Envoys and Agents of all the neighbouring Provinces and States, resident here in a public character, to

60 [*The Times*, 24 January 1822, p. 2, The Times Digital Archive. Accessed 4 June 2020].

whom I am ordered to declare in a positive manner, that these liberal dispositions of his Majesty extend to their respective governments.

And as in the said instructions official consideration is expressed for the Government of the State of Chili, I can no longer deny myself the satisfaction of communicating to your Excellency, as the Minister of that Supreme Government in these provinces, the generous sentiments of the Sovereign, in order that, in reporting them to your Government, you may at the same time declare that the subjects of the State of Chili shall be treated in the States of his Majesty with all the consideration enjoyed by the subjects of other Governments; and also that from henceforth the agents, whether mercantile or diplomatic, of that Government shall be received and treated at the Court of his Majesty with all the honours, consideration, and credit, which according to the general laws of nations are granted to similar Ministers or agents of other supreme Governments. I have, however, to inform your Excellency, that diplomatic agents only must be accredited to the Court of Lisbon, but that consuls and vice-consuls will be admitted into the ports of the Brazil by permission of his Royal Highness the Prince Regent, while he continues to execute the Royal authority.

I am happy to have the honour of being the medium through which the generous sentiments of my Court are declared, and in having an opportunity which affords me the pleasure of assuring your Excellency of my high esteem and consideration.

God preserve your Excellency many years.

JUAN MANUEL DE FIGUEIREDO

Buenos Ayres, Aug. 11, 1821

To His Excellency, Don Miguel Zanartu.

12. Cordoba treaties between Don Juan O'Donojú and Manuel [*sic*] Iturbide, Cordoba (Mexico), August 24, 1821[61]

LATEST FROM MEXICO

ARTICLES OF ADJUSTMENT ENTERED INTO BETWEEN THE PATRIOTS AND ROYALISTS, AT CORDOVA, ON THE 24TH OF AUGUST LAST.

Articles of adjustment entered into at Cordova between Don Juan O'Donojú, Vice King, and Don Manuel Iturbide, Commander-in Chief of the Imperial Mexican Forces:

1. America shall be sovereign and independent, and called the Mexican Empire.

2. Its Government shall be a moderate constitutional monarchy.

3. Ferdinand VIL, on coming to Mexico, shall reign; in default, his heirs or successors, in due order.

4. The Emperor shall fix his Court in Mexico, the capital of the Empire.

5. Two Commissioners from Senor Don Juan O'Donojú shall depart, and carry to the King of Spain this treaty; in the meantime the Cortes of the kingdom offer him the Crown under proper guarantees and forms, and request his compliance with the 3d article.

6. Conformable to the spirit of the plan of equality, there shall be formed a Junta of the chief persons of the empire for their virtues, their employments, their character, their riches, and the esteem they hold in public opinion, the number of whom are sufficiently considerable, that the re-union of their talents will assure obedience to their determination, that shall emanate from the authority and powers given them in the following articles:

7. The Junta shall be called a Provisional Government.

8. Senor Don Juan O'Donojú shall be a member of it; but it is indispensable to omit some persons named in the plan, in conformity with the spirit of its intentions.

9. The Junta shall elect a President, by a majority of votes, either from among its own members, or from the public in general.

---

61 [*The Times*, 3 November 1821, p. 2, The Times Digital Archive. Accessed 4 June 2020].

10. The first act of the Junta shall be to inform the people of its installation, motives of its re-union, and any further explanations they may think of public utility; and the mode to be adopted for electing Members to the Cortes.

11. The Junta, after electing its President, shall name a regency of three persons, chosen either from among themselves or the public, in whom shall be vested the executive power and government of the empire till the arrival of the Monarch.

12. The Provisional Government being installed, it shall govern according to the existing laws, excepting where they differ from a plan of equality, and until the Cortes form a constitution for the empire.

13. Immediately the Regency is named, the Cortes shall be called, conformably to the 24th article of the plan of equality.

14. The executive power resides in the Regency; the legislative in the Cortes; and in the interim of their meeting, the Provincial Junta shall exercise that faculty in cases which admit of no delay, and the Regency approve of the same; the Junta is also to form an auxiliary body and council to the Regency.

15. Every person shall be at liberty to remove himself and property to wherever he may think proper, excepting debtors and criminals; consequently Europeans who are in America, and Americans residing in the Peninsula, shall be at liberty to adopt the country they prefer, on these leaving this country paying the duties on the property they carry away.

16. In the foregoing article, public functionaries or military men, notoriously opposed to Mexican independence, are not included, but must necessarily leave the country within a period the Regency will prescribe, taking with them their property, on paying the export duty.

17. Senor Don Juan O'Donojú offers to use his authority, that the troops now in the city of Mexico shall quit it on an honourable capitulation, concurring with the wishes of the Commander-in-Chief to avoid the effusion of blood, and the use of force.

Cordova, August 24, 1821

13. Dispatch to the War Department in Lima on the state of affairs, by Bernardo Monteagudo, September 12, 1821[62]

MINISTRY OF WAR IN LIMA

SEPT. 12, 1821

SENOR,

The Spanish army which evacuated this capital on the 6th of July, after experiencing a considerable diminution of physical and moral force, having proceeded to the province of Jauja, and formed a junction with the division of Brigadier Canterac, put itself again in motion under the command of that officer on the 22d of last month, and directed its march towards this capital. General La Serna was left in Jauja with a squadron of cavalry, and the hospitals and stores of the army.

On the 3d instant, Brigadier Canterac advanced by the gap of Sicicaya, with his army, consisting, according to reports, of five battalions, and 700 horse.

The Protector of Peru having adopted, in anticipation, means for securing the best result to the warlike operations, as soon as the enemy approached, ordered the General in Chief, Camp Marshal Don Juan de Gregorio de las Heras, to march out with his troops and observe the movements of the Spanish force. On the following day, his Excellency proceeded to the army, and placed himself at it head.

As soon as the enemy had issued from the gap of Sicicaya, he took a position in the Hacienda de la Molina, at the distance of two leagues from the city, and one from our army in Mendoza. Since then, until the day before yesterday, both armies maneuvered in different positions, and the enemy manifested no inclination to fight, but, on the contrary, avoided any encounter. This was a consequence as well of the inferiority of his force, as of its being his plan to put himself in communication with Callao, which he accomplished yesterday at four in the evening, by a forced march from San Borja. His Excellency directed that a squadron of cavalry, and eight companies of Cazadores, under the command of Don Rudecindo Albardo, should pursue the rear-guard, which was done, but without effect, in consequence of the celerity of the enemy's march.

The enemy is now in Baquijano, and the Liberating Army is encamped near the Legua, watching his movements. The quantity of provisions necessary for

---

62 [We have been unable to locate the original source used by Parish].

subsisting the enemy's army, as well as the garrison of Callao, is very considerable, and we know by correct reports that the supply in the fortress is not sufficient for the remainder of this month. The enemy must, therefore, soon encounter our brave troops; for, besides this difficulty, it will be impossible to find forage for cavalry in the contracted position he now occupies. Thus it appears, that whatever may have been the enemy's plan in advancing on Callao, he cannot remain there many days, unless he can conquer the barrier which the superiority of our troops, in enthusiasm, numbers, and courage, presents.

Our naval force blockades the works of the fortress, and prevents any assistance reaching it, or any external communication with it. The progress made by the division under the command of Colonel Miller is also of great importance. It must now be in possession of Huamanga.

General La Serna remains in Jauja. The efforts which he may make with the small force under his command can produce no effect, as a considerable number of guerrillas watch his movements.

This is the present state of the campaign, and it is sufficient to give your Excellency a just idea of what may be hoped, it at the same time you take into consideration the heroic enthusiasm which, without exception of sex or of age, has been displayed in this capital in favour of the cause of the Continent.

I have the honour to communicate this to your Excellency, in order that the Supreme Director of your State, to whom the success of our arms is in a great measure due, may participate in the satisfaction created by the great hopes now about to be fulfilled, trusting thus in the destiny of the friendly States of America.

Accept the sentiments of my distinguished consideration, &c.

BERNARDO MONTEAGUDO
To Colonel Don Jose Ignacio Zenteno,
Minister of War

14. Act of the Independence of Guatemala, September 15, 1821[63]

GUATEMALA

We this day publish the Act of Independence agreed to by the capital of Guatemala, containing the regulations relative to the assembling of a Congress next March. It must have been a curious spectacle to see the people and Authorities of a country where Spanish Constitution has now been in force for some time, unanimously declaring that nothing short of a total Independence of Spain can satisfy their wants and wishes, and calmly, and with the smallest noise or commotion, proceeding to effect a change the most important that can be made by men in society.

The kingdom of Guatemala is situated between the province of Yucatan and Merida, belonging to the late Viceroyalty of Mexico, to the north, and the province of Veraguas, which forms part of New Granada, now Columbia, to the south. This geographical position is of extreme importance to the independence of Guatemala, from Columbia, on one side, and Mexico on the other, serving as points *d'appui*. In and near the Spanish part of the Bay of Honduras are the principal ports on the Atlantic, in which the productions of Guatemala are shipped; but this section has several good shipping ports on the Pacific. Guatemala was formerly a Captain-Generalship, and dependent on the Viceroy of Mexico in military concerns. It contains an Archbishopric, and a High Court of Justice. Its population exceeds one million, chiefly civilized Indians, European Spaniards, and Creoles, or descendants from the latter. It has six provinces; viz. Chiapa, where the celebrated historian of South America, Bartholomew de las Casas, was bishop; Paz, Guatemala, Honduras, Nicaragua, and Costa Rica. The province of Guatemala enjoys a fine climate, and is remarkable for the fertility of its soil. Its principal productions are indigo and cocoa. The latter is cultivated in the district of Soconusco, and though the quantity produced is not considerable, the quality is superior to any known. It was here the ancient Mexicans obtained their cocoa, the grains of which they used as money, in the same way as inhabitants of the Maldives Islands do shells. The indigo of Guatemala is superior to that of Carucas although the difference, since the commencement of the present century, is not so great as formerly, from the improvements introduce into this branch of cultivation in the latter. The quantity of Guatemala indigo annually made, is from 10 to 12,009 *quintals*, weighing 100 lbs. each, chiefly exported

<hr>

63 [*The Morning Chronicle*, 24 January 1822, British Library Newspapers. Accessed 4 June 2020].

to Spain, in serroons of 200 lbs. each. Guatemala abounds in mahogany, valuable resins, gums, medicinal plants, &c. It has not been much explored, although it is one of the finest botanizing countries in South America.

GUATEMALA, Sept. 16. At length, with heartfelt pleasure, I am enabled to announce to you that our independence is also declared, as you will see from the subjoined document.

Those anxious wishes to become independent of the Spanish Government, being public and indubitable, which in writing as well as verbally, have been manifested by the inhabitants of this capital, and several dispatches having also been received by the last post, from the Constitutional Municipalities of Ciudad Real, Comitan, and Jurtlan, in which they inform us that they have proclaimed and sworn to the said independence, and urge us to do the same in this city; and it being also well known that they have addressed similar dispatches to other corporations; it has been determined, in concurrence with the Provincial Deputation.

That, in order to treat of a matter of such great importance, the Members of the said Provincial Deputation, the Archbishop, the Members of the High Court of Justice, the venerable Dean and Ecclesiastical Chapter, the College of Lawyers, the regular Prelates, Military Commanders, and Public Functionaries, of all kinds, should assemble at the Town-hall, and deliberate there on.

The dispatches and papers above alluded to, having been read, and the subject fully discussed and meditated upon, and the loud and reiterated cries of 'Independence for ever' being heard from the people who had assembled in the streets, square, yard, and the galleries of the Town-hall, the following Resolutions were agreed upon:

1st. That as independence of the Spanish Government is the general wish of the people of Guatemala, and without detriment to what may thereupon be determined by the Congress that is to be formed, the political chief is ordered to proclaim the same, in order to avoid the consequences which might be dreaded if the people were to proceed to a declaration of that same independence themselves.

2d. That letters shall be immediately addressed to the provinces by extraordinary couriers, in order that without any delay they may be pleased to proceed to the election of deputies or representatives of their own, who will assemble in this capital and form Congress, which shall decide the point of general and absolute independence, and in case of agreeing to the same, determine what form of government and fundamental laws shall be put in force.

3. That in order to facilitate the nomination of Deputies, the Electoral Juntas

of the provinces which ought to have elected the last Deputies to the Cortes, shall themselves name the present ones.

4. That the number of Deputies shall be in proportion of one for every 15,000 persons, but without excluding from the rights of citizenship those who hold their descent from African blood.

5. That the Electoral Juntas of Provinces, in conformity to the last census, shall themselves determine on this basis, the number of deputies or representatives they are to elect.

6. That in consideration of the importance and urgency of the business, they will be pleased to close the elections in such manner, that on the 1st day of March in the ensuing year, 1822, the whole of the deputies may be assembled in this capital.

7. That, in the mean tine, no alterations shall take place in the Authorities already established, who shall continue to exercise their several functions, in conformity to the Constitution, Decrees and Laws now in force, till the aforesaid Congress shall determine what may be more just and advantageous.

8. That the Political Chief, Brigadier General Gavino Gainza shall remain in the superior Political and Military Government, and in order that he may possess the character suited to existing circumstances, a Consultive Provisional Junta shall be formed, composed of Messrs. Miguel de Larreinaga, Member of the High Court of Justice of this place; Jose Del Valle, Auditor of War; the Marquess de Aicinena, Jose Valdes, Treasurer of the Cathedral here; Dr. Angel Maria Candina, and Licentiate Antonio Robles, third Constitutional Alderman; the first for the province of Leon, the 2d for that of Comayagua, the 3d for Quesaltema, the 4th for Solala and Chemaltenango, 5th for Sonsonate, and the 6th for Ciudad Real de Chiapa.

9. That this Provisional Junta shall be consulted by the Political Chief on all economical and other matters deserving of their attention, and connected with the Government.

10. That the Catholic religion, which we have professed in former ages, and will profess in future ones, shall be preserved pure and unaltered, and that spirit of religion be maintained which has always distinguished Guatemala, the regular and secular Ministers shall be respected, and their persons and property respected.

11. That a letter of advice shall be forwarded to the worthy prelates of the religious communities, in order that by their cooperating in the maintenance of peace and tranquillity, the first duty of the people, when they effect a

transition from one government to another, they may take care that the persons under them may exhort to concord and fraternity among those united in the general sentiment of independence, ought equally to be so in other points, and all personal enmities waved.

12. That the municipality entrusted with the maintenance of order and tranquillity, shall take the most active measures for this purpose, as well in the capital as the surrounding towns.

13. That the political chief shall publish a manifesto, making known the real sentiments of the people, the opinion of the authorities and corporations, the measures of this new government, as well as the causes and circumstances which decided them to take the oath, in presence of the first Aldermen, and at the request of the people, to the independence and fidelity to the American Government, that may be established.

14. That the Provisional Junta shall take the same oath, as well as the Municipality, the Archbishop, the Tribunals, Political and Military Chiefs, the Regular Prelates, their Religious Communities, Chiefs, and persons employed in the revenues, authorities, corporations, and troops in their respective garrisons.

15. That the Political Chief, in concurrence with the Municipality, shall make the necessary arrangements, and name the day when the people shall also proclaim and swear to the said independence.

16. That the Municipality give orders for a medal to be struck, which may transmit to future ages the recollection of the 15th Sept. 1821, when we proclaimed our happy independence.

17. That the present act and aforesaid manifesto shall be printed, circulated, and sent to the provincial deputations, constitutional municipalities, and other authorities, ecclesiastical, regular, secular, and military, in order that agreeing in the same sentiments as those manifested by the people here, they may be pleased to act conformably to the stipulations therein contained.

18. That on the day the Political Chief may he pleased to appoint, a solemn mass of thanks shall be sung, in presence of the Provisional Junta and all the authorities, corporations, and Chiefs, with salutes of artillery, and three days of illuminations.

National Palace of Guatemala, this 15th day of Sept. 1821

[Here follow the signatures].

15. Declaration of the Independence of Mexico (1821)[64]

AMERICAN PAPERS

NEW SPAIN

DECLARATION OF THE INDEPENDENCE OF MEXICO
[From the *Charleston Gazette* of 27 September]

By the arrival yesterday of the brig Catherine Wellsman, in five days from Havannah, we have received some late accounts from Mexico, and particularly from the seat of war. A cessation of hostilities between the Patriots and Royalists has taken place. On the 11th of August, Colonel Santana had agreed to the proposition of the Viceroy, that the gates of La Vera Cruz should be thrown open the next day, the prisoners on both sides should be liberated, and that the country people be allowed to come unarmed, and in no great numbers.

Plan of the Government that is to be established provisionally for the purpose of securing our holy religion, and establishing the independence of the Mexican empire, under the title of the Administrative Junta of North America, proposed by Colonel Don Agustin de Iturbide, to his Excellency the Count de Venadito, Viceroy of New Spain:

1. The religion of New Spain is and shall be the Catholic Apostolic Roman religion, without toleration of any other.

2. New Spain's independent of Old Spain, and of every other Power, even upon our own continent.

3. Its Government shall be a limited monarchy conformably to the constitution that may be adopted by the kingdom.

4. Its Emperor shall be Don Ferdinand the Seventh; but in case he shall not personally appear in Mexico within the time that the Cortes shall specify, in order to take the oath, the most Serene Infant Don Carlos, Don Francisco de Paula, the Archduke Charles, or such other individual of the reigning family as Congress may think proper shall be called in his place.

5. Until the Cortes shall meet, there shall be a Junta for the purpose of bringing about such meeting, and causing the plan to be executed in its full extent.

---

64 [*The Times*, 3 November 1821, p. 2, The Times Digital Archive. Accessed 4 June 2020].

6. Said Junta, which shall be denominated administrative, is to be composed of the members named in the letter of his Excellency the Viceroy, by which its shall be convened.

7. Until Don Ferdinand the Seventh shall present himself in Mexico and take the oath, the Junta shall govern in his Majesty's name, in virtue of the oath of fidelity which the nation has taken. Nevertheless, the execution of all the orders that he may give previously to his taking the oath shall be suspended until then.

8. If Don Ferdinand the Seventh shall not condescend to come to Mexico, the Junta or the Regency shall govern in the name of the nation, until the Emperor who is to be crowned shall be fixed upon.

9. This Government shall be maintained by the army of the three guarantees hereinafter mentioned.

10. The Cortes shall determine upon the Constitution of a Regency, until the arrival of the person who is to be crowned.

11. The Cortes shall afterwards establish the Constitution of the Mexican Empire.

12. All the inhabitants of New Spain, without any distinction of Europeans, Africans, or Indians, are citizens of this monarchy, and eligible to every office, according to their merit and virtue.

13. The person and property of every citizen shall be respected and protected by the Government.

14. The secular and regular clergy shall be preserved in all their rights and pre-eminences.

15. The Junta shall take care that all the departments of the State remain without any alteration, and that all civil and military officer continue in their present situations; those only shall be removed who may refuse to concur in the plan, substituting in their place such persons as may be most distinguished for virtue and merit.

16. A protecting army shall be formed, which shall be denominated the Army of the Three Guarantees, inasmuch as it takes under its protection, in the first place, the preservation of the Catholic Apostolic Romish Religion, using all methods in its power that there may be no mixture of any other sect, and that the enemies that may threaten it be timely attacked; secondly, independence under the system above mentioned; thirdly, the intimate union of Europeans and Americans; and guarantees these fundamental bases of the felicity of New Spain, lo the infraction of which, rather than consent, it shall sacrifice itself, from the Commander in Chief to the last man.

17. The troops of the army shall observe the most exact discipline, to the very letter of the articles of war; and the chiefs and officers shall continue upon the footing on which they now are; that is to say, in their respective stations, with eligibility to the offices now vacant, and which may be vacated by such persons as may be unwilling to serve, and with eligibility to such new offices as may be considered necessary or convenient.

18. The troops of the said army shall be considered as of the line.

19. The same privilege shall be enjoyed by those who shall inlist without delay, and by those who, having borne arms in support of the former system of independence, shall immediately join the said army; and the peasants who may enlist shall be considered as troops of the national militia; and they shall all be employed for the internal and external security of the kingdom in such manner as the Cortes may direct.

20. The commission shall be granted according to real merit, as reported by the respective commanding officers, and in the name of the nation, provisionally.

21. Until the Cortes shall otherwise direct, proceedings in criminal cases shall be agreeably to the Spanish constitution.

22. In case of conspiracy against the Independence, the culprit shall be imprisoned until the Cortes shall determine upon the punishment of that greatest of all crimes, except those against the Divine Majesty.

23. Such persons as may attempt to foment disunion shall be watched, and reputed as conspirators against Independence.

24. As the Cortes who are to be installed are to frame a Constitution, it is necessary that the Deputies should receive powers sufficient for that purpose; and as it is also of much importance that the electors should know they are to be represented in the Congress of Mexico, and not in that of Madrid, the Junta shall prescribe just rules for the election, and shall designate the time of it, and the time of the opening of the Congress; and as the elections cannot now take place in March, the time shall be extended as much as possible.

16. Convocation of the National Constituent Congress, Mexico, November 17, 1821[65]

MEXICO

The Regency of the Empire has been pleased to address the following Decree to me:

The Regency of the Empire, entrusted with the temporary Government till an Emperor is chosen, to those who may see and know these presents: Know that the Sovereign Provisional Junta of Government has been pleased to decree the convocation of the national constituent Congress in the following manner.

The Sovereign Provisional Junta of Government for the Empire, from the first moment of their installation, were sensible of the importance and urgency of assembling the national and constituent Congress, in order that the latter, might be enabled to raise up the invaluable edifice of independence on the solid foundations contained in the plan of Iguala and the Treaty of Cordova, and after maturely deliberating on the doubts occurring on this subject, which prevented their earlier determination, they have been pleased to decree the following

ARTICLES FOR THE ELECTION OF THE DEPUTIES TO THE CONGRESS

1st. On the 16th of next December, Edicts shall be issued in all the towns of the empire having a Municipality, appointing the 21st for the election of the Electors, who are to name all the Aldermen, Members, and Sindics, conformably to the regulation of the Cortes of Spain of the 23d of May, 1812. On the ensuing 24th, the election is to be carried into effect, and immediately the former Municipality shall put the new one in possession of their respective seats. The electors are to bear in mind persons to be chosen ought to possess the requisites of good reputation, devotion to the independence of their country, and services performed to the cause; and in order that the edict of convocation may arrive in due time, it shall be published in an Extraordinary Gazette, the tenor of which is to be punctually observed; and if in the remote case of the election of Members of the Municipality having already been effected, in conformity to the regulation contained in the Spanish Constitution, it shall be done over again according to the enactment contained in these regulations. Half of those persons may be

---

65 [*The Morning Chronicle*, 4 September 1822, British Library Newspapers. Accessed 29 April 2020].

elected as Members of the Municipally who had previously been named, and would have kept their seats, if this general election had not been carried into effect, and this may also be serviceable as a guidance for the new Members. The citizens of all classes and clasts, even foreigners, in conformity to the plan of Iguala, shall be allowed to vote, after having attained 18 years of age.

2. In the edict it shall be announced that the electors are to be named by the people, on the express understanding that the new Municipality chosen shall have the necessary power to proceed to the election of electors for the district, province, and Deputies for the Constituent Congress about to be assembled.

3. On the 27th the new Municipality shall elect, as district elector, one of its own Members, who, besides possessing integrity, a fair name, suitable information, and adhesion to independence, shall have rendered services to the nation, and who on the 14th of the ensuing January, 1822, shall be in the head town of his respective district, in order to name an elector for the province, in union with the other electors of the same class, and the municipality of the said head town, at which election the mayor shall preside. The person elected may or not be a Member of the same.

4. The Provincial Electors shall assemble in the capital of the same on the 28th January, in order to elect, jointly with the rest and the municipality, presided by the Political Chief, if there should be one, and in defect thereof by the oldest Alderman, the Deputies for Congress corresponding to the province, which shall be expressed in the Edict of Convocation; it being borne in mind that in the latter reason requires there should be more particularly united fair reputation, information and devotion to independence, proved by positive acts, both previous and subsequent to its publication.

5. The District Electors shall by their municipality be provided with a corresponding credential, containing the express power to name an Elector for the province, and specifying that the latter are to name the Deputies to the Congress; and in like manner the municipality of the head town of the district, and the Electors who therewith jointly name those for the province to whom a similar credential shall be given, empowering him, with the others of the same class and the Provincial Municipality, to elect the respective Deputies for the Constituent Congress.

6. The District Electors shall present to the President of the Municipality of the head town their credential, those of the provinces shall do the same to the Political Chief, and in defect thereof to the oldest Alderman presiding over the Municipality, and the credentials shall be placed respectively in the archives of each.

7. The Provincial Electors, jointly with the Municipality of the capital, shall give to the Deputies they may name a suitable credential, containing the express power of naming Deputies for the Constituent Congress, they being answerable for any deficiency in this respect.

8. The Electors of the Provinces of Mexico, Guadalajara, Vera Cruz, Puebla, New Biscay, Sonora, Valladolid, Oajaca, Zacatecas, San Luis Potosi, Guanajuato, and Merida in Yucatan, shall name their respective Deputies according to the Prorata set down in the annexed statement, and of them three necessarily must be, one an Ecclesiastic of the secular order, another of the military, whether a native or foreigner, and the other a Magistrate, Judge, or Lawyer; the Magistrates and Judges being allowed to be named for the provinces in which they exercise their duties, a in the constituent Congress more information is required, and other arrangements can be made hereafter. In the Province of Chiapa, annexed to the Empire, and in the others that may gradually become incorporated, the same basis for the election of Deputies to the Congress shall be observed as in the other elections, that is, for every three districts two Deputies shall be elected.

9. As it is advisable, in order to promote the felicity of the Empire, that there should be in the Congress persons well informed in the important branches, besides the three Deputies pointed out in the preceding Article, the following Provinces shall be obliged besides to choose, viz. that of Mexico, a miner, one titled character, and a majorat; Guadalajara, a merchant; Vera Cruz, a merchant; Puebla, an artisan; New Biscay, a farmer; Sonora, an artisan; Valladolid, a farmer; San Luis Potosi, a public functionary; Merida in Yucatan, a public functionary; and Guanajuato, a miner. Public functionaries are not prevented from becoming Representatives for their respective Provinces; and in order to fill up the proportion of Deputies assigned to all, according to the annexed scale, those persons are to be named who may appear most eligible, and unite within themselves the recommendation of adhesion to the cause of Independence, services rendered to it, good character and information, provided they are not ecclesiastics, military persons, magistrates, nor lawyers; and the same is to be observed by the provinces of Oajaca and Zacatecas, after naming the three pointed out in Art. 8; it being understood that foreigners are to be possessed of fixed property, are to be married to Mexican women, and have the above requisites in order to be elected.

10. The provinces of Tlaxcala, New Kingdom of Leon, Santander, Coahuila, Texas, New Mexico, Upper and Lower California, as their proportion is only one deputy, they may be allowed to elect whomsoever they please, whether he be an ecclesiastic, of the secular clergy, a military person, judge, advocate, &c.

11. The city of Queretaro shall send to the capital of this province of Mexico a deputation of four members of its municipality, and the elector of the province chosen, who, jointly with the other electors and the municipality of the same, shall elect the 28 representatives corresponding to it, of whom two and one supernumerary shall bear the names of deputies for Queretaro, and the remaining 23 supernumeraries that of deputies for Mexico.

12. In the meetings of district and provincial electors, no formality of priority of seats shall be observed, as this does not in any way injure the rights of each.

13. The deputies shall be assembled in the capital of the empire at least by the 13th of February, although they may be waited for one or two days, if the badness of the roads require it, and they shall present their credentials to the Sovereign Junta on the 15th, in order that after they have been examined preparations may be made for the preparatory meetings, so that on the 24th the Congress may be opened by the members present, who, being one half, they shall proceed to solemnize the anniversary of the glorious day when liberty was first proclaimed in Iguala.

14. The Provincial Deputations shall subsist wherever they have been established, and besides they shall be established in the intendancies where there are none, and when the Congress divides the territory of the empire they shall establish such other representative bodies as may be necessary for the happiness of the people.

15. The existing Provincial Deputations shall be entirely changed and new members elected belonging to the province, one half of the former members may be allowed to continue on condition of their being re-elected.

16. In the new elections the members shall equally belong to the provinces respectively.

17. For this purpose the Provincial Electors shall assemble in the capital on the day following the election of Deputies to the Congress, and jointly with the municipality proceed to name the seven members, conformably to the regulations respectively. The elections being ended, the persons named shall appear before the municipality, and together with the members thereof proceed to the Cathedral Church, and there give thanks for the success of the new elections, when a solemn *Te Deum* shall be sung, and on the party returning to the Town Hall they shall inform the Regency of the elections, the municipality and electors signing the dispatch, in order that the Regency may notify the same to the Sovereign Junta at the first sitting.

18. The Deputies possessing patrimonial property, or a sufficient income, shall have no allowances for their attendance at Congress; but those who may be deficient in these respects, shall be provided for by the Provincial Deputations with what they may deem necessary for the journey, according to the distance, taking the same from any public fund that may exist, in order that their conveyance to the capital may not be delayed, and they shall besides propose the allowances they are to have, and the funds intended to meet the same.

19. That in the elections of the Municipality, as well as the following ones, the doubts that may occur shall be decided by the Electoral Juntas, and the Municipalities and Electors, without any other form being necessary.

20. As soon as the Congress is assembled, the Legislative Body shall divide into two Houses, having an equal number of Deputies, and with equal powers, and consequently dependent on each other, as regards all deliberations and

constitutional laws to be adopted; as in this manner the measures proposed in one House may be re-examined by the other, success will be more certain, and the public felicity will be provided with better support.

Mexico, 17th Nov. 1821
[Here follow the Signatures, &c.].

STATEMENT

SHEWING THE NUMBER OF EFFECTIVE AND SUPERNUMERARY DEPUTIES TO BE NAMED FOR THE CONSTITUENT CONGRESS OF THE MEXICAN EMPIRE.

Intendancies	Districts	Deputies	Supernumeraries
Mexico	43	28	4
Guadalaxara	28	17	2
Puebla	21	14	2
Vera Cruz	11	7	1
Merida	16	11	1
Oaxaca	22	14	2
Guanaxuato	10	7	1
Valladolid	21	14	2
St. Luis Potosi	10	7	1
Zacatecas	6	4	1
Government of Tlaxcala	1	1	1
Internal Eastern Provinces			
Govt. Of N. Kingdom of Leon	1	1	1
Id. Of New Santander	1	1	1
Id. Of Coahuila	1	1	1
Id. Of Texas	1	1	1
Internal Western Provinces			
Durango	34	23	3
Arizpe	12	8	1
New Mexico	1	1	1
Californias			
Government of Lower	1	1	1
Id. Of Upper	1	1	1
	242	162	29

Mexico, Nov. 17, 1821   A true Copy

17. Message of James Monroe, President of the United States, to the House of Representatives, March 8, 1822[66]

From the National Intelligencer, March 9 [1822]

The following important Message was yesterday transmitted by the President of the United States to the House of Representatives:

To the House of Representatives of the United States

In transmitting to the House of Representatives the documents, called for by the resolution of that House of the 30th of January, I consider it my duty to invite the attention of Congress to a very important subject, and to communicate the sentiments of the Executive on it, that, should Congress entertain similar sentiments, there may be such co-operation between the two Departments of the Government, as their respective rights and duties may require.

The Revolutionary movement, in the Spanish Provinces in this hemisphere, attracted the attention, and excited the sympathy of our fellow citizens, from its commencement. This feeling was natural and honourable to them from causes which need not be communicated to you. It has been gratifying to all to see the general acquiescence which has been manifested, in the policy which the constituted authorities have deemed it proper to pursue, in regard to this contest. As soon as the movement assumed such a steady and consistent form as to make the success of the Provinces probable, the rights to which they were entitled by the law of nations, as equal parties to a civil war, were extended to them. Each party was permitted to enter our ports with its public and private ships, and to take from them every article which was the subject of commerce with other nations. Our citizens, also, have carried on commerce with both parties, and the government has protected it, with each, in articles not contraband of war. Through the whole of this contest the United States have remained neutral, and have fulfilled with the utmost impartiality all the obligations incident to that character.

This contest has now reached such a stage, and been attended with such decisive success on the part of the provinces, that it merits the most profound consideration whether their right to the rank of independent nations, with all the advantages incident to it, in their intercourse with the United States, is

66 [We have been unable to locate the original source used by Parish. The original text was published in *Daily National Intelligencer* (Washington, U.S.), 9 March 1822].

not complete. Buenos Ayres assumed that rank by a formal declaration in 1816, and has enjoyed it since 1810 free from invasion by the parent country. The provinces composing the Republic of Colombia, after having separately declared their independence, were united by a fundamental law of the 17th of December, 1819. A strong Spanish force occupied, at that time, certain parts of the territory within their limits, and waged a destructive war. That force has since been repeatedly defeated, and the whole of it either made prisoners or destroyed, or expelled from the country, with the exception of an inconsiderable portion only, which is blockaded in two fortresses. The provinces on the Pacific have likewise been very successful. Chili declared independence in 1818. and has since enjoyed it undisturbed; and of late, by the assistance of Chili and Buenos Ayres, the revolution has extended to Peru. Of the movement in Mexico our information is less authentic, but it is, nevertheless, distinctly understood, that the new government has declared its independence, and that there is now no opposition to it there, nor a force to make any. For the last three years the government of Spain has not sent a single corps of troops to any part of that country; nor is there any reason to believe it will send any in future. Thus, it is manifest, that all those provinces are not only in the full enjoyment of their independence, but, considering the state of the war and other circumstances, that there is not the most remote prospect of their being deprived of it.

When the result of such a contest is manifestly settled, the new governments have a claim to recognition by other powers, which ought not to be resisted. Civil wars too often excite feelings which the parties cannot control. The opinion entertained by other powers as to the result, may assuage those feelings and promote an accommodation between them useful and honorable to both. The delay which has been observed in making a decision on this important subject, will, it is presumed. have afforded an unequivocal proof to Spain, as it must have done to other powers, of the high respect entertained by the United States for her rights, and of their determination not to interfere with them. The provinces belonging to this hemisphere are our neighbors, and have, successively, as each portion of the country acquired its independence, pressed their recognition by an appeal to facts not to be contested, and which they thought gave them a just title to it. To motives of interest this government has invariably disclaimed all pretension, being resolved to take no part in the controversy, or other measure in regard to it, which should not merit the sanction of the civilized world. To other claims a just sensibility has been always felt, and frankly acknowledged, but they in themselves could never become an adequate cause of action. It was incumbent on this government to look to every important fact and circumstance on which a sound opinion could be formed, which has been done. When we regard, then, the great length of time which this war has been prosecuted, the complete success which has attended it in favor of the provinces, the present condition of the parties, and the utter inability of Spain to produce any change in it, we are compelled to conclude that its fate is settled, and that the provinces which have declared their independence, and are in the enjoyment of it, ought to be recognized.

Of the views of the Spanish government on this subject, no particular information has been recently received. It may be presumed that the successful progress of the revolution, through such a long series of years, gaining strength, and extending annually in every direction, and embracing, by the late important events, with little exception, all the dominions of Spain, south of the United States, on this continent; placing thereby the complete sovereignty over the whole in the hands of the people, will reconcile the Parent country to an accommodation with them, on the basis of their unqualified independence. Nor has any authentic information been recently received of the disposition of other powers respecting it. A sincere desire has been cherished to act in concert with them in the proposed recognition, of which several were sometime past duly apprized, but it was understood that they were not prepared for it. The immense space between those powers, even those which border on the Atlantic, and these provinces, makes the movement an affair of less interest and excitement to them, than to us. It is probable, therefore, that they have been less attentive to its progress than we have been. It may be presumed, however, that the late events will dispel all doubt of the result.

In proposing this measure, it is not contemplated to change there by, in the slightest manner, our friendly relations with either of the parties, but to observe, in all respects, as heretofore, should the war be continued, the most perfect neutrality between them. Of this friendly disposition, an assurance will be given to the government of Spain, to whom it is presumed it will be, as it ought to be, satisfactory. The measure is proposed, under a thorough conviction that it is in strict accord with the law of nations; that it is just and right as to the parties; and that the United States owe it to their station and character in the world, as well as to their essential interests, to adopt it. Should Congress concur in the view herein presented, they will doubtless see the propriety of making the necessary appropriations for carrying it into effect.

JAMES MONROE

Washington, March 8, 1822

18. Report on the Recognition of the late Spanish Provinces in America, House of Representatives, United States, March 19, 1822[67]

FROM THE NATIONAL INTELLIGENCER

REPORT on the RECOGNITION of the late SPANISH PROVINCES in AMERICA.

HOUSE OF REPRESENTATIVES, MARCH 19 [1822]

The Committee on Foreign Affairs, to which was referred the Message of the President, concerning the recognition of the late Spanish Provinces in America, and the documents therewith communicated, have examined the same with the most profound attention, unanimously report:

That the Provinces of Buenos Ayres, after having, from the year 1810, proceeded in their revolutionary movements without any obstacle from the Government of Spain, formally declared their independence of that Government in 1816. After various intestine commotions, and external collisions, those provinces now enjoy domestic tranquillity and good understanding with all their neighbours; and actually exercise, without opposition from within, or the fear of annoyance from without, all the attributes of sovereignty.

The provinces of Venezuela and New Grenada, after having separately, declared their independence, sustained, for a period of more than ten years, desolating war against the armies of Spain, and having severally attained, by their triumph over those armies, the object for which they contended, united themselves, on the 19th of December, 1819, in one nation, under the title of 'the Republic of Colombia'.

The Republic of Colombia has now a well organised Government, instituted by the free will of its citizens, and exercises all the functions of Sovereignty, fearless alike of internal and foreign enemies. The small remnant of the numerous armies commissioned to preserve the supremacy of the parent state, is now blockaded, in two fortresses, where it is innoxious, and where, deprived, as it is, of hope of succour, it must soon surrender at discretion; when this event shall have occurred, there will not remain a vestage of foreign power in all that immense republic, containing between three and four millions of inhabitants.

---

67 [We have been unable to locate the original source used by Parish].

The province of Chili, since it declared its independence, in the year 1818, has been in the constant and unmolested enjoyment of the sovereignty which it then assumed.

The province of Peru, situated like Chili, beyond the Andes, and bordering on the Pacific Ocean, was, for a long time, deterred from making any effectual effort for independence, by the presence of an imposing military force, which Spain had kept up in that country. It was not, therefore, until the 18th of June, of the last year, that its capital, the city of Lima, capitulated to an army, chiefly composed of troops from Buenos Ayres and Chili, under the command of General San Martin. The greatest part of the Royal troops, which escaped on that occasion, retreated to the mountains, but soon left them to return to the coast, there to join the Royal garrison in the fortress of Callao. The surrender of that fortress soon after to the Americans, may be regarded as the termination of the war in that quarter.

When the people of Peru found themselves, by this event, free to express their will, they most unequivocally expressed in favor of independence, and with an unanimity and enthusiasm which have nowhere been excelled.

The revolution in Mexico has been somewhat different in its character and progress, from the revolutions in the other Spanish American provinces, and its result, in respect to the organization of its internal government, has, also, not been precisely the same. Independence, however, has been as emphatically declared and as practically established, since the 24th of August last, by the 'Mexican empire', as ever it has been by the Republics of the South; and her geographical situation, her population and her resources, eminently qualify her to maintain the independence which she has thus declared, and now actually enjoys.

Such are the facts which have occupied the attention of your Committee, and which, in their opinion, irresistibly prove, that the nations of Mexico, Colombia, Buenos Ayres, Peru and Chili, in Spanish America, are, in fact, independent.

It now remains for your committee to examine the right and the expediency, on the part of the United States, of recognizing the independence which those nations have, thus effectually achieved.

In this examination, it cannot be necessary to inquire into the right of the people of Spanish America, 'to dissolve the political bands which have connected them with another, and to assume, among the powers of the earth that separate and equal station to which the laws of nature and of nature's God entitle them'. The right to change the political institutions of the state has, indeed, been exercised equally by Spain, and by her colonies; and for us to deny to the people of Spanish America the right to independence, on the principles which alone sanction it here, would be virtually to renounce our own.

The political right of this nation to acknowledge their independence, without offending others, does not depend on its justice, but on its actual establishment. To justify such a recognition, by us, it is necessary only to show, as is already sufficiently shown, that the people of Spanish America are, within their respective limits, exclusively sovereign; and thus, in fact, independent. With them, as with every other government possessing and exercising the power of making war, the United States, in common with all nations, have the right of concerting the terms of mutual peace and intercourse.

Who is the rightful Sovereign of a country, is not an inquiry permitted to foreign nations, to whom it is competent only to treat with 'the powers that be'.

There is no difference in opinion, on this point, among the writers on public law; and no diversity, with respect to it, in the practice of civilized nations. It is not necessary, here, to cite authority for a doctrine familiar to all who paid the slightest attention to the subject; nor to go back, for its practical illustration, to the civil wars between the houses of York and Lancaster. Long since the chiefs of those conflicting houses alternately triumphed and ruled, and were alternately obeyed at home and recognized abroad, according as they successively exercised the powers without demonstrating the right -monarchies have become commonwealths or republics, and powerful usurpers have been recognized by foreign nations, in preference to legitimate and powerless pretenders. Modern history is replete with instances in point. Have we not, indeed, within the brief period of our own remembrance, beheld governments vary their forms, and change their rulers, according to the prevailing power or passion of the moment, and doing so in virtue of the principle now in question, without materially and lastingly affecting their relations with other Governments? Have we not seen the Emperors and Kings of yesterday receive on the Thrones of exiled Sovereigns, who claimed the right to reign there, the friendly embassies of other powers, with whom those exiled Sovereigns had sought an asylum -and have we not seen today those Emperors and Kings, thus courted and recognized yesterday, reft of their sceptres, and, from a mere change of circumstances, not of right, treated as usurpers by their successors, who, in their turn, have been acknowledged and caressed by the same foreign powers?

The peace of the world, and the independence of every member of the great political family, require that each should be the exclusive judge of its own internal proceedings, and that the fact alone should be regarded by foreign nations. 'Even when civil war breaks the bonds of society and of Government, or, at least, suspends their force and effect, it gives birth in the nation to two independent parties, who regard each other as enemies, and acknowledge no common judge'. It is of necessity, therefore, that these two parties should be considered, by foreign states, as two distinct and independent nations. To consider or treat them otherwise, would be to interfere in their domestic concerns, to deny them the right to manage their own affairs in their own way, and to violate the essential attributes of their respective sovereignty. For a nation to be entitled, in respect to foreign states, to the enjoyment of these attributes, 'and to figure directly in the great political society, it is sufficient that it is really sovereign and independent; that is, that it governs itself by its own authority and laws'. The people of Spanish America do, notoriously, so govern themselves, and the right of the United States to recognize the governments, which they have instituted, is incontestable. A doubt of the expediency of such a recognition can he suggested only by the apprehension that it may injuriously affect our peaceful and friendly relations with the nations of the other hemisphere.

Can such an apprehension be well founded?

Have not all those nations practically sanctioned, within the last thirty years, the very principle on which we now propose to act; or have they ever complained of one another, or of us, for acting on that principle?

No nation of Europe, excepting Spain herself, has, hitherto, opposed force to the independence of Spanish America. Some of those nations have not only constantly maintained commercial and friendly intercourse with them, in every stage of the revolution, but indirectly and efficiently, though not avowedly, aided them in the prosecution of their great object. To these the acknowledgment by the United States, of the attainment of that object, must be satisfactory.

To the other nations of Europe, who have regarded the events occurring in Spanish America, not only without interference, but with apparent indifference, such an acknowledgement ought not to be offensive.

The nations who have thus respectively favored, or never opposed, the Spanish American people, during their active struggle for independence, cannot, it is believed, regard with dissatisfaction the formal recognition of that independence by a nation, which, while that struggle lasted, has religiously observed, towards both conflicting parties, all the duties of neutrality. Your committee are, therefore, of opinion, that we have a right on this occasion, confidently to expect, from what these nations have done or forborne to do, during the various fortunes of the civil war which has terminated, that they will frankly approve the course of policy which the United States may now think proper to adopt in relation to the successful party in that war. It surely cannot be reasonably apprehended, that nations who have thus been the tranquil spectators, the apparent well-wishers, if not the efficient supporters of this party, and who have not made the faintest attempt to arrest its progress or to prevent its success, should be displeased with a third power, for merely recognizing the Governments which, owing to that success, have thus been virtually permitted, or impliedly approved, in acquiring the undisputed and exclusive control of the countries in which they are established. It is, therefore, on the consistency, as well as on the justice of these nations of Europe, that we may confidently rely, that the simple recognition, on the part of the United States, of the necessary effect of what has already been done, will not be considered as a just cause of complaint against them; while the interested and immediate agents, who have been directly and actively engaged in producing that effect, have neither been opposed nor censured.

Your committee, therefore, instead of seriously apprehending that the recognition, by the United States, of the independence of Spanish America, will be unacceptable to these nations, are not without hope, that they may practically approve it, by severally adopting a similar measure. It is not, indeed, unreasonable to suppose, that those Governments have, like this, waited only for the evidence of facts which might not only suffice to justify them, under the laws and usages of nations, but to satisfy Spain herself, that nothing has been prematurely done, or which could justly offend her feelings, or be considered as inconsistent with her rights. As their motives for not having hitherto recognized the independence of Spanish America, may thus be supposed to have been analogous to our own, it is permitted to presume that the facts and reasons which have prevailed on us no longer to hesitate, will, confirmed as they are by our example, have a like influence on them.

No nation can entertain a more sincere deference for the feelings of Spain, or take a more lively interest in her welfare, than the United States. It is to this deference, too evident to be doubted or misunderstood, that ought to be ascribed the hesitation of this Government, until now, to yield to the claims of Spanish America, although these claims were in perfect accordance with our own principles, feelings and interests. Having thus forborne to act, even at the hazard of having those principles and feelings misunderstood on this side of the Atlantic, we have, as your Committee believe, given at once satisfactory proof of our disinterestedness and moderation; and of our scrupulous respect to the principle which leaves the political institutions of every foreign state to be directed by its own view of its own rights and interests.

Your committee have been particularly anxious to show, in a manner satisfactory to Spain herself, that the measure, which this Government now proposes to adopt, has been considered with the most respectful attention, both in relation to her rights and to her feelings.

It is not on the laws and usages of nations, or on the practice of Spain herself on like occasions, that your Committee have relied for our justification towards her.

The fact that, for the last three years, she has not sent a single company of troops against her Transatlantic colonies, has not been used as evidence of their actual independence, or of her want of power to oppose it. This fact, explained as it is by the public acts of Spain herself, is regarded by your Committee as evidence only of her policy.

The last troops collected at Cadiz, in 1819, which were destined to suppress the revolutionary movements in Spanish America, not only rejected that service, but joined in the revolution, which has since proved successful in Spain itself. The declaration of the leaders in that revolution was, that 'Spanish America had a right to be free, and that Spain should be free'. Although the Constitution, which was re-established by that revolution, guaranteed the integrity of the Spanish dominions, yet the principles on which that Constitution was founded seem to discountenance the employment of force for the accomplishment of that object, in contempt of the equal rights and declared will of the American portion of the Spanish people. The conduct of the Government, organized under that Constitution, has uniformly been, in this respect, in conformity to those principles. Since its existence, there has not been even a proposal by that Government to employ force for the subjugation of the American provinces, but merely *recommendations of conciliatory measures for their pacification.*

The answer of the Cortes, on the 10th of July, 1820, to the address of the King, furnishes conclusive proof of this policy.

'The intimate union', says this answer, 'of the Cortes with your Majesty; the re-establishment of the Constitution; the faithful performance of promises, depriving malevolence of all pretext, will facilitate the pacification of the ultramarine provinces, which are in a state of agitation and dissension. The Cortes, on its part, will omit no opportunity to propose and adopt measures necessary for the *observance of the Constitution and restoration of tranquility in those countries, to the end that the Spain of both worlds may thus form a single and happy family'.*

Although the ultramarine provinces are not here encouraged to expect absolute independence, yet they are no longer treated as vassal colonies, or threatened with subjugation, but are actually recognized as brothers in the great constitutional and free family of Spain.

A report made to the Cortes, on the 24th of June, 1821, by a Committee appointed by that body, not only manifestly corroborates the policy above stated, but sufficiently intimates that the recognition of the independence of Spanish America by Spain herself, had nearly been the measure recommended by that Committee.

That report avers, that '*tranquility it not sufficient,* even if it should extend throughout America, with a prospect of permanency: No; *it falls short of the wishes of the friends of humanity'.*

In speaking of the measure demanded by the crisis, it says, that this measure was not only warmly approved by the Committee, but, *at first, entirely assented to by the Ministers,* with whom it had been discussed, and failed only to be proposed to the Cortes '*by these Ministers having, on account of peculiar occurrences, suspended their judgment'* It speaks of this measure as indicative of a new and glorious resolution; that it was demanded by America and the true interests of the Peninsula; that from it Spain might reap advantages which otherwise she could never expect; and that the *ties of kindred* and the uniformity of religion, with *commercial relations*, and those emanating from *free institutions*, would be the *surest pledge* of mutual harmony and close union.

Your committee do not feel themselves authorized to say, positively, what that measure was, but they do not hesitate to declare their entire conviction that no measure, short of a full recognition of unconditional independence, could have deserved the character, nor been capable of producing the effects ascribed to it.

It is, therefore, sufficiently manifest that Spain, far from wishing to call into action her means of prosecuting hostilities against the people of Spanish America, has *renounced even the feelings of an enemy towards* them, and, but for 'peculiar occurrences', had been prepared, nearly a year ago, to consent to their independence.

She has not only practically discontinued, and even emphatically deprecated, the employment of force to restore tranquility to Spanish America, but she has declared that even universal and permanent tranquility there 'falls short of the wishes of the friends of humanity'.

While she appeals to 'the ties of kindred', she undoubtedly feels them; and if she has not abandoned her desire, so often avowed, of mere constitutional union, and equal commercial intercourse with her former colonies, *as between provinces of the same empire,* a union and an intercourse which intervening Andes and oceans seem to render highly inconvenient, if not utterly impracticable, she evidently refers the accomplishment of this desire to the unawed deliberations, and to the congenial and kindred feelings of the people of those colonies, and thus substantially acknowledges their independence.

Whatever may be the policy of Spain, however, in respect to her former American colonies, our recognition of their independence can neither affect her rights, nor impair her means, in the accomplishment of that policy. We cannot, for this, be justly accused of aiding in the attainment of an independence which has already been established without our assistance. Besides, our recognition must necessarily be co-existent only with the fact on which it is founded and cannot survive it. While the nations of Spanish America are actually independent, it is simply, to speak the truth to acknowledge them to be so.

Should Spain, contrary to her avowed principles and acknowledged interests, renew the war for the conquest of South America, we shall, indeed, regret it, but we shall observe, as we have done, between the independent parties, an honest and impartial neutrality; but, on the other hand, should Spain, faithful to her own glory and prosperity, consent that her offspring in the new world should enjoy the right of self-government, equally with their brethren in the old, we shall sincerely rejoice; and we shall cherish, with equal satisfaction, and cultivate with equal assiduity, the friendship of regenerated Spain and of emancipated America.

Your Committee, in justice to their own feelings and to the feelings of their fellow-citizens, have made this declaration without disguise, and they trust that the uniform character and conduct of this people will save it from liability to misinterpretation.

Happy in our own institutions, we claim no privilege; we indulge no ambition to extend them to other nations; we admit the equal rights of all nations to form their own Governments and to administer their own internal affairs as they may judge proper; and, however they may, in these respects, differ from us, we do not, on that account, regard with the less satisfaction their tranquility and happiness.

Your Committee having thus considered the subject referred to them, in all its aspects, are unanimously of opinion, that it is *just and expedient* to acknowledge the independence of the several nations of Spanish America, without any reference to the diversity in the forms of their Governments; and, in accordance with this opinion, they respect fully submit the following resolutions:

Resolved. That the House of Representatives concur in the opinion expressed by the President, in his Message of the 8th March, 1822, that the American provinces of Spain, which have declared their independence, and are in the enjoyment of it, ought to be recognized by the United States, as independent states.

Resolved, That the Committee of Ways and Means be instructed to report a Bill appropriating a sum, not exceeding 100,000 dollars, to enable the President of the United States to give due effect to such recognition.

Bibliography

Archives

Archivo y Museo Histórico del Banco de la Provincia de Buenos Aires
Archivo Comercial de Hugh Dallas, Box 1.

Essex Record Office
John Parish to James Paroissien, Bath, 14 October 1822, James Paroissien
Papers (D-DOb C1–25).

Senate House Library, University of London
A concise account of the present state of the Spanish colonies of America, 1805
(MS149).

The Baring Archive
Buenos Aires and London: Letters from William and John Parish Robertson,
1817–1827.

The National Archives (TNA)
West Indies and South America. x. Miscellaneous Expedition to Buenos Ayres
[Buenos Aires] and Montevideo, 1806/1807, W.O. 1/161–162.
Alexander Mackinnon, and Domestic various, 1809, FO 72/90.
Colonel James Burke Papers, 1809, FO 72/81.
"Memorial from British Merchants resident at Rio de Janeiro", March 1809,
Board of Trade, 1–89.
Buenos Ayres. Alexander MacKinnon to Canning, 2 November 1809, FO
95/7/7.
Alexander Mackinnon, Don M. Yrigoyen, and various, 1810, FO 72/107.
Spanish America-South. Alexander McKinnon, Consul Robert P. Staples,
John C. Rawlinson, etc., Domestic, Messrs. Padilla Yrigoyen, Moreno,
and Guido, 1811, FO 72/126.
West Indies and South America. x. Miscellaneous. Papers and correspond-
ence on British policy towards Spanish America, 1811–1812, W.O. 1/164.
Robert P. Staples, Don Manuel Moreno, Don Luis Lopez Mendez, and
various, America, 1812–1813, FO 72/157.

Gregor McGregor, General Miranda, Robert P. Staples, and Domestic, America, 1812–1814, FO 72/171.
Memorials of merchants from London, Liverpool, Sheffield, Manchester, Exeter to South America, 18 May, 20 May, 23 May, 9 June and 13 June 1814, Board of Trade, 1–89.
Robert P. Staples, and Foreign various, 1817, FO 72/202.
Colonels J. P. Hamilton and Patrick Campbell, Joseph Cade. Consuls James Henderson, Thomas Tuper, Robert Sutherland, Edward Watts, and Malcolm MacGregor (October–December 1823), FO 18/1.

The Royal Geographical Society (TRGS)
The Sir Woodbine Parish Collection (SWP), 1807–1855.
SWP/1: Dalrymple's catalogue of authors who have written on the Rio de la Plata, Paraguay and Chaco, published in London in 1807, with manuscript annotations by Parish from 1807–1837.
SWP/3, South America. Volume containing printed and manuscript reports prepared for the Congress of Verona, 1822.

Newspapers [from British Library Newspapers, accessed 23 November 2019]

Caledonian Mercury.
Morning Chronicle.
Morning Post.
The Times.

Published sources

A Full and Correct Report of the Trial of Sir Home Popham. London: J. and J. Richardson, C. Chapple, 1807.
An Authentic and Interesting Description of the City of Buenos Ayres and the Adjacent Country: Situate on the River Plate, on the East Side of South America: Shewing the Manners, Customs, Produce and Commerce of That Most Important and Invaluable Country, Including an Account of the Capture of Buenos Ayres. London: John Fairburn, 1806.
An Authentic Narrative of the Proceedings of the Expedition under the Command of Brigadier-Gen. Craufurd, Operations against Buenos Ayres under the Command of Lieut-Gen. Whitelocke. London, 1808.
AGN, *Correspondencia de Lord Strangford y de la Estación Naval Británica en el Rio de la Plata con el Gobierno de Buenos Aires, 1810–1822.* Buenos Aires: G. Kraft, 1941.
AGN, *Misiones diplomáticas. Misiones de Matías Irigoyen, José Agustín de Aguirre y Tomás Crompton y Mariano Moreno, Vol. 1.* Buenos Aires: Kraft Ltd, 1937.
Antepara, J. M., *Documents, historical and explanatory shewing the designs wich have been in progress and the exertions made by the General Miranda for the South American Emancipation, during the last twenty-five years.* London: R. Juigné, 1810.
Artigas y Carrera. Viaje a América del Sur hecho por orden del gobierno americano en los años 1817 y 1818 en la Fragata Congress. London: F. and J. Allman, 1820.

Bonnycastle, R. H., *Spanish America, or a descriptive, historical, and geographical account of the dominions of Spain in the Western Hemisphere*. London: Longman, Hurst, Rees, Orme and Brown, 1818.

Brackenridge, H. M., *Voyage to South America performed by order of the American government, in 1817–18, in the US. Frigate Congress*, two volumes. London, 1820 (1st ed., Baltimore, 1819).

British and Foreign State Papers, 1818–1819, Compiled by the Librarian and Keeper of the Papers, Foreign Office. London: James Ridgway, Piccadilly, 1835.

Burke, W., *Additional Reasons for our Immediately Emancipating Spanish America deduced from the Present Crisis*. London, 1808.

Burke, W., *South American Independence, or the Emancipation of South America, the Glory and Interest of England*. London, 1807.

Castlereagh, R. S., Second Marquess of Londonderry and Viscount, *Correspondence, Despatches, and Other Papers of Viscount Castlereagh*. Edited by his brother Charles W. Vane, vol. XII. London: John Murray, 1853.

Colombia: being a geographical, statistical, agricultural, commercial, and political account of that country: adapted for the general reader, the merchant, and the colonist. London: Baldwin, Cradock, and Joy, 1822.

Davie, J. C., *Letters from Paraguay describing the settlements of Monte Video and Buenos Ayres*. London: G. Robinson, 1805.

"Death of Sir Woodbine Parish, K. C. H.", *Morning Post*, 21 August 1882, p. 5 [British Library Newspapers, accessed 2 February 2020].

Depons, F. J. R., *Travels in South America*. London, 1807.

Despatches, Correspondence, and Memoranda of Field Marshal Arthur, Duke of Wellington, K.G., vol. I. London: John Murray, 1867.

Foreign Office, Diplomatic, and Consular Sketches. London: W.H. Allen & Co., 1883.

Gentz, F. von, "Vienne, 15 janvier 1825" in *Dépêches inédites du chevalier de Gentz aux hospodars de Valachie: Dépêches adressées au prince Alexandre Soutzo janvier 1820–janvier 1821, et au prince Grégoire Ghika décembre 1822–juin 1825*. Paris: E. Plon et cie, 1877.

Gillespie, A., *Gleanings and Remarks; Collected during Many Months of Residence at Buenos Ayres, and Within the Upper Country...* Leeds: B. Dewhurst, 1818.

Gobierno de la Nueva Granada, Cuestión Mackintosh: Historia de ella y documentos. Publicación oficial del gobierno de la Nueva Granada, Bogotá, 1852.

Graham, J. and Rodney, C. A., *The reports on the present state of the United Provinces of South America; drawn up by Messrs. Rodney and Graham, commissioners sent to Buenos Ayres by the government of North America, and laid before the Congress of the United States; with their accompanying documents; occasional notes by the editor; and an introductory discourse, intended to present, with the reports and documents a view of the present state of the country, and of the progress of the independents*. London: Printed for Baldwin, Cradock and Joy, 1819 (1st ed. in the United States, 1818).

Helms, A. Z., *Travels from Buenos Ayres, by Potosi, to Lima, with notes by the translator*. London: Richard Phillips, 1807.

Henderson, J., *A history of the Brazil; comprising its geography, commerce, colonization, aboriginal inhabitants*. London: Longman, 1821.

Henderson, J., *A series of observations submitted to the Right Honourable Thomas Wallace, M.P., Vice President of the Board of Trade, on the expediency of Great Britain entering into commercial regulations with the South American States, accompanied by brief commercial notices of the five Republics.* London: J.M. Richardson, 1822b.

Henderson, J., *An Address to the South Americans and Mexicans: Chiefly Intended to Dissuade Them from Conceding Commercial Privileges to Other Nations, in Prejudice of Great Britain, on Account of the Delay by Her of Their Recognition; which Delay is Explained, on the Sound Principles of National Integrity and Honour: with a Cursory Review of Some of the Important Events and Traits of Patriotism which Have Distinguished Their Respective Revolutions.* London: J.M. Richardson and J. Hatchard, 1822a.

Henderson, J., *Observations on the Great Commercial Benefits that will result from the Warehousing-Bill, particularly as regards the free transit of foreign linens, silks & woolens, respectfully addressed to the consideration of the members of the British Parliament.* London: J.M. Richardson; Longman and Co.; J. Ridgway; Hatchard and Son; Budd and Calken; J. Harding, 1823.

Howell, J., *Journal of a Soldier of the 71st, or Glasgow Regiment Highland Light Infantry, from 1806–1815.* Edinburgh: William and Charles Tait, 1819.

Luccock, J., *Notes on Rio Janeiro [...] taken during a residence of 10 years in that country (from 1808 to 1818).* London: Leigh, 1820.

Mawe, J., *Travels in the Interior of Brazil, with notices, etc., including a voyage to the Rio de la Plata,* London, 1812.

"Obituary: Sir Woodbine Parish, K.C.H.F.R.S.", *Proceedings of the Royal Geographical Society and Monthly Record of Geography,* New Monthly Series, 4(10), October 1882, 612–613.

Palacio Fajardo, M., *Outline of the Revolution in Spanish America; or, an account of the origin, progress, and actual state of the war carried on between Spain and Spanish America, containing the principal facts which have marked the struggle, by a South-American.* London: Longman, Hurst, Rees, Orme and Brown, 1817.

Parish, W., *Buenos Ayres, and the Provinces of Rio de la Plata; their Present State, Trade, and Debt; with Some Account from Original Documents of the Progress of Geographical Discovery in Those Parts of South America during the Last Sixty Years.* London: John Murray, 1839.

Pazos, V., *Letters on the United Provinces of South America.* New York & London: J. Seymour, 1819.

Report of the Committee on Latin American Studies. London: Her Majesty's Stationery Office, 1965.

Robertson, J. P. and Robertson, W. P., *Letters on Paraguay: comprising an account of a four years' residence in that republic, under the government of the Dictator Francia,* two volumes. London: John Murray, 1838.

Robertson, J. P. and Robertson, W. P., *Letters on South America. Comprising travels on the banks of the Paraná and Rio de la Plata,* three volumes. London: John Murray, 1843.

Southey, R., *History of Brazil,* three volumes. London: Longman, Hurst, Rees & Orme, 1810.

Stapleton, A. G., *George Canning and His Times*. London: John W. Parker & Son, 1859.

Stapleton, A. G., *The Political Life of the Right Honourable George Canning*, three volumes. London: Longman, Rees, Orme, Brown and Green, 1831.

Stapleton, E. J. (ed.), *Some official correspondence of George Canning*, vol. II. London: Longmans, Green, and co., 1887.

The Foreign Office List for 1857. London: Harrison, 1857.

The Proceedings of a General Court Martial, Held at Chelsea Hospital, on Thursday, January 28, For the Trial of Lieut. Gen. Whitelocke, late Commander in Chief of the Forces in South America. Taken in Short-hand by Mr. Gurney, With the defense, copied form the original, by permission of General Whitelocke; also all the documents produced on the trial, two volumes. London, 1808.

Tucker, Maj. J. G., *A Narrative of the Operations of a Small British Force under the command of Brigadier-General Sir Samuel Auchmuty, employed in the Reduction of Monte Video*. London, 1807.

Vidal, E. E., *Picturesque illustration of Buenos Ayres and Monte Video with an account of the Costumes manners [...] of the inhabitants*. London: Ackerman, 1820.

Walton, W., *An exposé on the dissentions of Spanish America*. London, 1814.

Walton, W., *Present state of the Spanish colonies*, two volumes. London: Longman, Hurst, Rees, Orme and Brown, 1810.

Wilcocke, S. H., *History of the viceroyalty of Buenos Ayres*. London: Sherwood, Neely and Jones, 1807.

Secondary sources

AA.VV., *Modos de producción en América Latina*. Buenos Aires: Cuadernos de Pasado y Presente, No. 40, 1973.

Aguirre, R., *Informal Empire. Mexico and Central America in Victorian Culture*. Minnesota: University of Minnesota Press, 2005.

Alberich, J., "English Attitudes towards the Hispanic World in the Time of Bello, As Reflected by the *Edinburgh* and *Quarterly Reviews*" in J. Lynch (ed.), *Andrés Bello: The London Years*. Richmond: Richmond Publishing Company, 1982, 67–81.

Alison, A., *Lives of Lord Castlereagh and Sir Charles Stewart*, vol. III. Edinburgh & London: William Blackwood and Sons, 1861.

Anderson, P., "La naturaleza y el sentido de las guerras hispanoamericanas de liberación", in H. Bonilla (ed.), *La cuestión colonial*. Bogotá: Universidad Nacional de Colombia, 2011, 33–48.

Andrew, C., *Secret Service: The Making of the British Intelligence Community*. London: Sceptre, 1987.

Armstrong, W., "British Representation in Venezuela in 1826", *Caribbean Quarterly*, 6(1), 1960, 18–25.

Asquith, I., "Advertising and the Press in the Late Eighteenth and Early Nineteenth Centuries: James Perry and the *Morning Chronicle* 1790–1821", *Historical Journal*, 18(4), 1975, 703–724.

Baeza Ruz, A., *Contacts, Collisions and Relationships: Britons and Chileans in the Independence Era, 1806–1831*. Liverpool: Liverpool University Press, 2019.

Bartlett, C. J., *Castlereagh*. London: Palgrave Macmillan, 1966.

Barton, G. A., *Informal Empire and the Rise of One World Culture*. New York: Palgrave MacMillan, 2014.

Bayly, C. A., *Empire and Information: Intelligence Gathering and Social Communication in India, 1780–1870*. Cambridge: Cambridge University Press, 2000.

Bayly, C. A., *The Birth of the Modern World, 1789–1914: Global Connections and Comparisons*. Oxford: Blackwell, 2004.

Berruezo León, M. T., *La lucha de Hispanoamérica por su independencia en Inglaterra, 1800–1830*. Madrid: Ediciones de Cultura Hispánica, 1989.

Besseghini, D., "British Trade and the Fall of the Spanish Empire – Changing Practices and Alliances of Antony Gibbs & Sons in Lima during the Transition from Viceregal to Independentist Rule (1820–1823)", *Nuevo Mundo Mundos Nuevos*, https://journals.openedition.org/nuevomundo/79632, 2020a.

Besseghini, D., "Imperialismo informal e independencia: los británicos y la apertura del comercio en el Rio de la Plata (1808–1810)", *Illes i imperis*, 23, 2021, 41–68.

Besseghini, D., "The Anglo-American Conflict in the Far Side of the World: A Struggle for Influence over Revolutionary South America (1812–1814)", *Annals of the Fondazione Luigi Einaudi*, LIV, 2020b, 35–56.

Bew, J., *Castlereagh: A Life*. Oxford: Oxford University Press, 2012.

Bindoff, S. T., "The Unreformed Diplomatic Service, 1812–60 (The Alexander Prize Essay)", *Transactions of the Royal Historical Society*, 18, 1935, 152–153.

Black, J., *A History of Diplomacy*. London: Reaktion Books, 2010.

Black, J., *The English Press: A History*. London: Bloomsbury Academic, 2019.

Black, J., *The Power of Knowledge: How Information and Technology Made the Modern World*. New Haven & London: Yale University Press, 2014.

Blaufarb, R., "The Western Question: The Geopolitics of Latin American Independence", *Historical Review*, 112, 2007, 3–742.

Bonilla, H. (ed.), *La cuestión colonial*. Bogotá: Universidad Nacional de Colombia, 2011.

Bonpland, A., *Londres cuartel general europeo de los patriotas de la emancipación americana*. Buenos Aires: Coni, 1940.

Böttcher, N., *Monopol und Freihandel. Britische Kaufleute in Buenos Aires am Vorabend der Unabhängigkeit (1806–1825)*. Stuttgart: F. Steiner Verlag, 2008.

Brown, D., "Diplomacy and the Fourth Estate: The Role of the Press in British Foreign Policy in the Age of Palmerston" in J. Fisher and A. Best (eds.), *On the Fringes of Diplomacy: Influences on British Foreign Policy, 1800–1945*. London & New York: Routledge, 2011, 35–52.

Brown, M., *Adventuring through Spanish Colonies: Simón Bolívar, Foreign Mercenaries and the Birth of New Nations*. Liverpool: Liverpool University Press, 2006.

Brown, M., "Henderson, James (1782/3–1848), Diplomat and Hispanist", *Oxford Dictionary of National Biography*. Oxford: Oxford University Press, 2009.

Brown, M., *Informal Empire in Latin America: Culture, Commerce and Capital*. Oxford: Blackwell Publishing – SLAS, 2008.

Brown, M. and Paquette, G. (eds.), *Connections after Colonialism: Europe and Latin America in the 1820s*. Tuscaloosa: University of Alabama Press, 2013.

Bulmer-Thomas, V. (ed.), *Britain and Latin America: A Changing Relationship.* Cambridge: Cambridge University Press, 1989.

Busaniche, J. L., "Estudio preliminar" in W. Parish, *Buenos Aires y las provincias del Rio de la Plata. Desde su descubrimiento y conquista por los españoles.* Buenos Aires: Librería Hachette, 1958, 7–29.

Cámara de Comercio Argentino-Británica, *La influencia británica en el desarrollo de la Argentina.* Buenos Aires: Se-Bue S.A, 2014.

Camarda, M., "Circulación ultramarina de navíos del complejo portuario rioplatense (1779–1806)", *Anuario del Instituto de Historia Argentina,* 13, 2013, 1–19.

Cárcano, M. A., *La política internacional en la historia argentina. Libro III, Tomos I y II: La República unitaria, 1811–1828.* Buenos Aires: Eudeba, 1972.

Cardoso, F. H. and Faletto, E., *Dependencia y desarrollo en América Latina: ensayo de interpretación sociológica.* México: Siglo XXI Editores, 1969.

Cecil, A., "The Foreign Office" in A. W. Ward and G. P. Gooch (eds.), *The Cambridge History of British Foreign Policy, 1783–1919,* vol. III. New York: The Macmillan Company, 1923.

Chust, M. and Frasquet, I., *Tiempos de revolución. Comprender las independencias iberoamericanas.* Madrid: Fundación Mapfre, 2013.

Cibotti, E., *Queridos enemigos: de Beresford a Maradona, la verdadera historia de las relaciones entre ingleses y argentinos.* Buenos Aires: Aguilar, 2006.

Cline, H. F., "The Latin American Studies Association: A Summary Survey with Appendix", *Latin American Research Review,* 2(1), 1966, 57–79.

Cooper, F., *Colonialism in Question: Theory, Knowledge, History.* Berkeley: University of California Press, 2005.

Cozens, J., "The Making of the Peterloo Martyrs, 1819 to the Present" in Q. Outram and K. Laybourn (eds.), *Secular Martyrdom in Britain and Ireland: From Peterloo to the Present.* UK: Palgrave Macmillan, 2018.

Cutolo, V., "Parish, Woodbine" in *Nuevo Diccionario Biográfico Argentino (1750–1930),* vol. V. Buenos Aires: Editorial Elche S. A., 1978, 305–310.

Darwin, J., "Imperialism and the Victorians: The Dynamics of Territorial Expansion", *English Historical Review,* 112(447), 1997, 614–642.

Darwin, J., *The Unfinished Empire: The Global Expansion of Britain.* London, 2013.

Davies, H., "Integration of Strategic and Operational Intelligence During the Peninsular War", *Intelligence and National Security,* 21(2), 2006, 202–223.

Davis, T., *Carlos de Alvear. Hombre de revolución.* Buenos Aires: Emecé, 1964.

Dawson, F., *The First Latin American Debt Crisis: The City of London and the 1822–25 Loan Bubble.* New Haven: Yale University Press, 1990.

Day, R. B. and Gaido, D. (eds.), *Discovering Imperialism: Social Democracy to World War I.* Leiden: Brill, 2012.

De Gandía, E., "Lord Ponsonby, Woodbine Parish y la política argentina de 1827 a 1830", *Investigaciones y Ensayos,* 4, 1968, 21–43.

De Goey, F., *Consuls and the Institutions of Global Capitalism, 1793–1914.* London and New York: Routledge, 2014.

Deacon, R., *A History of the British Secret Service.* London: Muller, 1969.

Dittmer, J., *Diplomatic Material: Affect, Assemblage, and Foreign Policy.* Durham and London: Duke University Press, 2017.

Durey, M., *William Wickham, Master Spy: The Secret War against the French Revolution*. London: Pickering & Chatto Ltd., 2009.

Ehrenberg, R., *Das Haus Parish in Hamburg*. Jena: G. Fischer, 1925.

Elliott, J. H., *History in the Making*. New Haven: Yale University Press, 2012.

Escudé, C. and Cisneros, A. (eds.), *Historia general de las relaciones exteriores de la República Argentina. Tomo II: Desde los orígenes hasta el reconocimiento de la independencia formal*. Buenos Aires: Grupo Editor Latinoamericano, 1998.

Fast, J. J., "Parish, John" in *Neue Deutsche Biographie (NDB)*. Band 20. Berlin: Duncker & Humblot, 2001, www.deutsche-biographie.de/pnd123392632.html#ndbcontent (accessed 30 May 2020).

Fay, C. R., "The Movement towards Free Trade, 1820–1853" in J. H. Rose, A. P. Newton and E. A. Benians (eds.), *The Cambridge History of the British Empire. Volume 2. The Growth of the New Empire, 1783–1870*. Cambridge: Cambridge University Press, 1940, 388–414.

Ferns, H. S., *Britain and Argentina in the Nineteenth Century*. Oxford: Oxford University Press, 1960.

Fisher, J. and Best, A. (eds.), *On the Fringes of Diplomacy: Influences on British Foreign Policy, 1800–1945*. Surrey: Ashgate, 2011.

Fitte, E., *El precio de la libertad. La presión británica en el proceso emancipador*. Buenos Aires: Emecé, 1965.

Fitte, E., "Los comerciantes ingleses en vísperas de la Revolución de Mayo", *Investigaciones y Ensayos*, 2, 1967, 69–139.

Flores, R., "Británicos en la sociedad de Buenos Aires (1804–1810)", *Antíteses*, 4, 2011, 173–201.

Fontana, J., *De en medio del tiempo. La segunda restauración española, 1823–1834*. Barcelona: Crítica, 2006.

Fortescue, J. W., *A History of the British Army. Volume V. 1803–1807*. London: Macmillan and Co., 1921.

Frega, A. and Vegh, B. (eds.), *En torno a las "invasiones inglesas": relaciones políticas y culturales con Gran Bretaña a lo largo de dos siglos*. Montevideo: Universidad de la República, 2007.

Gallagher, J. and Robinson, R., "The Imperialism of Free Trade", *The Economic History Review*, 6(1), 1953, 1–15.

Gallo, K., *De la invasión al reconocimiento. Gran Bretaña y el Río de la Plata*. Buenos Aires: A-Z Editora, 1994.

Gleijeses, P., "The Limits of Sympathy: The United States and the Independence of Spanish America", *Journal of Latin American Studies*, 24(3), 1992, 481–505.

Godelier, M., "Colonialismo, cultura y política" in H. Bonilla (ed.), *La cuestión colonial*. Bogotá: Universidad Nacional de Colombia, 2011, 419–436.

Goodwin, G., "Henderson, James", *Dictionary of National Biography*, vol. 25. London: Smith, Elder & Co., [1885–1900], 1891.

Graham, G. S. and Humphreys, R. A., *The Navy and South America, 1807–1823: Correspondence of the Commanders-in-Chief on the South American Station*, vol. 104. London: Navy Records Society, 1962.

Graham-Yooll, A., *La colonia olvidada. Tres siglos de presencia británica en la Argentina*. Buenos Aires: Emecé, 2000.

Grainger, J. D., *British Campaigns in the South Atlantic, 1805–1807: Operations in the Cape and the River Plate and their Consequences*. South Yorkshire: Pen & Sword Books Ltd, 2015.

Green, J., "Castlereagh's Instructions for the Conferences at Vienna, 1822", *Transactions of the Royal Historical Society*, 7, 1913, 103–128.

Gregory, D., *Brute New World: The Rediscovery of Latin America in the Early Nineteenth Century*. London & New York: British Academic Press, 1993.

Guastavino, J. E., *Inglaterra y la Diplomacia de la Revolución de Mayo de 1810*. Buenos Aires, 1918.

Guevara, E., "Mensaje a la Tricontinental", *Pensamiento Crítico*, 9, 1967, 197–211.

Gutiérrez Ardila, D., *El reconocimiento de Colombia: Diplomacia y propaganda en la coyuntura de las restauraciones, 1819–1831*. Bogotá: Universidad Externado de Colombia, 2012.

Hall, C., *British Strategy in the Napoleonic War, 1803–15*. Manchester: Manchester University Press, 1992.

Halperín Donghi, T., *Storia dell' America Latina*. Turin: Einaudi, 1967.

Hanon, M., *Diccionario de Británicos en Buenos Aires (Primera Época)*. Buenos Aires: Edición del autor, 2005.

Harari, F. and Flores, J., "La diplomacia de la Revolución. Política diplomática y relaciones Internacionales (1810–1815)", *Conflicto Social. Revista del Programa de Investigaciones sobre Conflicto Social*, 10(18), 2017, 140–167.

Headrick, D. R., *When Information Came of Age: Technologies of Knowledge in the Age of Reason and Revolution, 1700–1850*. Oxford: Oxford University Press, 2001.

Heinowitz, R., *South American and British Romanticism, 1777–1826: Rewriting Conquest*. Edinburgh: University of Edinburgh Press, 2010.

Heredia, E., "El 'carlotismo', los ingleses y el comercio exterior", *Nuestra Historia. Revista de Occidente*, X(20), 1977, 80–100.

Herman, M., *Intelligence Power in Peace and War*. Cambridge: Cambridge University Press, 1996.

Hevia, J., *The Imperial Security State: British Colonial Knowledge and Empire-Building in Asia*. Cambridge: Cambridge University Press, 2021.

Historians in Records and Historical Department (RHD) of the Foreign and Commonwealth Office (FCO), "The FCO: Policy, People and Places (1782–1995)", *History Notes*, 2, April 1991.

Hobsbawm, E. J., *Industry and Empire: An Economic History of Britain since 1750*. London: Weidenfeld and Nicolson, 1968.

Hobsbawm, E. J., *The Age of Revolution: Europe, 1789–1848*. London: Weidenfeld and Nicolson, 1962.

Hopkins, A. G., "Informal Empire in Argentina: An Alternative View", *Journal of Latin American Studies*, 26(2), 1994, 469–484.

Howat, J., "Sir Woodbine Parish", *Dictionary of Falklands Biography*, September 2019, www.falklandsbiographies.org/biographies/parish_sir (accessed 2 February 2020).

Howe, S., "The Slow Death and Strange Rebirths of Imperial History", *Journal of Imperial and Commonwealth History*, 29(2), 2001, 131–141.

Hughes, B., *The British Invasion of the River Plate, 1806–7: How the Redcoats Were Humbled and a Nation Was Born*. South Yorkshire: Pen & Sword, 2013.

Humphreys, R. A., "Anglo-American Rivalries and Spanish American Emancipation", *Transactions of the Royal Historical Society*, 5, 1966, 131–156.

Humphreys, R. A., *British Consular Reports on the Trade and Politics of Latin America: 1824–1826*. London: Offices of the Royal Historical Society, 1940.

Humphreys, R. A., "British Merchants and South American Independence", *Proceedings of the British Academy*, 51, 1965.

Humphreys, R. A., "Latin American Studies in Great Britain: An Autobiographical Fragment", London, Institute for Latin American Studies, 1978.

Humphreys, R. A., *Liberation in South America, 1806–1827: The Career of James Paroissien*. London: University of London, Athlone Press, 1952.

Hunt, L., *The New Cultural History*. Berkeley: University of California Press, 1988.

Iñigo Carrera, J., *La formación económica de la sociedad argentina. De la acumulación originaria al desarrollo de su especificidad hasta 1930*. Santiago de Chile: Ariadna, 2022 (in press).

Iñigo Carrera, J., "La unidad mundial de la acumulación de capital en su forma nacional históricamente dominante en América Latina. Crítica de las teorías del desarrollo, de la dependencia y del imperialismo", *IV Coloquio Internacional de la Sociedad Latinoamericana de Economía Política y Pensamiento Crítico*, FaCE, UBA, 2008.

Jaramillo, J. D., *Bolívar y Canning, 1822–1827*. Bogotá: Banco de la República, 1983.

Jarret, M., *The Congress of Vienna and its Legacy: War and Great Power Diplomacy after Napoleon*. London & New York: I.B. Tauris, 2013.

Jiménez Codinach, G., *La Gran Bretaña y la independencia de México, 1808–1821*. México: FCE, 1991.

Jones, C., "Finance, Ambition and Romanticism in the River Plate, 1800–1892" in M. Brown (ed.), *Informal Empire in Latin America: Culture, Commerce and Capital*. Oxford: Blackwell Publishing – SLAS, 2008, 124–148.

Jones, R., "An Early Nineteenth-Century Patronage List: George Canning and the Consular Service, 1822", *Bulletin of the Institute of Historical Research*, 56(134), 1983a, 232–238.

Jones, R., *The British Diplomatic Service: 1815–1914*. London: Wilfrid Laurier University Press, 1983b.

Jones, R., *The Nineteenth-Century Foreign Office. An Administrative History*. London: London School of Economics and Political Science, 1971.

Jones, R., "The Social Structure of the British Diplomatic Service, 1815–1914", *Histoire Sociale / Social History*, 14(27), 1981, 49–66.

Jones-Parry, E., "Under-Secretaries of State for Foreign Affairs, 1782–1855", *The English Historical Review*, 49(194), 1934, 308–320.

Joseph, G. M., LeGrand, C. C. and Salvatore, R. D. (eds.), *Close Encounters of Empire: Writing the Cultural History of US–Latin American Relations*. London and Chapel Hill: Duke University Press, 1998.

Justo, L., "Una carta de H. S. Ferns" in *Nuestra Patria Vasalla. Historia del coloniaje argentino*, vol. I. Buenos Aires: Editorial Schapire, 1968.

Kaufmann, W., *British Policy and the Independence of Latin America, 1804–1828*. New Haven: Yale University Press, 1951.

Kay Shuttleworth, N., *A Life of Sir Woodbine Parish K.C.H., F.R.S. (1796–1882)*. London: Smith, Elder & Co., 1910.

Kennedy, P., *The Realities Behind Diplomacy: Background Influences on British External Policy, 1865–1980*. London: Fontana Press, 1981.

Knight, A., "Britain and Latin America" in A. Porter (ed.), *The Oxford History of the British Empire. Volume 3. The Nineteenth Century*. Oxford: Oxford University Press, 1999.

Knight, A., "Rethinking British Informal Empire in Latin America (Especially Argentina)" in M. Brown (ed.), *Informal Empire in Latin America: Culture, Commerce and Capital*. Oxford: Blackwell Publishing–SLAS, 2008, 23–48.

König, H. J., "¿Comercio libre a cambio de reconocimiento político? El caso especial de las negociaciones entre la Gran Colombia y las Ciudades Hanseáticas", *Anuario de Historia regional y de las fronteras*, 12, 2007, 321–337.

Kossok, M., *Historia de la Santa Alianza y la emancipación de América Latina*. Buenos Aires: Ediciones Sílaba, 1968.

Krasnyak, O., *National Styles in Science, Diplomacy, and Science Diplomacy*. Leiden & Boston: Brill, 2019.

Krasnyak, O. and Ruffini, P. B., "Science Diplomacy", *Oxford Bibliographies in International Relations*, 2020, www.oxfordbibliographies.com/view/document/obo-9780199743292/obo-9780199743292-0277.xml?rskey=Y84qJo&result=1&q=Science+Diplomacy#firstMatch (accessed 18 January 2021).

Laidlaw, Z., *Colonial Connections, 1815–45: Patronage, the Information Revolution and Colonial Government*. Manchester: Manchester University Press, 2005.

Larner, C., "The Amalgamation of the Diplomatic Service with the Foreign Office", *Journal of Contemporary History*, 7(1), 1972, 107–126.

Lenin, V. I., "El Imperialismo, fase superior del capitalismo", in *Obras completas*, vol. XXII. Buenos Aires: Cartago, 1960, 193–319 (1st ed., 1917).

Lewis, C. and Abel, C. (eds.), *Latin America, Economic Imperialism and the State: The Political Economy of the External Connection from Independence to the Present*. London: Athlone Press, 1985.

Lewis, C. M., "Britain, the Argentine and Informal Empire: Rethinking the Role of Railway Companies", in M. Brown (ed.), *Informal Empire in Latin America: Culture, Commerce and Capital*. Oxford: Blackwell Publishing–SLAS, 2008, 99–123.

Llorca-Jaña, M., *The British Textile Trade in South America in the Nineteenth Century*. New York: Cambridge, 2012.

Lloyd, E. M., "Canning and Spanish America", *Transactions of the Royal Historical Society, Royal Historical Society*, 18, 1904, 77–105.

Louis, W. R. (ed.), *El imperialismo. (La controversia Robinson-Gallagher)*. México: Nueva Imagen, 1978.

Lynch, J., "British Policy and Spanish America, 1783–1808", *Journal of Latin American Studies*, 1(1), 1969, 1–30.

Lynch, J. (ed.), *Andrés Bello: The London Years*. London: Richmond Publishing Company, 1982.

Lynn, M., "British Policy, Trade, and Informal Empire in the Mid-Nineteenth Century" in A. Porter (ed.), *The Oxford History of the British Empire. Volume 3. The Nineteenth Century*. Oxford: Oxford University Press, 1999.

Mackie, C. (ed.), *A Directory of British Diplomats*, four volumes. London: Foreign & Commonwealth Office, 2014.

Maffeo, S., *Most Secret and Confidential: Intelligence in the Age of Nelson*. Annapolis: Naval Institute Press, 2000.

Marchena Fernández, J., Chust, M. and Schlez, M. (eds.), *El debate permanente. Modos de producción y revolución en América Latina*. Santiago de Chile: Ariadna Ediciones, 2020.

Martínez Garnica, A., *Historia de la Primera República de Colombia, 1818–1831: "Decid Colombia sea, y Colombia será"*. Bogotá: Editorial Universitaria del Rosario, 2019.

Marx, K., *El Capital. Crítica de la economía política*. Tomo I. México: FCE, 1999.

McCarthy, M., *Privateering, Piracy, and British Policy in Spanish America, 1810–1830*. London, 2013.

McFarlane, A., "Relaciones internacionales y guerras coloniales: el contexto internacional de las independencias americanas", *Tempus*, 4, 2016, 256–275.

McLean, D., *War, Diplomacy and Informal Empire: Britain and the Republics of La Plata, 1836–1853*. London: British Academic Press, 1995.

Metford, J. C., "The Recognition by Great Britain of the United Provinces of Rio de la Plata", *Bulletin of Hispanic Studies*, XXIX(116), 1952, 201–244.

Middleton, C. R., *The Administration of British Foreign Policy, 1782–1846*. Durham, NC: Duke University Press, 1977.

Mikaberidze, A., *The Napoleonic Wars: A Global History*. Oxford. Oxford University Press, 2020.

Miller, N., *Republics of Knowledge: Nations of the Future in Latin America*. Princeton: Princeton University Press, 2020.

Miller, R., *Britain and Latin America in the Nineteenth and Twentieth Centuries*. London & New York: Longman, 1993.

Montaner Bello, R., *Historia diplomática de la independencia de Chile*. Santiago: Andrés Bello, 1961.

Muir, R., *Wellington. Waterloo and the Fortunes of Peace, 1814–1852*. New Haven & London: Yale University Press, 2015.

Munch-Petersen, T., "The Secret Intelligence from Tilsit in 1807", *Napoleonica. La Revue*, 18(3), 2013, 22–67.

Nichols, I. C., *The European Pentarchy and the Congress of Verona, 1822*. The Hague: Nijhoff, 1971.

Nicolau, J. C., *Correspondencia inédita sobre historia argentina: cartas entre Rosas y Parish*. Buenos Aires: Leviatán, 1990.

Nicolson, H., *Diplomacy*. London–New York–Toronto: Oxford University Press, 1939.

Nkrumah, K., *Neo-Colonialism: The Last Stage of Imperialism*. London: Thomas Nelson & Sons Ltd., 1965.

O'Brien, S., *Linguistic Diasporas, Narrative and Performance: The Irish in Argentina*. Cham: Palgrave Macmillan, 2017.

O'Connell, B., "Underground Alliances and Preventive Strikes: British Intelligence and Secret Diplomacy During the Napoleonic Wars, 1807–1810", *Intelligence and National Security*, 35(2), 2019, 179–196.

Ott, M., "Crossing the Atlantic: Bavarian Diplomacy and the Formation of Consular Services Overseas, 1820–1871" in M. Mösslang and T. Riotte (eds.), *The Diplomats' World: A Cultural History of Diplomacy, 1815–1914*. Oxford: German Historical Institute London – Oxford University Press, 2008, 381–405.

Otte, T. G., "'A Kind of Black Hole?': Commercial Diplomacy Before 1914" in J. Fisher, E. G. H. Pedaliu and R. Smith (eds.), *The Foreign Office, Commerce and British Foreign Policy in the Twentieth Century*. London: Palgrave Macmillan, 2016.

Otte, T. G., "Old Diplomacy: Reflections on the Foreign Office before 1914", *Contemporary British History*, 18(3), 2004, 31–52.

Otte, T. G., *The Foreign Office Mind: The Making of British Foreign Policy, 1865–1914*. Cambridge: Cambridge University Press, 2011.

Otte, T. G., *The Permanent Under-Secretary for Foreign Affairs, 1854–1946*. New York and London: Routledge, 2009.

Owen, R. and Sutcliffe, B., *Studies in the Theory of Imperialism*. London: Patrick Seale Books, 1972.

Paquette, G., "The Intellectual Context of British Diplomatic Recognition of the South American Republics, c. 1800–1830", *Journal of Transatlantic Studies*, 2(1), 2004, 75–95.

Paquette, G., "The 'Parry Report' (1965) and the Establishment of Latin American Studies in the United Kingdom", *The Historical Journal*, 62(1), 2019, 219–240.

Paquette, G., "Visiones británicas del Mundo Atlántico español, c. 1740–1830", *Cuadernos de Historia Moderna*, X, 2011, 145–154.

Parish, C. (revised by Malcolm Deas), "Parish, Sir Woodbine (1796–1882)", *Oxford Dictionary of National Biography*. University of London: Online Library, 2004.

Parry, B., "The Institutionalisation of Postcolonial Studies" in N. Lazarus (ed.), *The Cambridge Companion to Postcolonial Literary Studies*. Cambridge: Cambridge University Press, 2004, 66–80.

Pasino, A., "Publicitar la causa americana al otro lado del Atlántico. La labor de los representantes rioplatenses en Londres (1810–1816)", *PolHis*, 18(9), 2017, 13–52.

Paxson, F. L., *The Independence of the South American Republics: A Study in Recognition and Foreign Policy*. Philadelphia: Ferris and Leach, 1903.

Pearce, A. J., *British Trade with Spanish America, 1763–1808*. Liverpool: Liverpool University Press, 2007.

Peñaloza, F., "Appropriating the 'Unattainable': The British Travel Experience in Patagonia" in M. Brown (ed.), *Informal Empire in Latin America: Culture, Commerce and Capital*. Oxford: Blackwell Publishing–SLAS, 2008, 149–172.

Piccirilli, R., *Argentinos en Río de Janeiro, 1815–1820. Diplomacia. Monarquía. Independencia*. Buenos Aires: Editorial Pleamar, 1969.

Piccirilli, R., *Rivadavia*. Buenos Aires: Peuser, 1952.

Platt, D. C. M., *Finance, Trade, and Politics in British Foreign Policy, 1815–1914*. Oxford: Clarendon, 1968b.

Platt, D. C. M., "Further Objections to an 'Imperialism of Free Trade', 1830–60", *Economic History Review*, 26(1), 1973.

Platt, D. C. M., *Latin America and British Trade, 1806–1914*. London: Adam and Charles Black, 1972.

Platt, D. C. M., *The Cinderella Service: British Consuls since 1825*. Hamden: Archon Books, 1971.

Platt, D. C. M., "The Imperialism of Free Trade: Some Reservations", *The Economic History Review*, New Series, 21(2), 1968a, 296–306.

Platt, D. C. M. (ed.), *Business Imperialism, 1840–1930: An Inquiry Based on the British Experience in Latin America*. Oxford: Clarendon Press, 1977.

Pratt, E. J., "Anglo-American Commercial and Political Rivalry on the Plata, 1820–1830", *Hispanic American Historical Review*, XI, 1931, 315–316.

Pratt, M. L., *Imperial Eyes: Travel Writing and Transculturation*. London and New York: Routledge, 1992.

Pyne, P., "A Soldier Under Two Flags. Lieutenant-Colonel James Florence Burke: Officer, Adventurer and Spy", *Études irlandaises*, 23(1), 1998, 121–138.

Racine, K., "Commercial Christianity: The British and Foreign Bible Society's Interest in Spanish America, 1805–1830" in M. Brown (ed.), *Informal Empire in Latin America: Culture, Commerce and Capital*. Oxford: Blackwell Publishing – SLAS, 2008, 78–98.

Racine, K., *Francisco Miranda: A Transatlantic Life in the Age of Revolution*. Wilmington: Scholarly Resources, 2003.

Racine, K., "'This England and This Now': British Cultural and Intellectual Influence in the Spanish American Independence Era", *Hispanic American Historical Review*, 90(3), 2010, 423–454.

Ratto, H. R., *Los comodoros británicos de estación en el Plata 1810–1852*. Buenos Aires: Sociedad de Historia Argentina, 1945.

Reber, V. B., *British Mercantile Houses in Buenos Aires: 1810–1880*. Harvard: Harvard University Press, 1979.

Reeder, J., *The Forms of Informal Empire: Britain, Latin America, and Nineteenth-Century Literature*. Baltimore: Johns Hopkins University Press, 2020.

Rees Jones, R., *Bernardino Rivadavia y su negocio minero: Rio de la Plata Mining Association*. Buenos Aires: Librería Histórica, 2008.

Rippy, J. F., *Rivalry of the United States and Great Britain Over Latin America, 1808–1830*. New York: Octagon Books, 1972.

Roberts, C., *Las invasiones inglesas del Rio de la Plata (1806–1807) y la influencia inglesa en la independencia y organización de las provincias del Rio de la Plata*. Buenos Aires: Emecé Editores, 2006 (1st ed. 1938).

Robertson, W. S., "The Recognition of the Hispanic American Nations by the United States", *The Hispanic American Historical Review*, 1(3), 1918, 239–269.

Robinson, R., "Fundamentos no europeos del imperialismo europeo. Bosquejo para una teoría de colaboración" in W. R. Louis (ed.), *El imperialismo. (La controversia Robinson-Gallagher)*. México: Nueva Imagen, 1978, 185–215.

Robson, M., *Britain, Portugal and South America in the Napoleonic Wars: Alliances and Diplomacy in Economic Maritime Conflict.* London: I.B. Tauris & Co. Ltd., 2009.

Rock, D., *The British in Argentina: Commerce, Settlers and Power, 1800–2000.* London: Palgrave Macmillan, 2019.

Rock, D., "The British in Argentina: From Informal Empire to Postcolonialism" in M. Brown (ed.), *Informal Empire in Latin America: Culture, Commerce and Capital.* Oxford: Blackwell Publishing–SLAS, 2008, 49–77.

Roland, R., *Interpreters as Diplomats: A Diplomatic History of the Role of Interpreters in World Politics.* Ottawa: University of Ottawa Press, 1999.

Roldán Vera, E., *The British Book Trade and Spanish American Independence: Education and Knowledge Transmission in Transcontinental Perspective.* Aldershot: Ashgate, 2003.

Rosa, J. M., *La Misión García ante Lord Strangford: estudio de la tentativa de 1815 para transformar a la Argentina en colonia inglesa.* Buenos Aires: Instituto Juan Manuel de Rosas de Investigaciones Históricas, 1951.

Rosa, J. M., *Rivadavia y el imperialismo financiero.* Buenos Aires: A. Peña Lillo, 1964.

Ruiz-Guiñazú, E., *Lord Strangford y la Revolución de Mayo.* Buenos Aires: La Facultad, 1937.

Rydjord, J., "British Mediation between Spain and her Colonies", *The Spanish American Historical Review,* 21(1), 1941, 29–50.

Said, E. W., *Orientalism.* London: Routledge and Kegan Paul, 1978.

Salvatore, R., "Re-Discovering Spanish America: Uses of Travel Literature about South America in Britain", *Journal of Latin American Cultural Studies,* 8(2), 1999, 199–217.

Salvatore, R., "Reflections on Hiram Bingham and the Yale Peruvian Expedition", *Nepantla: Views from South,* 4(1), 2003, 67–80.

Schlez, M., "El tráfico comercial marítimo durante la invasión británica al Rio de la Plata (1806–1807)", *América Latina en la Historia Económica,* 27(1), 2019, 1–28.

Schlez, M., "La cuestión colonial en el siglo XXI. Balance y perspectivas del debate en torno a los modos de producción en América Latina", *Revista Eletrônica da ANPHLAC,* 2013, 65–83.

Schlez, M., *La necesidad es ley suprema. El capital mercantil en el Rio de la Plata: del monopolio comercial al industrial (1770–1825).* Castelló de la Plana: Publicacions de la Universitat Jaume I, 2021a.

Schlez, M., "Le commerce atlantique de Buenos Aires à l'ère révolution-naire (1778–1830). Bilan historiographique et perspectives de recherche" in D. E. Rojas (ed.), *Amérique latine globale. Histoire connectée, globale et interna-tionale.* París: L'Harmattan, 2017, 49–96.

Schlez, M. "Los comerciantes coloniales latinoamericanos en la transición al capitalismo. Un balance historiográfico", *REDE A. Revista de Estudos Afro - Americanos,* 5(1), 2015, 133–164.

Schlez, M., "Pensar, comprender y hacer la revolución. El debate en torno a las historiografías 'académica' y 'militante'" in M. Chust and J. A. Serrano (eds.), *¡Abajo la Tiranía! Las Revoluciones en América y España, 1776–1836.* Madrid: Sílex, 2018, 259–300.

Schlez, M., "*Que no se persuadan que las proposiciones que se hagan son por efecto de debilidad. Los fundamentos materiales del vínculo político entre Buenos Aires, España y Gran Bretaña durante el Trienio Liberal*" in M. Chust, J. Marchena Fernández and M. Schlez (eds.), *La ilusión de la Libertad. El liberalismo revolucionario en la década de 1820*. Santiago de Chile: Ariadna Ediciones, 2021b, 347–400.

Schlez, M., "*Tendrá una separación eterna*. Invasión territorial y construcción de un espacio del capital en *La Estrella del Sur* (Rio de la Plata, 1807)" in M. Tejerina and C. Cantera (eds.), *Implicar al otro: espacio, territorio y poder entre la colonia y las Provincias Unidas del Rio de la Plata*. Bahía Blanca: EDIUNS; La Pampa: EdUNLPam, 2021c, 45–70.

Schlez, M., "*Un fatal golpe a todos los de mi clase*. El combate en torno a la permisión provisoria de comercio con los extranjeros en el Rio de la Plata (1809–1810)" in J. A. Piqueras and J. von Grafenstein (eds.), *El pensamiento económico del reformismo criollo*. Santa Marta: Universidad del Magdalena; México: Instituto de Investigaciones Dr. José María Luis Mora, 2020b, 275–312.

Seiguer, P., "La Iglesia Anglicana en la Argentina y la colectividad inglesa. Identidad y estrategias misionales, 1869–1930", Doctoral Thesis, UBA, 2009.

Silva, H., "Economía, política y estrategia inglesa sobre el Rio de la Plata. Santa Catalina en los acuerdos británicos-portugueses", *Investigaciones y Ensayos*, 51, 2001, 97–127.

Silva, H., "La consolidación de los intereses comerciales británicos en el atlántico sur", *Minius*, 16, 2008, 261–290.

Silveira, A., "Comerciantes británicos en el Rio de la Plata. En torno a la construcción de una comunidad mercantil (1810–1860)", *Anuario del Centro de Estudios Históricos "Prof. Carlos S. A. Segreti"*, 15(15), 2015, 265–285.

Silveira, A., *Gran Bretaña en la Reina del Plata. Ingleses y escoceses en Buenos Aires, 1800–1880*. Buenos Aires: Biblos, 2017.

Silveira, A., "Nuevos actores entran en escena. Los británicos en el Rio de la Plata (1800–1850)" in M. Alabart, M. A. Fernández and M. Pérez (eds.), *Buenos Aires, una sociedad que se transforma*. Buenos Aires: Prometeo, 2011.

Smith, J., "New World Diplomacy: A Reappraisal of British Policy Towards Latin America, 1823–1850", *Inter-American Economic Affairs*, 32(2), 1978, 3–24.

Somarriva, M., "A Matter of Speculation: British Representations of Argentina, Chile and Perú during the Wars of Independence", *Bulletin of Latin American Research*, 36(2), 2016, 223–236.

Somarriva, M., "'An Open Field and Fair Play'. The Relationship Between Britain and the Southern Cone of America, c. 1808–1830", Doctoral Thesis, University College London, 2013.

Southern, J., "A Class of its Own? Social Class and the Foreign Office, 1782–2020", Occasional Paper No. 18, FCO Historians, Foreign and Commonwealth Office, 2020.

Steiner, Z., "Elitism and Foreign Policy: The Foreign Office Before the Great War" in B. J. C. McKercher and D. J. Moss (eds.), *Shadow and Substance in British Foreign Policy, 1895–1939*. Edmonton: The University of Alberta Press, 1984, 19–56.

Steiner, Z. S., *The Foreign Office and Foreign Policy, 1898–1914*. Cambridge: Cambridge University Press, 1969.

Steiner, Z., "The Old Foreign Office: From a Secretarial Office to a Modern Department of State" in *Opinion publique et politique extérieure en Europe. Actes du Colloque de Rome (13–16 février 1980)*. Rome: École Française de Rome, 1981, 177–195.

Stewart, I., *From Caledonia to the Pampas: Two Accounts of the Early Scots Emigrants to the Argentine*. East Lothian: Tuckwell Press, 2000.

Stoler, A. L., "On Degrees of Imperial Sovereignty", *Public Culture*, 18(1), 2006, 125–146.

Strang, W., *The Foreign Office*. London & New York: Allen & Unwin – Oxford University Press, 1955.

Street, J., *Gran Bretaña y la Independencia del Rio de la Plata*. Buenos Aires: Paidós, 1967.

Street, J., "Lord Strangford and Rio de la Plata, 1808–1815", *The Hispanic American Historical Review*, 33(4), 1953, 477–510.

Temperley, H., *The Foreign Policy of Canning, 1822–1827: England, the Neo-Holy Alliance, and the New World*. London: Bell and Sons, 1925.

Ternavasio, M., *Candidata a la corona. La infanta Carlota Joaquina en el laberinto de las revoluciones hispanoamericanas*. Buenos Aires: Siglo XXI, 2015.

Terragno, R., *Diario intimo de San Martín: Londres, 1824*. Buenos Aires: Debolsillo, 2013.

Terragno, R., *Maitland & San Martin*. Buenos Aires: Universidad Nacional de Quilmes, 1998.

Thompson, A., "Afterword: Informal Empire: Past, Present and Future" in M. Brown (ed.), *Informal Empire in Latin America: Culture, Commerce and Capital*. Oxford: Blackwell Publishing–SLAS, 2008, 149–172.

Thompson, A., "Informal Empire? An Exploration in the History of Anglo-Argentine Relations, 1810–1914", *Journal of Latin American Studies*, 24(2), 1992, 419–436.

Tilley, J. and Gaselee, S., *The Foreign Office*. London & New York: G. P. Putnam's Sons Ltd, 1933.

Topik, S., Marichal, C. and Frank, Z. (eds.) *From Silver to Cocaine: Latin American Commodity Chains and the Building of the World Economy, 1500–2000*. Durham: Duke University Press, 2006.

Van Hulle, I., "Britain's Recognition of the Spanish American Republics", *Tijdschrift voor Rechtsgeschiedenis / Revue d'Histoire du Droit / The Legal History Review*, 82(3–4), 2014, 284–322.

Vargas Garcia, E., "¿Imperio informal? La política británica hacia América Latina en el siglo XIX", *Foro Internacional*, XLVI(2), 2006, 353–385.

Waddell, D., *Gran Bretaña y la independencia de Venezuela y Colombia*. Caracas: Dirección de Información y Relaciones, 1983.

Warner, M., "Sources and Methods for the Study of Intelligence" in L. K. Johnson (ed.), *Handbook of Intelligence Studies*. New York: Routledge, 2007.

Warner, M., "Wanted: A Definition of 'Intelligence'", in Andrew, C., Aldrich, R. J. and Wark, W. K. (eds.) *Secret Intelligence: A Reader*. London & New York: Routledge, 2020.

Watt, D., "The Nature of the Foreign-Policy-Making Élite in Britain" in *Personalities and Policies: Studies in the Formulation of British Foreign Policy in the Twentieth Century*. Notre Dame, IN: University of Notre Dame Press, 1965.

Webster, C. K., "Castlereagh and the Spanish Colonies", *The English Historical Review*, 27(105), 1912, 78–95.

Webster, C. K., "Castlereagh and the Spanish Colonies II. 1818–1822", *The English Historical Review*, 30(120), 1915, 631–645.

Webster, C. K., *The Foreign Policy of Castlereagh, 1815–1822: Britain and the European Alliance*. London: G. Bell & Sons, 1925.

Webster, C. K. (ed.), *Britain and the Independence of Latin America 1812–1830: Select Documents from the Foreign Office Archives*, two volumes. London: Oxford University Press, 1938.

Whitaker, A. P., *The United States and the Independence of Latin America, 1800–1830*. Baltimore: Johns Hopkins University Press, 1941.

Williams, J. H., "Woodbine Parish and the 'Opening' of Paraguay", *Proceedings of the American Philosophical Society*, 116(4), 1972, 343–349.

Williams Álzaga, E., *Fuga del General Beresford, 1807*. Buenos Aires: Emecé, 1965.

Williford, M., *Jeremy Bentham on Spanish America*. Baton Rouge: Louisiana State University Press, 1980.

Yamada, N., "George Canning and the Concert of Europe, September 1822–July 1824", Doctoral Thesis, University of London–London School of Economics and Political Science, 2004.

Young, R., *Postcolonialism: An Historical Introduction*. Oxford: Blackwell, 2001.

Zoellick, R. B., *America in the World: A History of U.S. Diplomacy and Foreign Policy*. New York & Boston: Hachette Book Group, 2020.

Index